BUILDING DESIGN/ MATERIALS & METHODS

Caleb Hornbostel & John Raeber, FAIA, FCSI, CCS, Contributing Editor

President: Roy Lipner
Vice-President of Product Development and Publishing: Evan M. Butterfield
Editorial Project Manager: Jason Mitchell
Director of Production: Daniel Frey
Quality Assurance Editor: David Shaw
Creative Director: Lucy Jenkins

Published by Kaplan AEC Education
a division of Dearborn Financial Publishing, Inc.®
A Kaplan Professional Company
30 South Wacker Drive, Suite 2500
Chicago, IL 60606-7481
(312) 836-4400
http://www.kaplanAECarchitecture.com

CONTENTS

ARE OVERVIEW

Since the State of Illinois first pioneered the practice of licensing architects in 1897, architectural licensing has been increasingly adopted as a means to protect the public health, safety, and welfare. Today, all U.S. states and Canadian provinces require licensing for individuals practicing architecture. Licensing requirements vary by jurisdiction; however, the minimum requirements are uniform and in all cases include passing the Architect Registration Exam (ARE). This makes the ARE a required rite of passage for all those entering the profession, and you should be congratulated on undertaking this challenging endeavor.

Developed by the National Council of Architectural Registration Boards (NCARB), the ARE is the only exam by which architecture candidates can become registered in the United States or Canada. The ARE assesses candidates' knowledge, skills, and abilities in nine different areas of professional practice, including a candidate's competency in decision making and knowledge of various areas of the profession. The exam also tests competence in fulfilling an architect's responsibilities and in coordinating the activities of others while working with a team of design and construction specialists. In all jurisdictions, candidates must pass the nine divisions of the exam to become registered.

The ARE is designed and prepared by architects, making it a practice-based exam. It is generally not a test of academic knowledge, but rather a means to test decision-making ability as it relates to the responsibilities of the architectural profession. For example, the exam does not expect candidates to memorize specific details of the building code, but requires them to understand a model code's general requirements, scope, and purpose, and to know the architect's responsibilities related to that code. As such, there is no substitute for a well-rounded internship to help prepare for the ARE.

Exam Format

The ARE consists of nine divisions: three graphic and six multiple-choice. The multiple-choice divisions are timed and contain differing numbers of questions. The number of questions and time limit for each division is outlined in the table below. For detailed information on the graphic divisions, refer to the study guides for those divisions.

Division	Questions	Hours
Pre-Design	105	2.5
General Structures	85	2.5
Lateral Forces	75	2
Mechanical and Electrical Systems	105	2
Building Design/ Materials & Methods	105	2
Construction Documents & Services	115	3

The exam presents questions individually. Candidates may answer questions, skip questions, or mark questions for further review. Candidates may also move backward or forward within the exam using simple on-screen icons. The technique of marking questions for further review is a useful tool and is described in more detail below.

Actual appointment times for taking the exam are slightly longer than the actual exam time, allowing candidates to check in and out of the testing center. All ARE candidates are encouraged to review NCARB's *ARE Guidelines* for further detail about the exam format. These guidelines are available via free download at NCARB's Web site (*www.ncarb.org*).

ARCHITECTURAL HISTORY

Questions pertaining to the history of architecture appear in all of the multiple-choice divisions. The prominence of historical questions will vary not only by division but also within different versions of the exam for each division. In general, however, history tends to be lightly tested, with approximately three to seven history questions per division, depending upon the total number of questions within the division. One aspect common to all the divisions is that whatever history questions are presented will be related to that division's subject matter. For example, a question regarding Chicago's John Hancock Center and the purpose of its unique exterior cross bracing may appear on the Lateral Forces exam.

Though it is difficult to predict how essential your knowledge of architectural history will be to passing any of the multiple-choice divisions, it is recommended that you refer to a primer in this field—such as Kaplan's *Architectural History*—before taking each exam, and that you keep an eye out for topics relevant to the division for which you are studying. It is always better to be overprepared than taken by surprise at the testing center.

Question Format

It is important for exam candidates to familiarize themselves not only with exam content, but also with question format. Familiarity with the basic question types found in the ARE will reduce confusion, save time, and help you pass the exam. The multiple-choice divisions contain three basic question types.

The first and most common type is a straightforward multiple-choice question followed by four choices (A, B, C, and D). Candidates are expected to select the correct answer. An example of this type of question is shown below.

Which of the following cities is the capital of the United States?

A. New York

B. Washington, DC

C. Chicago

D. Los Angeles

The second type of question is a negatively worded question. In questions such as this, the negative wording is usually highlighted using all caps, as shown below.

Which of the following cities is NOT located on the west coast of the United States?

A. Los Angeles

B. San Diego

C. San Francisco

D. New York

The third type of question is a combination question. In a combination question, more than one choice may be correct; candidates must select from combinations of potentially correct choices. An example of a combination question is shown on the next page.

NEW TO THE EXAM

ARE 3.1

In November 2005 NCARB released *ARE Guidelines* Version 3.1, which outlines changes to the exam that are effective as of February 2006. These new guidelines primarily detail changes for the Site Planning division, which now combines the site design and site parking vignettes as well as the site zoning and site analysis vignettes. For more details about these changes, please refer to the study guides for the graphic divisions.

The new guidelines mean less to those preparing for multiple-choice divisions. Noteworthy points are outlined below.

- All division statements and content area descriptions are unchanged for the multiple-choice divisions.
- The number of questions and time limits for all exams are unchanged.
- The list of codes and standards candidates should familiarize themselves with has been reduced to those of the International Code Council (ICC), the National Fire Protection Association (NFPA), and the National Research Council of Canada.
- A statics title has been removed from the reference list for General Structures.

Rolling Clock

A rolling clock went into effect January 1, 2006. Candidates must now pass all nine ARE divisions within a five-year period. Additionally, NCARB has instituted a set of "transitional rules" for candidates already in the process of taking the ARE when the clock went into effect. See the new guidelines or visit the NCARB Web site for more detailed information.

Which of the following cities are located within the United States?

    I. New York

    II. Toronto

    III. Montreal

    IV. Los Angeles

A. I only

B. I and II

C. II and III

D. I and IV

Recommendations on Exam Division Order

NCARB allows candidates to choose the order in which they take the exams, and the choice is an important one. While only you know what works best for you, the following are some general considerations that many have found to be beneficial:

1. The Building Design/Materials & Methods and Pre-Design divisions are perhaps the broadest of all the divisions. Although this can make them among the most intimidating, taking these divisions early in the process will give a candidate a broad base of knowledge and may prove helpful in preparing for

subsequent divisions. An alternative to this approach is to take these two divisions last, since you will already be familiar with much of their content. This latter approach likely is most beneficial when you take the exam divisions in fairly rapid succession so that details learned while studying for earlier divisions will still be fresh in your mind.

2. The Construction Documents & Services exam covers a broad range of subjects, dealing primarily with the architect's role and responsibilities within the building design and construction team. Because these subjects serve as one of the core foundations of the ARE, it may be advisable to take this division early in the process, as knowledge gained preparing for this exam can help in subsequent divisions.

3. The General Structures and Lateral Forces divisions cover related and overlapping subjects. Take them consecutively, and take General Structures first, since it is broader and addresses fundamental principles necessary for success in Lateral Forces.

4. The three graphic divisions all use an identical software platform and employ similar graphic drawing tools. Because becoming fluent with this software is crucial to passing these exams, take the three graphic divisions sequentially.

5. The Mechanical & Electrical Systems and Building Technology exams cover loosely related material. As such, it is often beneficial to take these two exams consecutively.

6. Take exams that particularly concern you early in the process. NCARB rules prohibit retaking an exam for six months. Therefore, failing an exam early in the process will allow the candidate to use the waiting period to prepare for and take other exams.

EXAM PREPARATION

Overview

There is little argument that preparation is key to passing the ARE. With this in mind, Kaplan has developed a complete learning system for each exam division, including study guides, question-and-answer handbooks, mock exams, and flash cards. The study guides offer a condensed course of study and will best prepare you for the exam when utilized along with the other tools in the learning system. The system is designed to provide you with the general background necessary to pass the exam and to provide an indication of specific content areas that demand additional attention.

In addition to the Kaplan learning system, materials from industry-standard documents may prove useful for the various divisions. Several of these sources are noted in the "Supplementary Study Materials" section below.

Understanding the Field

The study of construction materials and methods is useful to architects in several ways. First, one must be aware of construction industry standards to determine what is safe and practical. Second, one must be able to communicate design ideas, through detailed drawings, to those in the field who will actually perform the work. Finally, one must recognize the limitations of skilled craftsmen while appreciating their ability to translate mere lines on paper into a real building.

In the past several years, building technology has become enormously complex and specialized, and new developments tend toward making past methods obsolete. While keeping up with all recent developments would be unrealistic, the goal should be to gain an understanding of the basic materials used in construction and to learn how these are put together to achieve strong, useful, and beautiful structures.

Understanding the Exam

The Building Design/Materials & Methods exam is among the broadest of all the ARE divisions. Since many of the subjects covered span other divisions, it is widely considered one of the more difficult and intimidating for which to prepare. However, the exam tends to focus on the general principles and properties of common building materials while avoiding specific data and calculations.

Many have found that this division places a particular emphasis on sustainable design, the properties of materials, and definitions of various materials and methods. The Kaplan flash cards should prove especially helpful in mastering the definitions.

Preparation Basics

The first step in preparation should be a review of the exam specifications and reference materials published by NCARB. These statements are available for each of the nine ARE divisions to serve as a guide for preparing for the exam. Download these statements and familiarize yourself with their content. This will help you focus your attention on the subjects on which the exam focuses.

Though no two people will have exactly the same ARE experience, the following are recommended best practices to adopt in your studies and should serve as a guide.

Set aside scheduled study time.
Establish a routine and adopt study strategies that reflect your strengths and mirror your approach in other successful academic pursuits. Most importantly, set aside a definite amount of study time each week, just as if you were taking a lecture course, and carefully read all of the material.

Take—and retake—quizzes.
After studying each lesson in the study guide, take the quiz found at its conclusion. The quiz questions are intended to be straightforward and objective. Answers and explanations can be found at the back of the book. If you answer a question incorrectly, see if you can determine why the correct answer is correct before reading the explanation. Retake the quiz until you answer every question correctly and understand why the correct answers are correct.

Identify areas for improvement.
The quizzes allow you the opportunity to pinpoint areas where you need improvement. Reread and take note of the sections that cover these areas and seek additional information from other sources. Use the question-and-answer handbook and CD-ROM test bank as a final tune-up for the exam.

Take the final exam.
A final exam designed to simulate the ARE follows the last lesson of each study guide. Answers and explanations can be found on the pages following the exam. As with the lesson quizzes, retake the final exam until you answer every question correctly and understand why the correct answers are correct.

Use the flash cards.
If you've purchased the flash cards, go through them once and set aside any terms you know at first glance. Take the rest to work, reviewing them on the train, over lunch, or before bed. Remove cards as you become familiar with their terms until you know all the terms. Review all the cards a final time before taking the exam.

Supplementary Study Materials

In addition to the Kaplan learning system, materials from industry-standard sources may prove useful in your studies. Candidates should consult the list of exam references in the NCARB guidelines for the council's recommendations and pay particular attention to the following publications, which are essential to successfully completing this exam:

- International Code Council (ICC) *International Building Code*
- *Standard on Accessible and Usable Buildings and Facilities* (ICC/ANSI A117.1-98)
- National Fire Protection Association *Life Safety Code* (NFPA 101)
- American Institute of Architects B141-1997 *Standard Form of Agreement Between Owner and Architect*
- American Institute of Architects A201-1997 *General Conditions of the Contract for Construction*
- American Institute of Steel Construction *Manual of Steel Construction: Allowable Stress Design*, Ninth Edition

Test-Taking Advice

Preparation for the exam should include a review of successful test-taking procedures—especially for those who have been out of the classroom for some time. Following is advice to aid in your success.

Pace yourself.

Each division allows candidates at least one minute per question. You should be able to comfortably read and reread each question and fully understand what is being asked before answering.

Read carefully.

Begin each question by reading it carefully and fully reviewing the choices, eliminating those that are obviously incorrect. Interpret language literally, and keep an eye out for negatively worded questions.

Guess.

All unanswered questions are considered incorrect, so answer every question. If you are unsure of the correct answer, select your best guess and/or mark the question for later review. If you continue to be unsure of the answer after returning the question a second time, it is usually best to stick with your first guess.

Review.

The exam allows candidates to review and change answers within the time limit. Utilize this feature to mark troubling questions for review upon completing the rest of the exam.

Reference material.

The General Structures and the Mechanical & Electrical Systems divisions include reference materials accessible through an on-screen icon. These materials include formulas and other reference content that may prove helpful when answering questions in these divisions. Note that candidates may *not* bring reference material with them to the testing center.

Calculator.

Candidates must bring their own calculator to the testing center. Note that only nonprogrammable, noncommunicating, nonprinting calculators are allowed. Candidates will need only a basic scientific calculator with trigonometry functions.

Best answer questions.

Many candidates fall victim to questions seeking the "best" answer. In these cases, it may appear at first glance as though several choices are correct. Remember the importance of reviewing the question carefully and interpreting the language literally. Consider the example below.

Which of these cities is located on the east coast of the United States?

A. Boston

B. Philadelphia

C. Washington, DC

D. Atlanta

At first glance, it may appear that all of the cities could be correct answers. However, if you interpret the question literally, you'll identify the critical phrase as "on the east coast." Although each of the cities listed is arguably an "eastern" city, only Boston sits on the Atlantic coast. All the other choices are located in the eastern part of the country, but are not coastal cities.

ACKNOWLEDGMENTS

This course was written by Caleb Hornbostel, a noted architect, teacher, and author. Mr. Hornbostel has taught at Pratt Institute, Columbia, Cornell, NYU, and Temple University.

The material in Lesson 10 was written by John A. Raeber, FAIA, FCSI, CCS. Mr. Raeber has been teaching classes for this division for 30 years.

The material in Lesson 11 was written by Jonathan Boyer, AIA. Mr. Boyer is a principal of the firm Farr Associates in Chicago, Illinois. He is a graduate of the University of Pennsylvania (BA) and Yale University (MArch). His practice has focused on sustainable design and environmental planning for more than 30 years with projects throughout the United States.

This introduction was written by John F. Hardt, AIA. Mr. Hardt is a principal of the firm Andrews Architects, Inc. in Columbus, Ohio. He is a graduate of Ohio State University (MArch) and has been in practice for more than 12 years.

ABOUT KAPLAN

Thank you for choosing Kaplan AEC Education as your source for ARE preparation materials. Whether helping future professors prepare for the GRE or providing tomorrow's doctors the tools they need to pass the MCAT, Kaplan possesses more than 50 years of experience as a global leader in exam prep and educational publishing. It is that experience and history that Kaplan brings to the world of architectural education, pairing unparalleled resources with acknowledged experts in ARE content areas to bring you the very best in licensure study materials.

Only Kaplan AEC offers a complete catalog of individual products and integrated learning systems to help you pass all nine divisions of the ARE. Kaplan's ARE materials include study guides, mock exams, question-and-answer handbooks, video workshops, and flash cards. Products may be purchased individually or in division-specific learning systems to suit your needs. These systems are designed to help you better focus on essential information for each division, provide flexibility in how you study, and save you money.

To order, please visit *www.KaplanAEC.com* or call (800) 420-1429.

SITE WORK

INTRODUCTION

A building project generally begins with the selection of a particular site. The exact location of the site, as well as its orientation, topography, existing vegetation, and subsoil conditions, all influence the design of the building, including the materials and methods of construction. In some cases, the client may contact the architect with property deed and survey in one hand and the building program in the other hand. At other times, however, the architect may be approached with several alternative sites, each of which satisfies the specific program. In those cases, the architect must examine the choices in order to recommend the site that will best meet the program's requirements.

In order for the architect to make this professional judgment, all potential sites should be verified for satisfactory size, topography, orientation, and access, and the availability of utilities, such as water, electricity, and gas. In addition, the site must be checked for all restrictions imposed by city, state, and federal regulations, such as zoning, easements, and subsurface rights. A final and perhaps most important criterion: one must verify that the soil is adequate to support the intended structure.

The geographical location of the site is most often established by the client. Thus, climatic

SITE CONSIDERATIONS

factors, such as sun, wind, precipitation, and temperature, are matters of fact rather than choice. However, the architect may consider such variables as topography, vegetation, sound, and orientation relative to sun and views. The land forms and ground slopes affect a building's foundation, drainage, and microclimate. Vegetation, too, affects the site's microclimate, as well as its views, solar radiation, and sound travel. Prevailing exterior sounds affect the orientation of the building mass, the choice of materials, and sound control methods employed. Finally, orientation affects solar radiation, natural ventilation, potential views, and ease of access to the site.

SOIL

Soil Composition

The stability of a building depends on the bearing capacity of the soil upon which it sits. The composition of soil is almost infinite in its variety, ranging from bedrock to loose organic material. While rock can easily support the enormous weight of multistory structures (as in midtown Manhattan), loose, wet sand may be incapable of supporting even a small animal unlucky enough to be caught in quicksand.

Soil composition determines a soil's bearing capacity. Soil is formed by the chemical decomposition of rock; water, air, and temperature action on rock; and the decay of vegetable and animal matter. A variety of these processes has resulted in the top layer of the earth's surface. Although the soil composition at a particular site is unique, soil types throughout the world are essentially similar, and they are identified in most soil classifications as bedrock, boulders, decomposed rock, hardpan, gravel, sand, silt, clay, and quicksand, or as mixtures of more than one soil type.

Soil Types

Rock, often referred to as *bedrock*, is the solid material that forms the crust of the earth. It is generally the strongest support for the foundation of a structure. *Slate* and *shale* are fine-textured soft rock. *Boulders* are rock detached from the bedrock of which they were once a part, and *decomposed rock* refers to disintegrated rock masses that were originally solid.

Hardpan is a consolidated mixture of gravel, clay, and sand, and it is a good foundation base for buildings.

Gravel consists of granular rock particles ranging in size from 1/4 inch to 3-1/2 inch. Any rock pieces that are larger are called cobblestones, and if still larger, boulders.

Sand consists of loose granular rock particles about .002 inch to 1/4 inch in size. Sand is neither plastic nor cohesive in its pure state. Sand and gravel are coarse-grained soils that provide an excellent base for building foundations, as well as excellent drainage properties, as they are relatively permeable.

Silt is a fine-grained sedimentary material deposited from running water. It is .002 inch or less in particle size. When mixed with water, it forms a soft, plastic, sticky material known as mud.

Clay is a fine-grained, firm cohesive material formed from the decomposition and hydration of certain rock. Clay is plastic when wet and relatively hard when dry. Clay is relatively impervious, and it may swell when it absorbs water and shrink when it dries, making it the least stable and predictable soil for the support of buildings. Clays and silts may provide satisfactory support for building foundations, but they require careful investigation.

Quicksand is a mixture of sand and moving water that is completely unsuitable for construction and a danger to any object falling, stepping, or resting on its surface.

Below is a table of allowable soil pressures reproduced from the Uniform Building Code (UBC). Soil bearing values from other sources are similar.

SOIL EXPLORATION AND TESTING

To understand a site's soil conditions, the architect generally requests a subsurface exploration of the site. Unless the entire site is

TABLE 18-I-A — ALLOWABLE FOUNDATION AND LATERAL PRESSURE

CLASS OF MATERIALS[1]	ALLOWABLE FOUNDATION PRESSURE (psf)[2] × 0.0479 for kPa	LATERAL BEARING LBS./SQ./FT./FT. OF DEPTH BELOW NATURAL GRADE[3] × 0.157 for kPa per meter	LATERAL SLIDING[4] Coefficient[5]	Resistance (psf)[6] × 0.0479 for kPa
1. Massive crystalline bedrock	4,000	1,200	.70	
2. Sedimentary and foliated rock	2,000	400	.35	
3. Sandy gravel and/or gravel (GW and GP)	2,000	200	.35	
4. Sand, silty sand, clayey sand, silty gravel and clayey gravel (SW, SP, SM, SC, GM and GC)	1,500	150	.25	
5. Clay, sandy clay, silty clay and clayey silt (CL, ML, MH and CH)	1,000[7]	100		130

[1]For soil classifications OL, OH and PT (i.e., organic clays and peat), a foundation investigation shall be required.
[2]All values of allowable foundation pressure are for footings having a minimum width of 12 inches (305 mm) and a minimum depth of 12 inches (305 mm) into natural grade. Except as in Footnote 7 below, increase of 20 percent allowed for each additional foot (305 mm) of width or depth to a maximum value of three times the designated value.
[3]May be increased the amount of the designated value for each additional foot (305 mm) of depth to a maximum of 15 times the designated value. Isolated poles for uses such as flagpoles or signs and poles used to support buildings which are not adversely affected by a 1/2-inch (13 mm) motion at ground surface due to short-term lateral loads may be designed using lateral bearing values equal to two times the tabulated values.
[4]Lateral bearing and lateral sliding resistance may be combined.
[5]Coefficient to be multiplied by the dead load.
[6]Lateral sliding resistance value to be multiplied by the contact area. In no case shall the lateral sliding resistance exceed one half the dead load.
[7]No increase for width is allowed.

Reprinted from *Uniform Building Code,* copyright International Conference of Building Officials, Whittier, California, 1997. All rights reserved.

an obvious outcrop of rock, guesswork is not advisable. More than one architect has excavated through firm-looking material only to discover alluvial silt or uncompacted fill extending down 10 or 20 feet or more.

There are a variety of soil exploration methods in common use, each of which may be appropriate, depending on the location, topography, depth of water table, and particularly on the magnitude of the structural loads anticipated. The test pit and soil load tests are two relatively uncomplicated methods that offer immediate results. Other tests that rely on boring into the earth include auger borings, wash borings, core borings, and dry sample borings.

Test Pits

Test pits are simple excavations that permit direct visual inspection of the actual soil conditions. Open pits allow close-up examination of the soil layers, as well as access to undisturbed samples for further laboratory testing. Excavating test pits to any substantial depth is costly, and they are generally not dug below the water table.

Soil Load Tests

Soil load tests employing a loading platform are empirical in nature and as old as the art of foundation design. A platform is erected on the site and incremental loads are applied; each load increment is maintained until the settlement becomes negligible for a period of several hours. The test continues until the measured settlement becomes regular under subsequent loadings. The total test load is usually double the contemplated design load.

Borings

Auger borings are designed to bring up soil samples by means of an ordinary 2- or

LOADING PLATFORM

The auger usually stops at the first obstruction, which may be rock, hardpan, or the stump of a tree. This method is most effective in sand or clay and for depths not exceeding 50 feet.

Wash borings are useful in locating bedrock when the soil is too compact to use an auger. These borings are made with a two- to four-inch diameter pipe that is driven into the soil and contains a smaller jet pipe through which water is forced. The material washed up is often thoroughly mixed, thus reducing the dependability of the samples. Another problem in the use of wash borings is that boulders may be mistaken for bedrock. This system can penetrate all other materials, however, and the test can be extended downward 100 feet or more.

Core borings are more costly than most other methods, but they are the most reliable. They can penetrate through all materials, to great depths, and bring up complete cores of the material through which they pass. Core borings are made with a diamond drill that is sufficiently hard to cut through rock. The results of these borings are usually recorded, according to standard practices, in a test boring log book, shown on page 6.

Dry sample borings utilize a drive pipe with a special split sampling pipe at the tip instead of a drill. The sampling pipe is driven down approximately five inches, then lifted out, and the contents removed and stored. Soil samples are taken every five inches, and the removed soil is tested in a laboratory.

With each of the methods above, it is important to check a sufficient number of locations over the building area in order to determine the depth and extent of good bearing material. For large structures, a site plan with the building outline is often used by a structural engineer to indicate the number, size, and location of the test borings to be made. Soil analysis is performed by a soils engineer or agency that is generally subject to approval by the local building department.

Soil Properties

Some properties for which soil may be tested include the following:

Specific gravity, to determine void ratio.

Grain size (for granular soils), to estimate permeability, frost action, compaction, and shear strength.

Grain shape, to estimate shear strength.

Liquid and plastic limits (in cohesive soils), to obtain compressibility and compaction values.

Water content (in cohesive soils), to obtain compressibility and compaction values.

Void ratio, to determine compressibility.

Unconfined compression (in cohesive soils), to estimate shear strength.

Based on the field exploration and laboratory tests, a written soils report is prepared in which the soils engineer recommends the type of foundation to be used and the allowable soil bearing pressure.

SOIL AND SITE PROBLEMS

There are enough problems on the earth's crust to ruin the good night's sleep of many an architect. These soil problems may involve inadequate bearing capacity, subsurface water, shrinkage, slippage, and—in some parts of the country—unpredictable earth movement due to seismic forces. Architects like to think of the earth as stable, just as clients prefer to think of their buildings as immovable; the fact is, however, that neither is permanently fixed forever.

Settlement

Settlement of buildings must be carefully considered, except when the structure's foundations are on solid bedrock where little or no settlement can occur. As dead load is added to the structure, it compresses the soil beneath the footings, reducing the void volume and causing settlement.

A slight amount of settlement that is uniform throughout the structure is of little concern. However, uneven or *differential settlement* may cause serious cracks or even failures. While a building is under construction, constant checking with surveying instruments should be performed to note any settlement and make certain that it is uniform.

TYPICAL PAGE FROM TEST BORING LOG BOOK		

BORING LOG NO. 5

Drilling date: September 10, 1997   Elevation: 597

DEPTH IN FEET	DESIGNATION	DESCRIPTION
1	GM	FILL: Silty Gravel, dark grey-brown, very moist, loose
	GM	ALLUVIUM: Silty Gravel, light grey-brown, moist, medium dense
	SC	Clayey Sand layer, light grey-brown, moist, dense, porous
5	GM	continues Silty Gravel, coarser, drier 2' diameter boulder
10	GC	WEATHERED BEDROCK: Clayey gravel, light brown, damp, very dense, grades to Slate Bedrock at 10 feet
		End at 10.0 feet No water, no caving

Note: The designations GM, SC, etc. are standard classification symbols that are in general use. For example, GM indicates silty gravel, or a gravel-sand-silt mixture.

INADEQUATE BEARING   SUB-SURFACE WATER   SEISMIC FORCES

SOIL PROBLEMS

For a number of reasons, settlement may continue for several years after a building is completed. Some soils take a long time to consolidate, the moisture content of the soil may change, or movement may occur within the earth itself.

Frost Action

In cold climates, the freezing and subsequent thawing of soil may cause the ground to heave. This places stress on a building's foundation, which can lead to serious damage.

The extent of frost action depends on the soil type and geographic location. In all areas subject to frost action, footings must be placed at least one foot below the *frost line*, which is the depth below which the soil does not freeze. Frost line levels vary throughout the country, ranging from zero in San Diego to more than six feet in Fargo, North Dakota.

Earth Movement

Earth movement is a prevalent condition with clay subsoils, as clay may swell when wet and shrink when dried. Near the surface, where variations in moisture are common, there may be considerable earth movement. At a depth of about five feet, however, movement will be slight. Thus, serious structural problems can result where some footings are close to the ground surface and other footings are quite deep.

The moisture content of clay may be affected by an adjacent excavation. This could cause settlement or slippage of the subsurface clay, either of which can lead to serious damage. Sloping layers of earth may also cause problems, as they tend to move as a mass when subjected to excessive rain or moisture. Evidence of this phenomenon can be seen in older structures that have a slight tilt, or in rows of sloping power poles.

SOIL DRAINAGE

Many severe soil problems are caused by the presence of moisture, both at and below grade. The presence of moisture can lead to reduction of a soil's load bearing capacity, leakage of water into a building, or disintegration of certain building materials. Therefore, the location of subsurface water and the control of surface water must both be considered prior to beginning any construction.

Water Table

The level below which all soil is saturated with ground water is known as the water table. In general, the water table roughly follows the ground surface, but its level may fluctuate because of seasonal variations, precipitation, or developmental changes on the ground surface, such as paving a large parking area.

In practice, building foundations should be located well above the site's water table to avoid potential damage from hydrostatic pressure or capillary action. In addition, subsurface water should be diverted away from the foundation by means of a drain tile system. Drainage tiles have a minimum diameter of six inches and are laid in gravel, or another kind of porous bed, at least six inches below the lowest floor slab. Open joints between tiles should be covered with wire screening to prevent clogging, and then covered by coarse gravel or stone backfill.

Slabs on grade not subject to hydrostatic pressure are often placed over a gravel fill several inches thick, which prevents water from being drawn into the slab by capillary action.

In place of solid pipes laid with open joints, round or half-round drainage tiles with perforations on the bottom may be used.

TOPSOIL

WALL

FINE GRAVEL

WATERSTOP

SLAB

COARSE GRAVEL

DRAIN TILE

FOOTING

6" MIN.

DRAINAGE TILE INSTALLATION

A preformed *waterstop* may be used between the slab on grade and the foundation wall to seal the joint against water penetration.

Drainage

Drainage of surface water involves directing water away from all structures. This is accomplished by grading or shaping the contours of the site to provide a gradual transition from high to low elevations. Gutters, flumes, berms, and the gentle warp of paved surfaces collect and conduct water to yard drains, catch basins, and underground storm drainage lines from which it is finally discharged.

SOIL MODIFICATION

Soil can be altered in a variety of ways in order to improve its consistency, dependability, and bearing capacity. Under normal conditions, bearing capacity may be increased by simply deepening or increasing the bearing area of the footing. Drainage is another common method used to improve the physical characteristics of soil, especially where the soil is affected by subterranean water flow.

If the subsoil is unusually soft or contains organic fill, the undesirable material should be removed and replaced with compacted granular materials. If this excavation and replacement process is too costly, other methods of soil consolidation may be used. For example, a compressible soil can be improved by covering it with a porous layer of sand, gravel, or crushed rock and blending it into the natural material. Thus, hardpan-type soil material can be artificially produced.

Because density of soil is a rough measure of its strength, soil improvement often involves a reduction in the void volume. This can be achieved by adding a compacted layer of cinders or ash, by subsurface drainage, or by the ancient method of using a large number of short piles in the ground to compress the upper layer of the earth.

Soils may also be compacted by the use of heavy machinery, such as sheepsfoot rollers. In such cases, the control of density can be critical. Overcompaction will improve soil strength, but it may produce an unstable structure within the soil, resulting in serious heaving of the earth.

All soil modification methods intended to increase load-bearing capacity should be reviewed by the local building department prior to starting any work.

SITE PREPARATION

Prior to construction, a site must be cleared of all undesirable materials. These might include existing structures that must be demolished, their footings and foundation walls, and existing utility lines that must be disconnected, capped, or relocated.

Plant material that is to remain undisturbed must be protected. Other vegetation must be removed, and root systems and tree stumps must be completely dug out, or grubbed, because in time they will decay and leave undesirable voids in the ground.

Corner stakes, placed in the ground to locate building lines, may be moved or lost when the excavation begins. Therefore, batter boards, which are offset from the building line, are often used instead. The structure is thus located by means of strings or wires stretched between batter boards, shown below.

BATTER BOARD
STRING LINES
NAIL
PLUMB LINE
EXCAVATION LINE
BUILDING LINE

BATTER BOARDS

Before grading begins, the top six inches or so of soil (topsoil) are removed and stockpiled on the site. At the conclusion of construction, this topsoil is spread over the area as a final landscape base, which forms the finish grade. On sites where the topsoil is not worth saving, such material may have to be imported at the end of construction.

EARTHWORK

Earthwork consists of all grading work, including excavation, rough grading, and finish grading.

Excavation

Excavation is the removal of existing soil to permit construction of the foundation and substructure. Excavation may be performed by hand or more generally by machines, and includes the digging of basements, trenching for footings, and all other required removal of soil.

Permanently cut slopes should not exceed a slope of 1-1/2 horizontal to 1 vertical, and permanently filled slopes should be no steeper than 2 to 1, unless substantiated by soil tests or geological data. A cubic yard of earth weighs more than a ton, and therefore unstable earth slopes represent a danger that must be avoided or corrected.

Grading

Grading is the alteration of a site's contours, usually by means of power equipment. *Rough grading* is the addition or removal of earth prior to the start of construction. *Finish grading* is the final distribution of earth at the conclusion of construction. It is generally a more precise operation and may include the placement of topsoil for landscaping. Finish grades are usually accurate to within one inch and represent the final shaping of a site's contours.

Backfill

Backfill is earth that is replaced around a foundation or retaining wall after the concrete forms have been removed. Backfill material should be deposited in layers 6 to 12 inches in depth and thoroughly tamped and compacted to

EXISTING TOPSOIL

ROUGH GRADING

FINISHED GRADE

6" MIN. TOPSOIL

NEW BUILDING

EXISTING GRADE

ROUGH GRADING

FINISHED GRADE

EXCAVATION FOR FOOTINGS, FOUNDATIONS, AND SUB-STRUCTURE OF NEW BUILDING

BACKFILL AFTER FOOTINGS AND FOUNDATIONS HAVE BEEN INSTALLED

EXCAVATION, ROUGH AND FINISH GRADING, AND BACKFILL

avoid settlement. Backfill used over drain lines should be devoid of rock or other material that could crack or displace tiles. It should also be free of any debris that might later disintegrate and form voids.

FOUNDATIONS

The *foundation* of a building is the part of its structure that transmits the building's loads to the soil, while *footings* are those parts of a foundation that are widened to spread the load over a large area of soil.

In every case, the load of a building must not exceed the safe bearing capacity of the underlying soil, in order to avoid distress such as settlement cracks, uneven structural movement, or even failure of the structure.

Shallow Foundations

If the soils close to the ground are of adequate strength, the most economical foundation system generally consists of shallow spread footings, of which there are several basic types. A *column footing* is a square or rectangular pad of concrete that spreads the column load over a sufficiently large area so that the bearing capacity of the soil is not exceeded. A *wall footing* is a continuous spread footing that serves the same purpose under a wall. When a column footing abuts the property line, a *combined footing* or a *cantilever footing* may be used that connects the exterior column footing to the first interior column footing. A *mat footing* is essentially one large footing under the entire building that distributes the load over the entire building area. Also called a *raft foundation*, it is used when soil conditions are poor. A *boat footing* is similar to a mat footing, except that it is placed at a depth such that the weight of the soil

PAD IS CENTERED
UNDER COLUMN

COLUMN FOOTING

EXTERIOR
COLUMN

1ST INTERIOR
COLUMN

PROP.
LINE

COMBINED FOOTING

FOOTING IS
CENTERED
UNDER WALL

WALL FOOTING

EXTERIOR
COLUMN

1ST INTERIOR
COLUMN

PROP.
LINE

COLUMN
FOOTINGS

CONCRETE BEAM (STRAP)

CANTILEVER FOOTING

removed from the excavation is equal to the load of the building, and thus little or no new load is added to the underlying soil.

Deep Foundations

If the upper soils have insufficient bearing capacity to support spread footings, the building loads are often transmitted to deeper, firmer soils by *piles*, which are driven into the ground.

A pile may transfer the load to the soil by skin friction between the pile and the surrounding soil, or by end bearing, where the load is supported by the rock or firm subsoil under the pile tip.

Piles may be made of wood, steel, concrete, or a composite of two materials. The choice of pile material depends primarily on the size of the load and the presence of moisture, with its potential for deterioration. Concrete piles are generally most suitable under all conditions, particularly where permanence is a factor.

Piles are driven into the earth by steam, air, or diesel hammers that drop from one to four feet. Piles may also be jetted into place with high-pressure water jets, but this method, because of the danger of overexcavating, is rarely advised. In driving a pile, care must be taken with respect to position, alignment, and possible drift, so that its predetermined location in the ground relative

THE TOTAL LOAD OF
THE BUILDING MUST
BE LESS THAN THE
BEARING CAPACITY
OF SOIL

MAT FOOTING
USED FOR HEAVY LOADS AND
LOW BEARING SOIL CAPACITY

BOAT FOOTING
USED IN AREAS OF LOW
BEARING SOIL CAPACITY

Caissons and Cofferdams

Box-like structures used where very wet or soft soils are encountered are also called caissons. They provide a method of constructing foundations below water level, and may be formed from timber; steel (sheet piling); or concrete. Excavation is performed within the caisson. For bridge piers or similar construction located in water, the entire area is surrounded with watertight sheet piling, the water is pumped out, and the foundations are then constructed. Such an installation is known as a cofferdam.

TEMPORARY SUPPORTS

During the construction of a foundation, it is often necessary to provide temporary support, or shoring, for excavated earth or existing structures. This is commonly achieved by means of sheeting, bracing, and/or underpinning.

Sheeting is a temporary wall of wood, steel, or precast concrete to retain the soil around an excavation.

to other piles and its verticality are both kept within tolerable limits.

The safe carrying capacity of a pile can be determined by pile-driving formulas, static pile formulas, or pile load tests, which are the most dependable.

Another type of deep foundation is a vertical shaft drilled into the ground and then filled with concrete. If it transmits its load to the soil by skin friction, it often is called a *drilled pile*. If it transfers the load by end bearing, it is called a *drilled caisson*. Frequently the bottom of the shaft is enlarged, or belled, to form a larger bearing area. Drilled piles and caissons sometimes require a steel casing, which is removed as the concrete is poured.

TYPES OF PILING

A *slurry wall* is a type of sheeting in which a narrow trench is filled with a slurry, or soupy mixture, of bentonite clay and water, which resists the pressure of the earth. After the trench excavation is completed, reinforcing steel is lowered into the trench, concrete is placed from the bottom up, and the slurry is pumped out. The site is now excavated, and the reinforced concrete wall is tied back as the excavation progresses to resist the earth pressure.

Bracing is used to brace the sheeting to resist the soil pressure. One common method is the use of diagonal braces called *rakers*.

However, rakers interfere with the excavation process. Therefore, where soil conditions permit, tiebacks into the surrounding soil or rock can be used in place of rakers, thus keeping the excavation clear and more accessible.

Underpinning is employed to support existing foundations or walls being extended downward to the level of a new, deeper foundation. The two most common methods of underpinning involve *needle beams* or pipe cylinders with hydraulic jacks.

PILING CHART	
Type of Pile	**Remarks**
1. Wood	Must be below permanent ground water level
2. Precast concrete	Round, square, or octagonal, often prestressed
3. Cast-in-place concrete	Driven with mandrel core, removed before pouring
4. Concrete-filled steel pipe	Driven with sealed tip, then filled with concrete
5. Structural steel	For dense earth and heavy loads—H section
6. Sheet piling	May be used as a water dam

DRILLED PILE

DRILLED & BELLED CAISSON

NEEDLING

SITE IMPROVEMENTS

Site work invariably involves many kinds of improvements that are not part of the structure. These include roads and walks, fences, walls, lighting, and other such common landscape features. Roads and parking areas are most frequently constructed from concrete, which is discussed in the following lesson, or from asphalt, which is discussed below.

Asphalt Paving

Asphalt paving is a term that encompasses several bituminous paving products, all of which derive from asphaltic petroleum. Asphalt is applied, either hot or cold, in a single layer over a prepared foundation. A sub-base course of crushed stone or gravel is covered by a base course of finer aggregate. After rolling and tamping, the final asphalt surface is applied, two to three inches in thickness, depending on the amount of wear expected. The surface drainage of asphalt paved surfaces is critical, for even the slightest depression will result in unsightly and harmful ponding of water. Following are several types of asphalt paving in common use:

Asphaltic concrete consists of asphalt cement and graded aggregates, proportioned and mixed in a plant, transported to the site, spread over a firm foundation, and rolled while still hot.

Cold laid asphalt is the same as asphaltic concrete, except cold liquid asphalt and aggregates are used.

Asphalt macadam begins with a base of crushed stone, gravel, or slag compacted to a smooth surface. It is then sprayed with asphalt emulsion or hot asphalt cement in controlled quantities, covered with fine aggregate, and finally rolled until the smaller aggregate fills the voids in the coarse aggregate.

Other Paving Materials

Paving materials other than concrete or asphalt are used principally for pedestrian walks and may include brick, stone cobbles, granite setts, and flagstones.

Brick paving is a very popular and durable surface for pedestrian traffic. The material can be laid over a sand or cement/sand bed, but it is far more permanent when laid on a concrete slab foundation. Smooth bricks or bricks that are often wet may become slippery underfoot; this disadvantage, however, may be overcome to some extent with proper drainage.

Stone cobbles are mainly used for decorative effect. The best cobbles are rounded river-bed stones, from two to four inches in diameter, that are closely set in cement mortar. Cobbles can be set in a variety of patterns or in a random fashion.

Granite setts are small, rectangular or square blocks of granite that are set in a cement mortar to produce a very durable paved surface. Many years ago, city streets were often paved in this manner, but due to their high cost, granite setts are used today only in small areas and mainly for decorative purposes.

Flagstones refer to thin slabs of slate, bluestone, or soapstone. They are available with various

BRICK BASKET WEAVE

BRICK HERRINGBONE

RUNNING BOND BRICK

FLAGSTONES WITH ALL FACES SAWED & SQUARED

FLAGSTONES WITH ONLY TWO EDGES SAWED

FLAGSTONES WITH NO SIDES SAWED (RANDOM SHAPES)

PAVING PATTERNS

surface textures, rough to smooth, and in various colors. Flagstones are installed over a sand bed or with mortar on a concrete slab.

Grade Changing Devices

Grade changing devices are the means by which earth is shaped or retained in order to modify the finish grade of a site. The most obvious device, of course, is a concrete or masonry retaining wall. In addition, however, there are other devices in common use, some of which are illustrated below.

MASONRY OR CONCRETE
RETAINING WALL

CONCRETE OR STONE
BATTERED WALL

CRIBBING

STONE RIPRAP

METHODS TO ACCOMMODATE VERTICAL
GRADE CHANGES

LESSON 1 QUIZ

1. Which of the following will most effectively divert subsurface water away from a building's foundation?

    A. Place the foundation below the water table

    B. Modify the contours of the site during finish grading

    C. Install drainage tiles adjacent to the bottom of footings

    D. Provide a bed of coarse gravel at the perimeter of the foundation

2. Underpinning an existing wall might involve

    A. cribbing.

    B. needle beams.

    C. cofferdams.

    D. sheet piling.

3. If the loads of a proposed structure are high relative to the bearing capacity of the soil, one would likely provide

    A. a mat footing.

    B. continuous wall footings.

    C. combined footings.

    D. shallow spread footings.

4. A system of piles may be appropriate for supporting a structure when

    A. moisture in the soil is detected.

    B. the piles can be placed below ground water level.

    C. dense earth makes conventional excavation difficult.

    D. the surface soil has low bearing capacity.

5. Asphalt paving should generally be applied

    A. in no less than a four-inch thickness.

    B. over an aggregate base.

    C. in small sections separated by dividing joints.

    D. while hot, as it is more durable than cold-laid asphalt.

6. Frost line refers to the level of earth

    A. at which the soil bearing value is affected by weather.

    B. at which the building foundation should be located.

    C. below which the footings will not freeze.

    D. below which the soil does not freeze.

7. In what sequence are the following construction procedures generally performed?

    I.   Excavate for footings

    II. Stockpile topsoil

    III. Grub roots

    IV. Erect batter boards

    V.   Rough grade

    A. III, II, V, IV, I

    B. V, II, III, IV, I

    C. III, V, II, I, IV

    D. II, III, V, I, IV

8. For a structure with very heavy loads resting on dense earth, which of the following would be most appropriate?

   A. Boat footings

   B. Jetted piles

   C. Wood piles

   D. Structural steel piles

9. Placing load on a footing results in

   A. reduced soil bearing capacity.

   B. differential settlement.

   C. a reduction of the soil's void volume.

   D. shrinkage of the soil.

10. The principal purpose of all soil exploration and testing is to determine

    A. the bearing capacity of the soil.

    B. the intrinsic character of the soil.

    C. the depth of the water table.

    D. the depth of the bedrock.

CONCRETE

INTRODUCTION

Concrete is a manufactured construction material that is a mixture of fine aggregate (sand); coarse aggregate (gravel or crushed rock); portland cement; and water.

The aggregates in concrete are the inert ingredients, while cement and water are the active ingredients. The aggregates, usually sand and gravel, are first mixed thoroughly with the cement. As water is added, a chemical reaction takes place between the water and cement that creates heat and causes the concrete to harden.

It is this chemical reaction, called *hydration*, rather than the drying out of the mix, that causes hardening of the concrete. In fact, during the curing process, concrete must be kept moist for satisfactory hydration of the cement. Confirmation of this chemical process is the fact that concrete will harden just as well under water as in the air.

TYPES OF THIN-SHELL AND RIGID FRAME CONCRETE FORMS

The use of concrete as a building material has greatly increased in recent years to a point where all types of structures, from simple bus shelters to multistory buildings, are constructed from essentially this one material. Concrete is used for foundations, floors, columns, walls, beams, and roofs, for precast panels in floors and walls, in thin-shell structures, in rigid frames, in decorative cast shapes, and for bricks and blocks that are used in concrete masonry construction. Concrete, it would appear, is a material for all purposes and all times.

BACKGROUND

More than 2,000 years ago, in some ancient province, a Roman citizen mixed slaked lime with pozzolana (volcanic ash), added stone and water, and thus created the world's first concrete. The development was very likely an accident, and the material was, by today's standards, relatively primitive. However, the discovery of concrete changed the shape of the ancient world, and after 20 centuries, it

continues to influence the appearance of our world today.

The Romans admired concrete for many of the same reasons that we continue to do so today. First of all, it is a material that can be used almost anywhere, as the basic ingredients are virtually universal. Secondly, it requires a minimum of highly skilled labor to prepare and place. Finally, concrete is as strong as natural stone, it is durable and resistant to exposure, and the design of its final shape is unusually flexible, limited only by the designer's imagination and the ability of workers to construct the required formwork. The hundreds of monumental Roman structures that survive today confirm the durability and ancient popularity of this remarkable material.

After the fall of the Roman Empire, the knowledge of concrete construction was either lost or more likely abandoned by subsequent civilizations, which had neither the manpower nor inclination to build in the Roman fashion. The technology of the Industrial Revolution, however, changed that outlook. In 1824, portland cement became a manufactured product, and the result was readily available cement that was cheap, strong, and uniform. However, as concrete by itself has virtually no tensile strength, there were numerous European experiments with *ferroconcrete*, in which iron reinforcement was embedded in the concrete to provide the needed tensile strength. By 1900, reinforced concrete had come into widespread use nearly everywhere. Concrete remains today one of the most important materials in the world of construction.

COMPOSITION OF CONCRETE

Cement

Any adhesive substance capable of uniting non-adhesive materials is called cement. In concrete construction, that substance is portland cement, the most widely used cement in existence.

Portland cement is manufactured from lime, silica, iron oxide, and alumina. The ingredients are properly proportioned, ground, and burned to form clinkers, which are then pulverized to produce cement. This final step is strictly controlled, as the fineness of grinding has a direct bearing on the strength of the cement. Portland cement hardens by reacting to water. The two materials first form a paste that loses its plasticity as it begins to set. The initial set occurs within an hour, and the final set takes about ten hours. The cement continues to harden, however, over a long period of time. Cement paste is the chemically active ingredient in concrete, and is referred to as the matrix.

The table below summarizes the various types of portland cement used in building construction.

Aggregates

Aggregates are the chemically inert ingredients that are combined with cement and water to make concrete. Aggregates affect the quality of the concrete, reduce shrinkage of the concrete, and serve as a filler, for economy.

Aggregates are classified by size: *fine aggregate* (usually sand) is material 1/4 inch or less in diameter, while *coarse aggregate* (gravel or crushed rock) varies in size from 1/4 to 1-1/2 inches in diameter. For economy, concrete used in massive structures, such as dams, may contain natural stones or rocks ranging up to six inches in size.

The general requirement for natural aggregates is that they should be hard, durable, clean, and free from any harmful matter which would adversely affect the concrete mix. Bank-run gravel aggregates consist of completely rounded shapes that vary in strength, whereas crushed rock aggregates consist of irregular and

Portland Cement	Type of Concrete	Primary Use
Type I	Standard	For general all-purpose use
Type II	Modified	For slow setting and less heat
Type III	High Early Strength	For quick setting and early strength
Type IV	Low Heat	For very slow setting (little heat)
Type V	Sulfate Resisting	For alkaline water and soils

LARGE
AGGREGATE
(ECONOMICAL)

SMALL
AGGREGATE
(LESS
ECONOMICAL)

LARGE + SMALL
AGGREGATE
(MOST
ECONOMICAL)

AGGREGATE COMBINATIONS

angular shapes, the strength of which is consistent with the type of rock that is crushed. Irregular or angular-shaped particles are preferred for maximum strength, as water-rounded pebbles may not bond properly with the cement paste. Rounded particles, on the other hand, require less cement paste and improve workability. Most important, the grading of aggregates (the distribution of particle sizes) is critical to a proper mix.

A concrete mix is basically composed of large, coarse aggregate particles between which smaller and finer particles are fitted until all the voids in the mixture are as solidly filled as possible. This requires predetermined percentages of particle sizes, implemented by various sieve tests. Ultimately, when the cement paste is added to a well-graded aggregate mixture, each particle is coated with the paste and forever bonded to the adjacent particles.

The maximum aggregate size should be no greater than 1/3 the thickness of concrete slabs, or 3/4 of the minimum space between reinforcing bars.

Admixtures

Sometimes, materials other than portland cement, water, and aggregates are added to concrete mixes to alter certain characteristics or to achieve some special qualities. These materials are called admixtures, some of which are listed in the table on the following page. In addition to those listed, there are also surface applications or finishes for concrete, which include hardeners, pigments, special aggregates, sealers, abrasives, and fillers for patching. (See later discussion on finishes.) Some portland cements are manufactured with admixtures as part of the cement, such as air-entraining agents, accelerators, and retarders.

CONCRETE MIX DESIGN

Proportioning

The proportioning of the ingredients that comprise concrete is referred to as the *mix*. It involves determining the optimum combination of ingredients to produce concrete that is workable, economical, and has the required strength and other properties when hardened. To satisfy these requirements, several trial mixes may be prepared in which relative amounts of ingredients are varied until the optimum proportions are determined.

The unit of volume for concrete is the cubic foot, and ordinary concrete weighs about 150 pounds per cubic foot. A standard sack of portland cement contains one cubic foot and weighs 94 pounds.

Aggregates are measured either by weight or volume (dry sand and gravel weigh about 100 pounds per cubic foot), and water is measured by the gallon, which weighs about 8 pounds.

For small, relatively uncontrolled concrete work, the mix is generally expressed by volume. For example, a 1:3:5 mix consists of one part cement; three parts fine aggregate (sand); and five parts coarse aggregate (crushed rock or bank-run gravel).

Type of Admixture	Ingredients	Principal Use
Accelerators	Calcium chloride	Speed up setting time
Air-entraining agents	Resins, fats, and oils	Resist freezing action
Retarders	Starches, sugars, and acids	Slow down setting time
Waterproofing	Stearate compounds	Decrease permeability
Water-reducing	Organic compounds	Reduce water content
Workability agents	Powdered silicas and lime	Improve workability

Water-Cement Ratio

A number of factors are important in concrete mix design, including the grading and proportioning of aggregates. But perhaps most important is the water-cement ratio. This ratio, expressed as the number of gallons of water for each sack of cement, is the major factor controlling concrete strength, and to a large extent, its durability. Maximum strength is obtained by using the minimum amount of water required to complete hydration of the cement, but a mix of this type would be too dry and unworkable. Thus, a plastic or workable mix always contains more water than the amount needed to attain maximum strength. In other words, concrete strength decreases as the extra water required for workability increases.

The optimum water-cement ratio provides the minimum amount of cement paste that will coat each aggregate particle and fill all voids while providing the required concrete strength and adequate workability. Excess water not only reduces the concrete's strength and durability, but it may also produce *laitance*, which is a chalky surface deposit of low strength. If laitance does appear, it must be removed before any new concrete is poured, in order for the new concrete to bond to the old.

Strength

The compressive strength of concrete always refers to its strength 28 days after being placed. Concrete develops a wide range of compressive strength values, depending primarily on the water-cement ratio. For example, a mix using about seven gallons of water for each sack of cement will develop a compressive strength of about 3,000 psi after 28 days. While it is possible to obtain concrete with a compressive strength of 10,000 psi or greater, the usual range for structural concrete is 3,000 to 6,000 psi, with values around 4,000 psi being the most common. High-early-strength concrete can develop a compressive strength in 7 to 14 days equal to that developed by normal concrete in 28 days.

MIXING

All concrete should be thoroughly mixed until it is uniform in appearance and all ingredients are evenly distributed. For small jobs, concrete may be mixed at the job site, but this method is slow, relatively imprecise, and generally not recommended for quantities in excess of a few cubic yards. More commonly, concrete is mixed in a plant, a truck, or a combination of both.

Ready-mixed concrete is mixed completely at a central mixing plant and transported to the building site in an agitator truck with a revolving chamber. Ordinarily this type of concrete must be placed within one and a half hours after water is added to the mix. Therefore, jobs using ready-mixed concrete are limited to those relatively close to the mixing plant.

Transit-mixed concrete is mixed completely in a truck mixer. The dry materials are picked up at a central plant and placed in a mixer truck that carries a water tank. The mixer continues to revolve the dry mix while en route to the site; after arrival, water is added and mixed, and the concrete is deposited.

The transit-mix truck may also pick up the concrete at the plant in a partially mixed state and complete the mixing in the truck.

FORMWORK

Forms are the molds into which the concrete is placed and held in shape until it has hardened and developed sufficient strength to support its own weight. Formwork may be job-constructed or prefabricated units of standard lumber, plywood, metal, fiberboard, paper pulp, or a variety of reinforced synthetics.

FORMWORK FOR WALL

4'-0" x 8'-0" PLYWOOD FORMS   FORM TIE HOLES

DESIGN FEATURE OF FORM TIE HOLES

The most important requirement for all formwork is that it be strong and stiff enough to support the considerable weight and fluid pressure of wet concrete. Forms must also be tight so that there will be no significant loss of cement paste. Finally, as the plastic concrete will take on the shape, texture, and peculiarities of the forming material, the choice of formwork should be carefully considered from the standpoint of aesthetics.

SLAB AND BEAM FORM
(VIEWED FROM BELOW)

PANELS

WEDGES

BOLT

YOKE

COLUMN FORM

CONCRETE

FORMS

STEEL FORMS FOR
WAFFLE PATTERN CEILING

FORM

REMOVED FORMS
AND 2" X 4" FORM STUDS

2" X 4"
FORM
STUDS

CONSTRUCTION
REMOVED

WALER

FLAT STRAP
(BREAK OFF)

SHE-BOLT TIE
(SCREW OFF)

PULL-OUT TIE
(BREAK OFF)

CONSTRUCTION
REMOVED

2" X 4" FORM
STUDS AND FORM

REMOVED DRIVE
WEDGES, WALER, 2" X 4"
FORM STUDS, AND FORM
BOARDS

WIRE TIE
(TWIST OFF)

HE-BOLT TIE
(SCREW OFF)

DRIVE-WEDGE TIE
(SAW OFF)

FORM TIES

Form ties are metal devices used to prevent concrete forms from spreading. The location of form ties is an important design factor in wall surface appearance, as shown in the illustration on page 24.

Forms, or parts of forms, are often omitted where there is a firm earth surface capable of supporting or molding the concrete. In footings, for example, the bottom of the footing is generally cast directly against the undisturbed earth and only the sides are molded in forms.

Before concrete is placed, the forms are usually coated with a suitable oil or other material to prevent water absorption or bond between the form and the concrete. Excessive oiling should be avoided, however, as it may permanently stain the concrete or otherwise interfere with the final concrete finish. It is important that the oil or other coating material be applied to the forms before setting the steel reinforcement in order to avoid accidental coating of the steel, which would prevent satisfactory bonding between the concrete and steel.

All formwork is expensive, often representing the major cost of concrete work. For this reason, forms should be designed and constructed so that they are practical to erect, simple to strip, and capable of being reused. In many areas, the formwork for large buildings is designed by a structural engineer.

REINFORCED CONCRETE

Concrete is strong in compression but weak in tension. By embedding reinforcing steel in concrete to resist tension, while the concrete itself resists compression, we have a composite material known as reinforced concrete.

Concrete and reinforcing steel are compatible materials: they have almost the same coefficient of thermal expansion so that temperature changes do not introduce significant stresses, concrete is sufficiently impervious and fire-resistant to protect the reinforcing steel from corrosion and fire, and concrete bonds well to steel.

Reinforcing steel is usually in the form of round bars or welded wire fabric. Reinforcing bars (rebar) are deformed, which means they have regular deformations, or projections, which interlock and bond with the concrete. Reinforcing bars are designated by numbers representing the bar diameter in eighths of an inch. The standard sizes are #3 (3/8-inch diameter) through #11 (1-3/8-inch diameter); #14 (1-3/4-inch diameter); and #18 (2-1/2-inch diameter).

Reinforcing bars are specified by their ASTM designation, such as ASTM A615 (billet steel); ASTM A616 (rail steel); A617 (axle steel); or ASTM A706 (low-alloy steel). In addition, a grade designation is used: grades 40, 50, 60, and 75 have minimum specified yield strengths of 40,000, 50,000, 60,000, and 75,000 psi, respectively. The most common designation for reinforcing bars used in buildings is ASTM A615 Grade 60.

REINFORCING BAR

Reinforcing bars are furnished with rolled-in markings that identify the rolling mill, the bar size number, the type of steel, and an additional marking for identifying the higher strength steels, as shown on page 26.

Welded wire fabric (WWF) is a grid of smooth or deformed cold-drawn steel wires welded at all points of intersection. This type of reinforcement may be used for floors, walls, roofs, or other large expanses of concrete.

Welded wire fabric is designated by the size and spacing of the longitudinal and transverse wires. For example, WWF $6 \times 6 - W2.9 \times W2.9$ indicates welded wire fabric with wires at six inches on center in each direction, with each wire having a cross-sectional area of $2.9 \div 100$ or 0.029 square inches (which is six-gauge wire).

Steel used in prestressed concrete will be discussed later in this lesson.

Steel reinforcement must be clean, accurately placed, and have a sufficient protective covering of concrete. Before placement, reinforcing steel should be cleaned of all loose rust, oil, mud, paint, or any other foreign matter that might reduce the bond between the bars and the concrete.

Reinforcing bars are generally spliced by lapping them a specified number of bar diameters. In some cases, bars may be butted end-to-end and spliced by welding or using mechanical devices.

Reinforcing bars may be pre-assembled. Column reinforcement, for example, is often completely assembled as a cage before being placed within the formwork. The proper placement of reinforcement is shown on the structural drawings, which are then used as the

basis for preparing shop drawings. When concrete is placed over a network of steel reinforcement, the pressures may tend to dislodge the steel. Therefore, the reinforcement must be held rigidly in place, with sufficient supports and ties, so that the steel will end up in precisely the right location. For this purpose there are a number of devices, such as ties, chairs, and supports, that hold the reinforcing steel in its exact location.

HIGH CHAIR   CONTINUOUS HIGH CHAIR

SLAB BOLSTER   BEAM BOLSTER

REBAR SUPPORT DEVICES

Steel reinforcement must have adequate concrete coverage to protect it from corrosion. For example, footings should have at least three inches of concrete between the steel and the ground. Retaining walls require two inches of concrete cover; beams and columns, 1-1/2 inches; and slabs, 3/4 inch.

Where concrete structures are exposed to chlorides, such as deicing salts or seawater, reinforcing bars may be epoxy-coated or galvanized to resist corrosion.

LIGHTWEIGHT CONCRETE

Structural Lightweight Concrete

One of the principal disadvantages of concrete construction is its great weight. By using lightweight aggregates made from expanded shale or clay instead of natural aggregates, structural lightweight concrete can be produced. Its weight of 90 to 115 pounds per cubic foot is substantially less than that of normal concrete, which weighs 150 pounds per cubic foot.

Structural lightweight concrete with strength, workability, and appearance comparable to normal concrete can usually be obtained. There are some differences, however.

For structural lightweight concrete, the maximum size of coarse aggregate is generally 3/4 inch; and air entrainment is almost always used. Handling and placing are easier; the modulus of elasticity is lower (and thus deflections are greater); drying shrinkage is slightly greater; thermal insulation properties are better, and the cost is almost always greater than that of normal-weight concrete.

Insulating Lightweight Concrete

Another type of lightweight concrete is insulating lightweight concrete, used primarily for thermal insulation in roof construction. It has a weight of 15 to 90 pounds per cubic foot and relatively low compressive strength. It is usually made with aggregates of expanded materials such as perlite or vermiculite, although other lightweight aggregates may be used. Some mixtures are made without fine aggregate (no-fines), which creates voids in the concrete.

Another way of producing insulating lightweight concrete is to incorporate a uniform cellular structure of air voids into a cement paste or cement-sand mortar by using preformed or formed-in-place foam.

PLACEMENT OF CONCRETE

Prior to placing concrete, trenches and formwork should be thoroughly cleaned out, reinforcement should be checked for position, and wood forms should be moistened. Concrete may be placed by spouts or chutes; pumped; placed pneumatically (gunite); or even deposited under water with the use of a tremie. In any event, concrete must be placed evenly, continuously, and—most important—in a manner that avoids segregation of the aggregates.

When new concrete is placed on hardened concrete, precautions must be taken to ensure a

PLACING CONCRETE UNDER WATER WITH A TREMIE

well-bonded, watertight joint. The surface of the hardened concrete should be thoroughly moistened and prepared using sandblasting, water jets, pneumatic tools, or other methods.

Concrete should be placed as close as possible to its final location. A load of concrete should not be dumped at one point and permitted to flow over long distances, as this will lead to the segregation of water and fine particles from the rest of the mass.

Dropping the mixture from excessive heights will also cause it to separate. Vertical drops should generally be limited to four feet.

When concrete is placed, air bubbles are frequently trapped in the body of the mixture. If allowed to remain, these air bubbles will produce a honeycomb effect that can cause a substantial reduction in concrete strength and watertightness, as well as an unsightly finish. To eliminate this condition, concrete should be compacted or consolidated by hand tools or by the use of mechanical vibrators. The formwork

can be vibrated externally, or vibrators can be immersed in the mix itself. Vibration of concrete results in greater density, homogeneity, durability, and more complete contact with the reinforcing. Vibration also allows the use of stiffer mixes with a reduced cement content. However, vibration does not make the concrete stronger, and excessive vibration may result in segregation.

Concrete may be placed during almost any weather condition, but special methods and procedures are required during both extremes of hot and cold weather. Concrete must not be allowed to dry out too rapidly or to freeze.

Pneumatically applied concrete, often called gunite, is shot into place using compressed air. It may be used for repair work as well as new construction. It is especially useful for placing concrete that has a large surface area and thin sections, such as the sides and bottoms of swimming pools and thin sections used to strengthen existing masonry walls for seismic forces.

TESTING

In order to verify that the concrete used on a project has the required quality, several tests may be performed. Among these are the *slump test* and the *cylinder test.*

Slump Test

The slump test measures the consistency and workability of the concrete mix and is usually performed in the field.

The test employs a standard slump cone mold that is set on a level surface and filled with concrete taken directly from the mixer, in three layers of approximately equal volume.

POOR PRACTICE

GOOD PRACTICE

PLACING CONCRETE IN FORMS

PROCEDURE FOR SLUMP TEST

Each layer is rodded and after the top layer is leveled, the mold is carefully lifted and the wet concrete is permitted to slump. The mold is then placed alongside the slumped concrete and the difference in height measured directly. In general, the acceptable slump for concrete in building construction ranges from two to six inches. If the slump is less than two inches, the mix is probably too stiff and unworkable, and if it is greater than six inches, it may be too wet and loose.

After the measurement is completed, the slumped concrete may be tapped gently, which will give some indication of its workability.

Cylinder Test

The cylinder test measures the compressive strength of concrete and utilizes standard test cylinders 6 inches in diameter and 12 inches long. From each batch of concrete, at least two cylinders are cast, laboratory-cured for 7 and 28 days, and tested in a crushing machine. If the cylinders fail to attain the specified strength, cores 2 inches to 4 inches in diameter may be cut from those areas in the actual structure

where the concrete is suspected of being deficient and tested in a laboratory for compression.

Other Tests

Other tests that may be performed include the *Kelly ball test*, the *impact hammer test*, and *tests for air content*.

The Kelly ball test, like the slump test, measures workability. In this test, a 30-pound, six-inch diameter hemisphere is dropped from a standard height onto the surface of the fresh concrete, and its penetration into the concrete is measured. When properly calibrated, the results of the Kelly ball test can be directly related to slump.

The impact hammer test is a common nondestructive test, in which the rebound of a spring-loaded plunger is measured after it strikes a smooth concrete surface. The rebound reading gives an approximate indication of the concrete strength. This test is simple and nondestructive, but it is not a substitute for standard cylinder tests.

There are various methods for determining air entrainment in concrete that measure the volume of air contained in the mix. These tests should be regularly made immediately after the concrete is discharged from the mixer, and frequently after the concrete has been placed and consolidated.

CURING

The curing of concrete consists of maintaining the proper humidity and temperature for some period of time after it is placed, to assure satisfactory hydration of the cement. Excessive evaporation of water can retard the hydration process and reduce the strength of the concrete, as well as causing the concrete to shrink and develop surface cracks. Exposed surfaces must therefore be protected against moisture evaporation.

Concrete may be cured by the following methods:

1. Supplying additional moisture to the concrete surface, by ponding or sprinkling

2. Using a wet covering, such as moist sand, burlap, or straw

3. Covering the surface with a membrane or curing compound that prevents evaporation

4. Leaving wood forms in place and keeping them moist

The length of the curing period varies from 3 to 14 days or more, depending on many factors. As all the desirable qualities of concrete are improved by curing, the curing period should be as long as possible, consistent with other project requirements.

The most favorable temperature for curing concrete is between 50 and 70°F. The chemical reaction of hydration generates internal heat in the concrete, which must be considered, especially in hot weather. In very hot weather special care may have to be taken, such as cooling the concrete ingredients or adding ice to the mixing water. Wind and sun tend to dry out concrete, and temporary windbreaks and/or shading may be required.

During cold weather, additional heat may be required, from heaters, heating coils, or live steam. It may even be necessary to temporarily enclose and heat portions of the building during and after concrete placement.

CONCRETE JOINTS

Construction Joints

The horizontal or vertical joints between two successive concrete pours are called

VERTICAL REINFORCING RODS IF REQUIRED   REINFORCING ROD

KEYED   STEPPED   ROUGHENED   KEYED
               HORIZONTAL   VERTICAL

CONCRETE CONSTRUCTION JOINTS

FACE OF WALL

EXTRUDED METAL COVER ASSEMBLY

COMPRESSIBLE MATERIAL

FINISH FLOOR

ANCHOR BOLT

EXPANSION JOINT FILLER

JOINT AT FLOOR AND WALL

COVER PLATE SECURED ONE SIDE SLIDES ON OTHER PLATE

PLATE SECURED

BRICK

BLOCK

VINYL WATER STOP

JOINT FILLER

FOAM INSULATION

ALUMINUM PLATE SECURED TO ONE SIDE

INTERIOR FINISH ON METAL FURRING

PLATE SECURED AND SLIDES ON PLATE

WALL

COMPRESSIBLE MATERIAL

BED PLATE WITH ANCHOR

COVER PLATE SECURED ONE SIDE

MASTIC FILLER

COPPER WATER STOP

EXPANSION JOINT FILLER

FLOOR

COPPER CAP WITH EXPANSION LOOP

RIGID INSULATION

ROOFING

FLASHING

COPPER CLEAT

PREMOLDED EXPANSION JOINT FILLER

ROOF

EXPANSION JOINTS

construction joints. These joints exist whenever concreting is interrupted, or when new concrete is placed against old. Joints should be straight, and their form and location should be designed carefully.

To ensure the maximum bond between old and new pours, the old surface should be roughened, cleaned, and wetted before placing the new concrete. In many cases, reinforcing bars extend through the joint and help to connect the new and previously poured concrete. Construction joints are always planes of weakness, and therefore should be located at sections of minimum shear. They are often keyed to provide some shear strength.

Expansion Joints

Expansion joints are designed to allow free movement of adjacent parts due to expansion or contraction of the concrete. This movement may be caused by shrinkage or changes in temperature. Expansion joints provide complete separation through a structure, from the top of the footings to the roof. They are waterproof, weather tight, and generally filled with an elastic joint filler. The placement and size of joints is a function of the size of the building and the maximum expected temperature differential.

Expansion joints are required in buildings more than 200 feet long, at joints of building wings, and at additions to existing buildings.

Control Joints

Control joints are tooled, sawed, or premolded joints to allow for the shrinkage of large concrete areas. Control joints create a weakened section that induces cracking to occur along the joint, rather than in a random fashion.

- (A) LOW BLDG. ABUTTING HIGH BLDG.
- (B) CONCRETE BLDG. OVER 200' LONG
- (C) INTERSECTION OF BLDG. WINGS
- (D) NEW BLDG. ADJOINING EXISTING BLDG.

EXPANSION JOINTS

CONCRETE JOINTS (PLAN)

80'-0", 100'-0" AND 120'-0"

20'-0" TO 36'-0"

—6'-0", 8'-0" AND 10'-0"

4'-0"

TEE SECTION

DEPTHS VARY WITH SPAN

DOUBLE-TEE SECTION

PRESTRESSED CONCRETE SECTIONS

Isolation Joints

Isolation joints provide a separation between a slab on grade and columns or walls, so that each can move independently.

PRESTRESSED CONCRETE

Prestressed concrete is concrete placed in compression by applying a tensile force to prestressing steel *before* the external loads are applied. The purpose is to cause stresses in the concrete that are opposite in direction from those caused by the external loads.

The combined effect of the prestress and the external dead and live loads usually results in compression over the entire cross-section of the beam, in contrast to the relatively small compression area of conventional reinforced concrete beams. Prestressing thus results in more efficient and economical use of material, especially in repetitive long-span applications. Concrete members can be smaller, span greater distances, and support greater loads.

Because prestressed members are completely in compression, tension cracks are prevented, which is particularly advantageous in structures exposed to the weather. In addition, prestressed concrete members are stiffer (because the entire section is effective) and have greater shear strength.

However, offsetting these advantages are greater material and labor costs and the need for closer quality control than with conventional reinforced concrete.

There are two procedures used to apply prestress: *pretensioning* and *posttensioning*.

In pretensioning, the prestressing steel is stretched between abutments, usually at a casting yard away from the building site, and tensioned by jacks *before* placing the concrete. After the concrete is placed and has attained its required strength, the prestressing steel is cut, and its tensile force is applied as a compressive force to the concrete through bond between the concrete and steel.

Some loss of prestress occurs because of creep and shrinkage, slip, and friction.

Pretensioning lends itself to mass production, as the casting beds can be hundreds of feet long, the entire length can be cast at one time, and individual beams can be cut to the required lengths.

In a posttensioned beam, the concrete is cast with a hollow duct or sleeve to encase the prestressing steel and prevent bond between the concrete and steel. This is usually done on the site. The concrete is cured and after it has acquired sufficient strength, the steel is tensioned by jacking against anchorages at the ends of the beam, which compresses the concrete. The prestressing steel is permanently locked under stress by special end anchors and grouted. The losses after tensioning, caused by friction, elastic shortening, and shrinkage, are usually less than with pretensioning.

Both the concrete and steel used in prestressed concrete construction must have greater strength than required for conventional reinforced concrete. For example, the concrete is generally required to have a compressive strength of 5,000 psi or greater.

There are three types of prestressing steel: high-strength bars, single wires, and wire strands, all of which are called tendons. Wire strands have seven wires each: one central wire enclosed tightly by six helically placed outer wires.

PRECAST CONCRETE

Precasting is the casting of concrete members at a location other than its final position in the structure, as opposed to cast-in-place concrete, which is produced in the exact location it will occupy. Precasting can be done almost anywhere, unless the handling and transportation of members become unfeasible. Thus, it is good practice to verify the manufacturing location, the size of precast elements, trucking sizes, and highway clearances relative to the site location.

HOLLOW CORE

TONGUE AND GROOVE

CHANNEL

DOUBLE-TEE

PRECAST CONCRETE PLANKS

Precast concrete has the greatest economic advantage when there are many identical members to be cast, as the same forms can be reused many times. There are other advantages to precasting:

1   Better quality control of concrete

2. Better control over curing (may be steam cured)

3. Members castable in all weather

4. Members erectable in all weather

5. Faster actual construction time

Precast Floor and Roof Systems

Precast floor and roof systems, which are often prestressed, consist of a variety of precast planks that may be used with precast beams, joists, and purlins. Curtain wall panels may also be precast. Once on the job, precast members are handled in much the same way as other

CONCRETE PLANKS · LIGHTWEIGHT CONCRETE PLANKS · NAILABLE CONCRETE PLANKS · TONGUE & GROOVE CONCRETE PLANKS · WOOD NAILER · DOVETAIL ANCHOR

PRECAST CONCRETE JOIST SYSTEMS

building components as they are integrated with the structure.

Tilt-Up Construction

Tilt-up construction involves casting a wall panel in a horizontal position and then tilting it to its final vertical position. Usually, these panels are solid, reinforced slabs five to eight inches thick and long enough to span between the supporting columns or footings. Various casting platforms may be used, the most

common of which is the slab on grade, which serves as the bottom form. It is important to prevent bonding of one surface to another, and therefore bond-breaking agents, patented liquid solutions, and various sheet materials are used between the slab and the tilt-up panel.

The upper or exterior surface of the panel may be finished by floating, troweling, or with special decorative finishes, such as pebbled, grooved, polished, colored, etc. Tilt-up panels

PRECAST CONCRETE PANEL · INSULATION · CAST-IN ANCHORS · SLOTTED HOLES IN CLIP ANGLES

WALL PANEL · INSULATION · METAL FURRING · CLIP ANGLE WITH SLOTTED HOLES · PIN · CONCRETE WALK · THREADED ROD

PRECAST WALL TO SLAB

PRECAST WALL AT FOUNDATION

PRECAST CURTAIN WALL PANELS

TILT-UP PANEL SYSTEMS

TILT-UP PANELS WITH CAST-IN-PLACE COLUMNS

may be load or non-load-bearing, may rest on a foundation wall or span between footings, and are connected to cast-in-place columns.

Lift-Slab Construction

Lift-slab construction consists of casting floor and roof slabs of a multistory building, one upon another, with a membrane or bond-breaking agent between, to prevent bonding of the separate slabs. Jacks, which are attached to the structure's columns, lift the slabs to their final position where they are welded into place, using special steel collars. This method of construction eliminates practically all formwork, and greatly shortens the overall construction time.

A great advantage of lift-slab construction is that all mechanical pipes, conduits, and ducts can be installed on grade. Thus, when the floors are raised into their permanent positions, all electrical, heating, plumbing, ventilating, and air-conditioning have been completely roughed in.

Tube-Slab

Tube-slab refers to a system in which paper tube fillers are embedded in the section to obtain a flat ceiling with no exposed beams. This allows mechanical and duct spaces to be integrated within the thickness of the system.

CONCRETE FINISHES

Concrete finishing is performed in many different ways, depending on the final surface effect desired. In general, finishes are limited only by the designer's imagination and the properties of the concrete. Finishes for walls and ceilings are generally applied to concrete that has already set, while finishes on floor slabs are applied while the concrete is still plastic and workable.

PAPER TUBE FILLERS

CONCRETE BEAM   FINISH PLASTER CEILING   DUCT SPACE   REINFORCEMENT

TUBE - SLAB SYSTEM

Walls and Ceilings

Walls can be finished in a variety of ways: rough; smooth; with a rubbed finish; sand-blasted; with textured formwork; bush hammered; with exposed aggregate; or with an applied finish such as stucco, plaster, ceramic tile, or concrete paint. They may also be furred and insulated and then covered with a variety of materials such as plasterboard, composition panels, and plywood.

Ceilings may be finished in many of the same ways as walls, in addition to adhesive-applied acoustical tile.

Floors

Floor surfaces may be finished with a wood float finish; a smoother and harder steel troweled finish; an applied texture, such as brooming; or an applied finish, such as nonslip, pigmented, heavy duty, etc. The finishing operation of all slabs involves screeding or leveling, floating, and troweling; and at any point in the process a final finish can be produced. The final finishing of a slab, however, is not done until all surface water has disappeared.

Terrazzo

Terrazzo is not, strictly speaking, a concrete finish, but rather a topping material that is applied over concrete slabs. Terrazzo is a mixture of portland cement and water, known as the matrix, to which are added colored marble granules. After the mixture has set, it is ground and polished to a smooth finish. Terrazzo can be applied to floors, walls, wainscots, and stairs; and it is also precast as stair treads, window stools, saddles, and floor tiles.

Seamless terrazzo floors and precast terrazzo tile use a synthetic resin matrix instead of cement and water. Further information can be found in Lesson Eight under Flooring.

LESSON 2 QUIZ

1. If you are pouring a large concrete slab and wish to avoid random cracks caused by shrinkage, you would likely provide

    A. expansion joints.

    B. isolation joints.

    C. control joints.

    D. construction joints.

2. When pouring concrete in hot weather, what kind of agent would one add to the mixture?

    A. Retarding agent

    B. Air-entraining agent

    C. Hardening agent

    D. Workability agent

3. The purpose of a concrete slump test is to

    A. determine the plasticity of the mix.

    B. measure the consistency and workability of the mix.

    C. test the compression of the mix.

    D. define the compression strength of the mix.

4. Which of the following qualities are normally associated with lightweight concrete?

    I. Good thermal insulation

    II. High density

    III. Excellent fire resistance

    IV. Low cost

    V. Difficulty of handling

    A. I and III　　　C. I, III, and V

    B. II and III　　　D. II, IV, and V

5. The principal determinant of concrete strength is the

    A. amount of air entrained.

    B. type of portland cement used.

    C. volume of aggregate in the mix.

    D. water-cement ratio.

6. In curing concrete slabs, which of the following procedures is rarely used?

    A. Overlay with plastic membrane

    B. Spray with moisture

    C. Blow with fans

    D. Cover with sand

7. While observing a concrete pour, an architect notices that the entire concrete load has been deposited from a 6-foot height at the middle of a 40-foot-long form. The architect should direct the contractor to

    A. spread the concrete throughout the length of the form.

    B. pour the next two concrete loads at each end of the form.

    C. pour the next load in exactly the same location.

    D. remove and discard the concrete.

8. The steel in reinforced concrete

    A. furnishes rigidity.

    B. provides tensile strength.

    C. increases bond strength.

    D. adds ductility and durability.

9. The size of coarse aggregate in a concrete mix is governed by the

   I.   type of cement used.

   II. strength of concrete desired.

   III. thickness of concrete section.

   IV. water-cement ratio.

   V.   space between reinforcing bars.

   A. V only

   B. I and IV

   C. II and III

   D. III and V

10. All of the following are advantages of using precast concrete sections, *EXCEPT*

    A. better quality control.

    B. faster curing.

    C. all-weather construction.

    D. greater economy.

MASONRY

INTRODUCTION

Masonry construction consists of walls and other building elements made of individual masonry units that are joined together with mortar. Small masonry units are either solid or hollow and include brick, structural clay tile, concrete block, gypsum block, and glass block. Larger units include terra cotta, ceramic veneer, precast concrete, and various types of stone.

HISTORY

Masonry construction began when prehistoric people first piled up rocks to create protection from wind, rain, and wild animals. Where stone was not available, mud from nearby river beds was fashioned into convenient building units. These primitive bricks were at first sundried and later burned by fire to make them hard and more durable. As civilization progressed, builders learned how to span great distances using small shaped units, first by corbeling, and later by the use of compressive structures, such as arches, vaults, and domes.

Every civilization has employed some form of masonry construction. Through centuries of exposure, in all types of climate, magnificent masonry monuments remain today, from the ancient Egyptian pyramids to the glorious Gothic cathedrals.

Masonry construction continues to be a popular building method. Despite our technical advances, there remains an admiration for this ancient way of building, which no doubt results from its ageless character, distinctive texture, and human scale.

BRICK

A brick is a rectangular masonry unit that is molded from clays and shales, dried, and then fired in a kiln. The physical and chemical characteristics of the ingredients vary considerably, and this, along with the temperatures at which they are fired, accounts for the variations in color and hardness. The differences among finished bricks are also dependent on the method of molding used.

Molding Methods

There are three main methods of molding brick. The *soft mud process* uses molds into which moist clay is pressed by hand or machine into rectangular molds.

The widely used *stiff mud process* forces the mixture through a die, extruding a clay ribbon that is cut into bricks by tightly stretched wires (wire-cut brick).

The *dry-press process* uses a relatively dry mixture that is pressed into gang molds by plungers under high pressure. This process produces the most accurately formed brick.

Bricks are produced in solid, cored, and hollow units, although cored brick is classified as solid if at least 75 percent of its total cross-sectional area is solid. In hollow brick, at least 60 percent of the total cross-sectional area is solid. Most natural brick colors are in the red or buff ranges, while the commonly available surface textures are smooth, water-and sand-struck, scored, wire-cut, combed, and roughened. Brick can also be finished with a fire-bonded ceramic glaze in either a satin or gloss finish.

Brick Types

Building brick, sometimes referred to as *common brick*, is the type most widely used in construction. It is made from clay fired at about 1,850°F, usually red in color, and available in various sizes. Although there is no U.S. standard brick size, the closest thing to it is the standard building brick, which has the approximate dimensions shown below.

STANDARD BUILDING BRICK

Brick is specified in accordance with the use and exposure to which it will be subjected, as follows:

Grade SW   (Severe weathering) Used in areas of heavy rain, snow, or continual freezing.

Grade MW   (Moderate weathering) Used in areas of average rain and moderate freezing.

Grade NW   (No weathering) Used in areas of minimal rain and no freezing, as in sheltered or indoor locations.

Face brick is brick that will be exposed to view, and it is made from controlled mixtures of clay or shale and carefully manufactured to produce high quality units in specific sizes, textures, and colors. Face brick, too, is specified according to exposure, and is available in SW and MW grades. In addition, it is classified according to factors affecting its appearance, as follows:

Grade FBX High degree of mechanical perfection, narrow color range, and minimum size variation.

Grade FBS Greater size variation and wide color range.

Grade FBA Nonuniform in size, color, and texture.

Hollow brick is available in SW and MW grades, and is classified by factors affecting its appearance, similar to face brick, as follows:

Grade HBX High degree of mechanical perfection, minimum size variation, and narrow color range.

Grade HBS Greater size variation and wide color range.

Grade HBA Nonuniform in size, color, and texture.

Other types of brick include the following:

Backup brick. Inferior brick used behind face brick.

Paving brick. Very hard and dense brick used in pavements.

Fire brick. Brick made with great resistance to high temperatures, as in a fireplace.

Sewer brick. Low absorption brick for use in sewerage and storm drains.

Adobe brick. Brick made from a mixture of natural clay and straw, placed in molds, and dried in the sun. Requires protection from rain and subsurface moisture.

Nail-on brick. Flat brick generally used on interiors where solid masonry cannot be structurally supported.

Hollow brick. Brick whose net cross-sectional area is at least 60 percent of its gross cross-sectional area.

Most bricks are manufactured in standard sizes, but there are dimensional variations, based on the region and the manufacturer. Some variations are caused by the differences in clays used and the amount of shrinkage that occurs when bricks are fired.

Modular bricks have dimensions such that one or more brick courses plus the mortar joints produce courses with an exact dimension, which is usually a multiple of 4 inches. For example, an Economy-8 modular brick 3-1/2 inches × 7-1/2 inches × 3-1/2 inches in size laid with 1/2 inch joints will produce regular courses exactly 4 inches in height and 8 inches in length. Other modular bricks include Roman (1-1/2 inches high) and Economy-12 (3-1/2 inches high).

Brick Nomenclature

Special terms are used to identify, classify, and describe brick shapes, surfaces, and placement within a wall. For example, the six surfaces of a brick are called the *face, side, cull, end,* and *beds,* as shown below.

SURFACES OF A BRICK

Frequently, the mason must cut bricks into various shapes in order to fill in the spaces at corners and other places where a full brick will not fit. The more common cut shapes are shown below.

SHAPES OF CUT BRICK

Bricks may also be identified by their placement within a wall. For example, if they are laid with the end or cull (short sides) exposed, they are called *headers*; but if they are laid with the face (long side) exposed they are called *stretchers*. Various other positions are illustrated in the next column.

Bricklaying

Bricklaying has always been a manual, rather than a mechanical, process, and therefore, the quality of brickwork depends to a large extent on workmanship. In this regard, there are several standard practices with which one should be familiar. For example, bricks should be laid when the temperature is between 40 and 90°F, for best results.

In addition, bricks should be wetted prior to setting in order to minimize absorption of water from the mortar. Loss of water will cause the mortar to set too soon, and the bond between brick and mortar will be weak. Wetting bricks will also wash dust from the brick surface,

BRICK POSITIONS AND COURSES

resulting in better bond. Tests have indicated that the absorption rate of wetted brick should not exceed 0.7 ounces of water per minute. If the absorption rate exceeds this amount, the bricks should be rewetted until the desired value is achieved.

Bricks should always be set in a full bed of mortar with mortar solidly filling all vertical head joints. Standard joint thicknesses vary, although they usually range between 1/4 and 1/2 inch. In general, three bricks plus three joints equals eight inches in height.

MASONRY JOINTS

Few brick walls today are laid solid. Most walls are cavity walls, in which two tiers, or wythes, of masonry are separated by two or three inches of air space. Rigid foam insulation, applied to the inside wythe, occupies about half this space, thus increasing the insulation value of the wall.

Reinforced brick masonry consists of two wythes of brick separated by a two- to four-inch space in which horizontal and vertical reinforcing bars are placed. The space is filled solidly with grout, which is a mixture of portland cement, sand, water, and sometimes pea gravel. A small amount of lime is also permitted in the grout mix. Reinforced brick masonry is much stronger than unreinforced brick masonry, for both vertical loads and lateral loads from wind or earthquake.

Brick Bonding

Brick bonding refers to the pattern in which bricks are laid to tie the wythes together into a structural unit. Some of the common bond patterns are shown on the following page. *Common bond* has a header course every sixth course, *English bond* alternates header and stretcher courses, *Flemish bond* alternates headers and stretchers in each course, and *running bond* and *stacked bond* have

mesh reinforcing every sixth course. Reinforced brick masonry is generally laid in running bond or stacked bond, and as the cavity between the brick wythes contains reinforcing bars, mesh reinforcing is unnecessary.

Veneering

Veneering is the term used for exposed masonry that is attached, but not structurally bonded, to the backing. The veneer units are held in place by metal wires, clips, or anchors.

Efflorescence

Efflorescence is a white, powdery deposit on the masonry surface caused by soluble salts in the units or in the mortar. These salts are leached out by water that penetrates the masonry and results in unsightly patches of discoloration.

Efflorescence can be prevented, or at least minimized, by selecting materials free of harmful salts and by preventing water from penetrating the masonry. This may be accomplished by the use of solid and tight mortar joints, capped walls, effective flashing, and adequate weather protection of the masonry during the course of construction.

When efflorescence appears, it can be removed by washing with high pressure water, by light sandblasting, or most commonly by washing with a 5 percent solution of muriatic acid in water.

Expansion Joints

Expansion joints are required in all masonry structures more than 200 feet in length, or where there are two or more wings in a building. Temperature and moisture changes cause expansion and contraction, but in masonry walls much of the movement is accommodated by the wall itself because of the flexibility in the many mortar joints. Nevertheless, to avoid harmful cracking,

BRICK BONDING PATTERNS

CONCRETE MASONRY

expansion joints such as those shown on the next page should be used. In these joints, the sealant adheres to the two masonry surfaces to prevent air and water infiltration, while permitting movement parallel to the wall face. The compressible filler is used to maintain the required depth of the sealant.

CONCRETE MASONRY

A wide variety of concrete masonry units are made from concrete, using either normal or lightweight aggregates. The units are manufactured by consolidating a stiff concrete mixture in steel molds. The molds are immediately removed and the units cured at an accelerated rate and dried. Units include concrete bricks, concrete blocks, concrete tile, and cast

(concrete) stone. The most widely used of these masonry products is *concrete block*, which has become increasingly important as a construction material.

Concrete blocks are easy and relatively inexpensive to manufacture in a variety of patterns, textures, and colors. They are light, strong, and have good fire resistance, and they can be used for foundations, partitions, and load-bearing or non-load-bearing walls. Concrete blocks are modular, so that a nominal 8 × 8 × 16 block actually measures 7-5/8 × 7-5/8 × 15-5/8 inches to allow for 3/8 inch mortar joints, both horizontally and vertically.

Individual blocks are manufactured with two or three cores (cells), as well as solid. As compared

ELASTIC JOINT SEALANT

PREMOLDED COMPRESSIBLE FILLER

METAL TIES 16" O.C. VERT

COVER PLATE (OPTIONAL)

BUILDING FELT TO BREAK BOND

EXPANSION JOINT IN STRAIGHT BRICK WALL

ELASTIC JOINT SEALANT

FLEXIBLE ANCHORS

CONCRETE COLUMN

PREMOLDED COMPRESSIBLE FILLER

JOINT SEALANT

METAL TIES 16" O.C. VERT.

EXPANSION JOINT AT CONCEALED COLUMN

EXPANSION JOINTS

WEB

END SHELL

FACE SHELL

$15\frac{5}{8}$"

$7\frac{5}{8}$"

$7\frac{5}{8}$"

2-CORE STRETCHER WITH TYPICAL DIMENSIONS

3 CORE STRETCHER

2- OR 3-CORE CORNER BLOCK

JAMB BLOCK

WINDOW JAMB BLOCK

LINTEL BLOCK

CONCRETE BLOCK SHAPES

to solid units, two-cell concrete blocks reduce heat conduction, are lighter, and have more space for mechanical pipes and conduits.

Load-bearing concrete block is classified in two grades: N for more severe exposures and S for block requiring protection from the weather.

Concrete block walls are normally constructed one block thick and laid with staggered vertical joints (running bond). Steel reinforcing bars are often placed vertically in the middle of grout-filled cells. Horizontal reinforcement consists of either thin welded grids laid in bed joints or reinforcing bars placed in blocks with channeled webs, called bond beam blocks. Lintels over door and window openings can be made of steel or reinforced concrete, or solid-grouted lintel or bond beam blocks with horizontal reinforcing bars.

Block walls may be left unfinished, thus displaying the color of the cement used in the manufacturing process, or they may receive a coating of cement plaster, cement paint, or clear waterproof sealer. Concrete block can also be used as a backup wall behind a facing of brick, stone, or tile.

Concrete block masonry is usually less expensive per square foot of wall than brick or stone masonry. Although concrete blocks can be saw cut on the job, it is more economical if the architect lays out the dimensions of the building to correspond with the block module, which is generally eight inches.

STRUCTURAL CLAY TILE

Structural clay tiles are hollow, burned-clay masonry units with parallel cells. They are made from the same clays as brick, and may be load-bearing or non-load-bearing (partition tile). Clay tiles are divided into two broad groups accord-

END-CONSTRUCTION TILE (8"x12"x12")

SIDE-CONSTRUCTION TILE (3¾"x5"x12")

STRUCTURAL CLAY TILE

ing to function: backup tile and facing tile. They are available in a variety of textures, in natural colors (usually in the range of brick reds), or in various glazed finishes.

Structural clay tile is used for interior partitions, or, in combination with other masonry, as back-up for exterior walls. Depending on the orientation of the cells, the tile is referred to as a side-construction tile (cells horizontal) or an end-construction tile (cells vertical).

Architectural terra cotta is clay tile that is available in various colors, textures, and shapes. It is used primarily for multicolored decorative designs.

Ceramic veneer is terra cotta available in large face dimensions, thin sections, and a variety of natural and glazed finishes. It is applied with a mortar setting bed, or by using metal anchors and mortar.

CERAMIC VENEER
(TERRA COTTA)

GYPSUM BLOCKS

GYPSUM BLOCK

Gypsum blocks, often referred to as gypsum tiles, are solid or cored units manufactured from gypsum plaster. They are available in thicknesses from 2 to 6 inches, and in standard panels 12 × 30 inches in size.

Gypsum block is used for interior non-load-bearing partitions and, because of its chemical properties, for lightweight fireproofing protection. For example, two inches of gypsum block has the same fire rating as four inches of concrete block. Gypsum block cannot be used on the exterior or in areas subject to continuous dampness. It is always set with gypsum mortar on top of a base course of water-resistant material.

GLASS BLOCK

Glass blocks are either solid or hollow units that have the same general chemical composition as window glass. They are used where light transmission, glare, or solar heat must be controlled, or where a specific decorative effect is desired. Glass blocks are available in several standard sizes, which are based on a four-inch module.

Walls of glass block are limited in length, height, and area, and they may never be used to support structural loads. The blocks are always set in a stacked bond pattern. When using glass block, one must give special consideration to the mortar mix, because of the poor bond between glass and mortar. In addition, control joints are critical because of the high coefficient of thermal expansion for glass. Also critical are the joints with other materials, which should be filled with resilient expansion joint material.

Glass blocks were very popular following their introduction in the 1930s; however, due to overuse and frequent misuse, their popularity waned in the post-war period. In recent years, there has been increased interest in glass block for decorative purposes and because of the demand for greater insulation values in exterior wall materials.

INSIDE FACE: PRISMED, ETCHED CLEAR, RIBBED, SCULPTURED, OR FLUTED

WITH OR WITHOUT GLASS FIBER INSERT

DEHYDRATED PARTIAL VACUUM

OUTSIDE FACES: CLEAR, RIBBED, SCULPTURED, OPAQUE OR SMOOTH

3⅞"

SIZES: SQUARES 5¾" 7¾" AND 11¾"
RECTANGULAR 3¾" X 11¾"

GLASS BLOCK

STONE

Stone is one of the original natural materials used in construction by prehistoric people. As such, it has served literally as the foundation of all architectural efforts, from prehistory to the turn of the last century. Today stone is used for aggregates or as a surface finish material, in the form of veneer, paving, shingles, counter tops, and various decorative items.

Classification

Stone consists of small or quarried pieces of rock, of which there are three types: *igneous*, *sedimentary*, and *metamorphic*, based on how the rock was formed. The principal building stones in each type that are commonly used in construction are listed above right.

Stone Forms

Stone is available in a number of forms and used in construction in a variety of ways. Some of the most common forms are as follows:

Type of Rock	Name of Stone
Igneous	Granite
Sedimentary	Limestone
	Sandstone
	Bluestone
	Brownstone
Metamorphic	Marble
	Soapstone
	Slate

Rough stone (fieldstone)—natural stone used decoratively

Rubble stone—irregular stone with at least one good face used for ashlar veneers, copings, sills, curbs, etc.

Dimension stone—cut stone, used for surface veneers, toilet partitions, flooring, stair treads, etc.

Flagstone—thin slabs used for paving, treads, counter tops, etc.

Monumental stone—used for sculpture, monuments, gravestones, etc.

Crushed stone—used as aggregate for concrete, asphaltic concrete, terrazzo, built-up roof surfacing, etc., as well as granular fill

Stone dust—used as filler in asphalt flooring, shingles, paints, etc.

The properties of natural stone vary considerably, and therefore, one must choose carefully with regard to strength, porosity, absorption, and permeability. It is also important to select a surface finish that will be appropriate to the stone type and suitable for the function it must perform. Surface finishes range from very rough (quarry face, split face, or sawed finish) to quite smooth (rubbed finish, honed finish, or polished finish). All stone is affected by rapid temperature change, and therefore, it should not be used where fire resistance is important.

Stone Masonry

Stone masonry is classified in two principal groups: *rubble masonry*, in which the stones are left in their natural rough state, and *ashlar masonry*, in which the stones are shaped and smoothed (dressed) into rectangular blocks. Stone masonry is further categorized as *coarsed*, which has continuous horizontal joints, and *uncoarsed* or *random*, which does not. A *bond stone* is a stone with its longest dimension perpendicular to the wall face to tie the wall to its backing. Several stone masonry patterns are shown in the right column.

Stone masonry may be laid in mortar, similar to brick and concrete block, or it may be in the

UNCOURSED   COURSED

FIELDSTONE

COURSED ASHLAR   BROKEN ASHLAR

POLYGONAL   RANDOM COURSED

ASHLAR STONEWORK

BROKEN JOINTS   STACKED JOINTS

DIMENSION STONE VENEER

STONEWORK PATTERNS

form of thin veneer mechanically anchored to the backup wall or frame.

Stone masonry should be set with nonstaining portland cement mortar, and care should be taken to avoid moisture penetration of the stone. This is usually accomplished by dampproofing the backup material. There are many varieties of anchors and ties used to secure stone veneer or stone trim, and several of these are shown on the following page.

MORTAR

All masonry units are bonded with mortar, the purpose of which is to join the units to each other, or to their supporting members, while preventing moisture penetration of the joints. Mortar is composed of varying quantities of portland cement, sand, lime, and water. Mortar sand should be clean and free from organic

STONE VENEER JOINTS

STONE VENEER ANCHORING DETAILS

SECTION OF STONE LINTEL

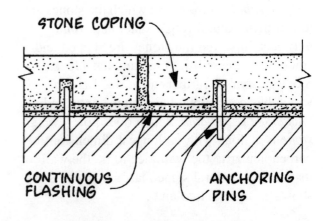

PARALLEL SECTION THROUGH STONE COPING

TABLE 21-A — MORTAR PROPORTIONS FOR UNIT MASONRY

MORTAR	TYPE	PROPORTIONS BY VOLUME (CEMENTITIOUS MATERIALS)								AGGREGATE MEASURED IN A DAMP, LOOSE CONDITION
		Portland Cement or Blended Cement	Masonry Cement[1] M	S	N	Mortar Cement[2] M	S	N	Hydrated Lime or Lime Putty	
Cement-lime	M	1	—	—	—	—	—	—	$1/4$	
	S	1	—	—	—	—	—	—	over $1/4$ to $1/2$	
	N	1	—	—	—	—	—	—	over $1/2$ to $1\,1/4$	
	O	1	—	—	—	—	—	—	over $1\,1/4$ to $2\,1/2$	
Mortar cement	M	1	—	—	—	—	—	1	—	Not less than $2\,1/4$ and not more than 3 times the sum of the separate volumes of cementitious materials.
	M	—	—	—	—	1	—	—	—	
	S	$1/2$	—	—	—	—	—	1	—	
	S	—	—	—	—	—	1	—	—	
	N	—	—	—	—	—	—	1	—	
Masonry cement	M	1	—	—	1	—	—	—	—	
	M	—	1	—	—	—	—	—	—	
	S	$1/2$	—	—	1	—	—	—	—	
	S	—	—	1	—	—	—	—	—	
	N	—	—	—	1	—	—	—	—	
	O	—	—	—	1	—	—	—	—	

[1]Masonry cement conforming to the requirements of U.B.C. Standard 21-11.
[2]Mortar cement conforming to the requirements of U.B.C. Standard 21-14.

material, and its grading is based on the thickness of the mortar joint. Lime putty or hydrated lime is used to improve workability and water retentivity, although it reduces the strength of the mortar. Admixtures are permitted, but except for powdered coloring agents, they are not recommended where high bond strength is desired.

Masonry cement or mortar cement may be used instead of, or in addition to, portland cement, in which case no lime may be added. However, only portland cement-lime mortar should be used where high strength and low permeability are required.

Mortars may be tested for slump or flow, similar to concrete, in order to insure a proper mix. Mixes that have lost water through evaporation may be retempered (water added); however, mortar should not be used more than three hours after it is mixed.

A table of mortar proportions reproduced from the Uniform Building Code is shown above. For masonry that is load-bearing and/or exposed to the weather, type M or S mortar is generally specified. Types N and O mortars are used where a lesser compressive strength is required.

High-strength mortars are used for preassembled masonry units, and as such they have greater compressive and tensile strength. These mortars consist of portland cement, sand, a high-bond additive, a plasticizer, and water.

In severe climates, special precautions may be necessary when masonry work is performed during the winter. These may include protecting the masonry units and mortar ingredients from the weather, heating the water used in the mortar mix, and providing temporary enclosures while the work is being done and for several days after.

MORTAR JOINTS

The exterior surface of mortar joints, which is exposed to the weather, is finished to make the masonry more waterproof and/or to achieve a specific aesthetic appearance. Joints may be made with a trowel, a special jointing tool, or a raking device. In each case, the joint should be

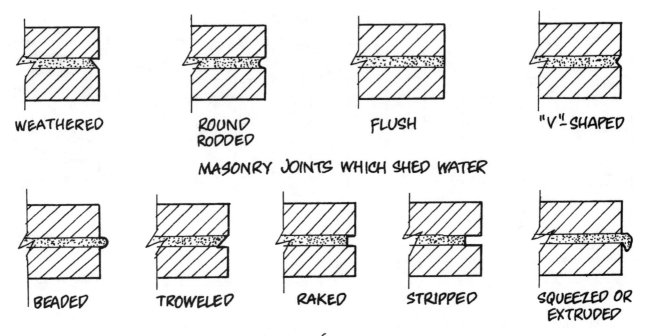

WEATHERED   ROUND RODDED   FLUSH   "V"-SHAPED

MASONRY JOINTS WHICH SHED WATER

BEADED   TROWELED   RAKED   STRIPPED   SQUEEZED OR EXTRUDED

MASONRY JOINTS (INTERIOR USE OR
EXTERIOR USE IN DRY CLIMATES)
THAT DO NOT SHED WATER

COMMON MORTAR JOINTS

entirely filled with mortar to begin with, and the face of the joint should be smooth and dense when the joint is completed. Shown above are several common masonry joints used in construction.

Masonry accessories are readily available for each type of masonry unit; they include anchors, ties, reinforcing, fillers, wire mesh, and so on, as well as various accessories for installing masonry ceilings, as shown on the following page.

CONCLUSION

The use of masonry has been called an anachronism in the modern world of construction. As most masonry work is performed very much as it has been for centuries, there is no doubt that it is labor intensive, and that means expensive. However, recent innovations, including prefabricated units, preassembled panels, and high bond adhesives, have led to decreased costs and expanded use.

There is also a psychological factor associated with masonry work; its warmth, scale, and handcrafted appearance are pleasing and cannot be replaced by factory-produced materials. Perhaps one day the stone wall and brick-paved patio will go the way of the cobbled street, but that day still appears to be in the distant future.

STRAP ANCHORS

DOVETAIL ANCHORS

CRAMP   PIN   THREADED
ANCHORS   DOWEL

HANGERS

EXPANSION JOINTS
WATER STOPS

MASONRY ACCESSORIES

LESSON 3 QUIZ

1. In a situation that requires a lightweight, fire-resistant interior partition, which of the following materials would be preferred?

   A. Concrete block

   B. Glass block

   C. Gypsum block

   D. Common brick

2. If a project required a nonbearing exterior wall to minimize solar heat gain while transmitting some light, which of the following materials would be appropriate?

   A. Glass block

   B. Face brick

   C. Modular brick

   D. Grade MW brick

3. Face brick differs from building brick in that it is generally

   A. more resistant to severe weathering.

   B. harder and more durable.

   C. more uniform in size and color.

   D. available in a variety of sizes.

4. To construct an eight-inch-thick masonry wall, concrete block might be selected instead of brick because it is

   I. less expensive.

   II. easier to handle.

   III. easier to reinforce.

   IV. faster to erect.

   V. more attractive.

   A. I and IV   C. I, II, and IV

   B. I and III   D. II, III, and V

5. Which of the following has little effect in preventing efflorescence?

   A. Using solid, tight mortar joints.

   B. Wetting the masonry units prior to setting.

   C. Furnishing adequate weather protection during construction.

   D. Providing a continuous weatherproof cap on walls.

6. A mortar mixture of portland cement, sand, and water, but no hydrated lime, would probably produce a mortar with

   A. greater strength and workability.

   B. insufficient bonding strength.

   C. little resistance to moisture penetration.

   D. insufficient water retention.

7. The considerable variation found in natural brick colors is caused by the

   I. preference of the manufacturer.

   II. clays from which they are made.

   III. pigmented admixtures used.

   IV. temperatures at which they are fired.

   V. length of time they are stored.

   A. II only   C. I, III, and IV

   B. II and IV   D. II, III, and V

8. A masonry course in which the long dimension of the exposed ends is placed vertically is called a

   A. header.   C. stretcher.

   B. soldier.   D. rowlock.

9. During a weekly job-site visit, the architect notices that a mason has used troweled joints on an exposed exterior masonry wall, instead of the weather-struck joints that were specified. In the interest of practicality, the architect should

    A. accept the change, because there is little difference in the two joints.

    B. accept the change, because there is no practical way to modify troweled joints.

    C. reject the work and have the mason trowel additional mortar over every horizontal joint.

    D. reject the wall and have the wall rebuilt.

10. The most reasonable alternative solution to the problem stated in the previous question would be to

    A. paint the entire wall with a waterproof sealer.

    B. spray the entire wall with a clear lacquer.

    C. fill each joint with expansion joint filler.

    D. plaster the masonry wall.

WOOD

INTRODUCTION

Wood is unique, as it is the only building material that grows and is renewable. Each year a new layer of wood develops naturally on a tree, with no need for human intervention. Therefore, with intelligent planning and forestry management, wood should remain available to us forever.

Because wood is organic, it does not have the precise properties of a manufactured product. On the contrary, wood has numerous and varied imperfections, such as checks, knots, pitch pockets, and shakes. To overcome some of these natural defects, wood used in construction is often modified to create more precisely engineered products, such as glued laminated lumber, panel products, and chemically treated wood with improved resistance to fire and decay.

Wood, mud, and stone were the first natural building materials used by prehistoric people. As civilizations advanced, trees were cut and the logs used for protective walls, lintels, and roofs. Some form of wood architecture was developed by every civilization with access to forests. Often, these historic structures displayed great imagination and beauty, such as the Norwegian stave churches of the 12th century.

In the New World, the westward movement and the development that followed would have been impossible without the virgin forests, which provided the material for log cabins, farm buildings, and eventually, whole towns.

In the past two centuries, wood construction has evolved from the relatively crude use of logs, poles, and heavy timbers to sophisticated structural systems employing engineered timber products never dreamed of by the early pioneers. Wood and wood products today constitute an important building material that continues to be highly regarded by architects and builders in much the same way it was by their predecessors.

TERMINOLOGY AND CLASSIFICATION

The terms *wood, lumber,* and *timber* are often used interchangeably, but each term has a distinct meaning.

Wood is the hard fibrous substance lying beneath the bark of trees.

Lumber is wood that has been sawn into construction members.

Timber is lumber that is five inches or larger in its least dimension.

Wood is classified as *softwood* or *hardwood,* depending on the type of tree from which it comes. Softwoods, such as pine, fir, and spruce, come from needle-leaved conifers, which are evergreen. Hardwoods, such as maple, oak, and sycamore, come from broad-leaved deciduous trees, which shed their leaves annually.

These terms are botanical, not structural, and they do not necessarily indicate the relative hardness or strength of a particular wood. For example, Douglas fir, a softwood, is much harder and stronger than basswood, which is a hardwood. And balsa, one of the most spongy and lightweight woods, is also a hardwood. Softwoods are used structurally in general construction for framing, sheathing, bracing, and so on, while hardwoods are mainly used for flooring, paneling, interior trim, and furniture.

CHARACTERISTICS

Wood is the handiest and most accommodating of all construction materials. It is available almost everywhere, readily transported, and easily worked with simple carpenters' tools. Wood-framed structures are strong, durable, and usually lower in cost than comparable concrete, masonry, or steel structures.

Although wood is combustible, heavy timber construction can resist fire better than unprotected steel construction. In addition, wood construction has great popular appeal, as light wood framing requires relatively little technical knowledge, and it may easily be worked with small, simple tools. Wood also has a unique beauty and warmth that people have enjoyed through the ages.

Wood consists of approximately 70 percent cellulose and 18 to 28 percent lignin, which is the adhesive imparting strength to the wood. The remainder is made up of minerals and extractives, which give wood its color, odor, and resistance to decay.

STRENGTH OF WOOD

Wood is generally stronger in compression than tension. Unlike most other building materials, the strength of wood is not the same in every direction: for both tension and compression, wood is much stronger when the load is applied parallel to the grain than perpendicular to the

CROSS SECTION OF A TREE

grain. In fact, the strength of wood in tension perpendicular to the grain is so low that this type of loading can easily cause the wood to split and should therefore be avoided.

For shear, wood is very strong perpendicular to the grain and relatively weak parallel to the grain. Therefore, horizontal shear stress (parallel to the grain) is often a design consideration, while vertical shear stress (perpendicular to the grain) is not.

SEASONING OF WOOD

Making wood suitable for construction involves more than simply cutting down a tree, shaking out the squirrels, and sawing the wood to size. Wood in the living tree is *green*; that is, it contains a large amount of water. If green lumber is used in construction, it will shrink as it dries out, which can cause a variety of problems. To minimize shrinkage, lumber should be *seasoned* (dried) before installation, until it reaches the moisture content it will have in service. This can be accomplished either by *air drying*, which takes several months and leaves 10 to 20 percent moisture in the lumber, or *kiln drying*, which takes only a few days and leaves less than 10 percent moisture. Framing lumber is

considered seasoned if its moisture content is 19 percent or less.

Even with seasoned lumber, however, moisture changes can occur. Dry members in a humid space will absorb moisture and conversely, members with a high moisture content will lose moisture in a dry environment. Between zero moisture content and the *fiber saturation point* (about 30 percent), wood swells as it absorbs moisture and shrinks as it loses moisture. Consequently, construction details should allow for some shrinkage or swelling of lumber members.

TANGENTIAL SHRINKAGE (GREATEST)

LONGITUDINAL SHRINKAGE (NEGLIGIBLE)

RADIAL SHRINKAGE (ABOUT HALF OF TANGENTIAL)

SHAPE AFTER SHRINKAGE

OUTLINE INDICATES SHAPE BEFORE SHRINKAGE

TYPICAL SHRINKAGE

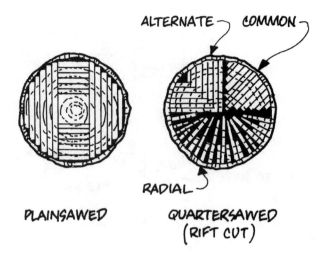

ALTERNATE   COMMON

RADIAL

PLAINSAWED   QUARTERSAWED (RIFT CUT)

LUMBER CUTTING

Not only does seasoned lumber have less tendency to shrink, but it is also stronger, stiffer, and lighter in weight than green, unseasoned lumber. In addition, seasoned lumber is less susceptible to warping; more resistant to fungi, decay, and insects; and has greater nail-holding power and ability to hold paint.

CUTTING AND SAWING LUMBER

Shrinkage, distortion, and warpage of lumber depend partially on the way lumber is cut from a tree. Wood shrinks most in the direction of the annual growth rings (tangentially); less across

these rings (radially); and very little parallel to the grain (longitudinally).

Lumber can be cut from a log in two different ways: tangent to the annual rings, called *plain-sawed* in hardwoods and *flat-grained* or *slash-grained* in softwoods; and radially to the rings, called *quartersawed* in hardwoods and *edge-grained* or *vertical-grained* in softwoods. *Rift-grained* and *comb-grained* are other terms sometimes used for quartersawed.

In actual practice, however, this is not strictly true, and so lumber is classed as quartersawed if the grain is 45° to 90° to the wide face and plainsawed if the grain is 0° to 45° to the wide face.

The characteristics of plainsawed lumber include:

1. Distinct grain pattern
2. May twist, cup, and wear unevenly
3. Tends to have raised grain
4. Shrinks and swells more in width, less in thickness
5. Less waste in cutting, and therefore less expensive

Quartersawed lumber has the following characteristics:

1. Relatively even grain pattern
2. Wears evenly with less warpage
3. Shrinks and swells more in thickness, less in width
4. More waste in cutting and therefore more costly

WOOD DEFECTS

There are a variety of defects that affect the strength, appearance, use, and grading of lumber. Defects may be natural or caused by manufacturing. In addition to these defects, wood can be damaged by insects, decayed by fungus, and of course, destroyed by fire.

Natural Defects

Natural defects are those resulting from natural causes. Some of these are listed below:

Knot—branch embedded in a tree and cut through in manufacture

Peck—pitted area sometimes found in cedar and cypress

Pitch pocket—opening between growth rings containing resin

Shake—lengthwise grain separation between or through growth rings

Manufacturing Defects

Manufacturing defects are those arising from the seasoning or processing of lumber. Some of these are listed below:

Check—lengthwise grain separation caused by seasoning

WOOD DEFECTS

Split—lengthwise separation of wood extending from one face to another

Wane—lack of wood on the edge or corner

Warp—shrinkage distortion of a plane surface; includes bow, crook, cup, and twist

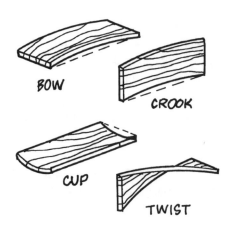

TYPES OF WARPAGE

GRADING LUMBER

As products of nature, no two pieces of wood are alike: they vary in strength, appearance, and other characteristics. In order to establish uniform standards of quality, lumber is graded for appearance or strength depending on its end use.

Grading for strength (stress grading) is done either visually or by machine, using standardized lumber grading rules. Visual grading is based on the number, size, type, and location of visible defects, such as knots, shakes, and wane. The grade assigned to a piece of lumber is then stamped on it, along with the mill identification and other information. During construction the grade is easily verified by checking the grade mark.

The best grades of lumber are practically free from imperfections, while in each lower grade, the imperfections increase in quantity.

In machine stress rating, lumber is subjected to bending, and the values of modulus of elasticity (E) and allowable fiber stress (f) are computed and automatically stamped on each piece.

Softwood Grades

Guidelines for softwood grading have been established by the National Bureau of Standards according to use, size, and manufacturer. The classification of principal uses is as follows:

Yard lumber is used in general construction.

Factory and shop lumber is used for remanufacture into products such as sash and doors, and the grades are based on the amount of clear wood in each piece.

There are three lumber size classifications: *boards, dimension lumber*, and *timbers*, as shown above right.

LUMBER SIZE CLASSIFICATION

Boards are graded for appearance and used as siding, subflooring, and trim. They are classified as *select* and *common*. Select lumber has a good appearance and is graded from A to D; A and B grades are of the highest quality and are suitable for natural finishes, while C and D are considered paint grades. Common lumber has more blemishes than select and is classified into five grades of descending quality, from number 1 to number 5.

Dimension lumber and timbers are called *structural lumber*, used for load-bearing members, and graded for strength. Dimension lumber is further classified according to its size as *joists and planks, light framing*, and *decking*. Timbers include *beams and stringers* and *posts and timbers*.

Three classifications based on manufacture are *rough, dressed*, and *worked lumber*. Rough lumber has visible saw marks, dressed or surfaced lumber is planed smooth to uniform sizes, and worked lumber is dressed and then tongue-and-grooved, shiplapped, or shaped to a pattern. Some examples of worked lumber are shown on the following page.

Hardwood Grades

Hardwood grades are based on the amount of clear, usable lumber in a piece. Standard lengths vary from 4 to 16 feet, and the standard grades

DROP SIDING   FINISH FLOORING   SHIPLAP SHEATHING FLOORING & SIDING   EXPOSED ROOF SHEATHING

WORKED LUMBER

are firsts, seconds, selects, sound wormy, and numbers 1, 2, 3A, and 3B common.

Lumber Sizes

All lumber is specified according to its nominal dimensions, which are the rough or unfinished sizes. The dressed, surfaced or finished size is always smaller due to the seasoning and surfacing of lumber before its use. For example, a nominal 2" × 4" is actually 1-1/2 by 3-1/2 inches in size.

Lumber is measured, computed, and priced in board feet. This is a conventional, standard unit in which a board foot is defined as a nominal 1" × 12" board one foot in length.

PLYWOOD

Description

Plywood is a manufactured wood panel consisting of several thin wood veneer sheets (plies) that are permanently bonded together with adhesive under high pressure, with the grain of each ply perpendicular to the grain of the adjacent plies. The center ply is known as the *core*, while the outer plies are called *face* and *back*. When there are five or more plies, the additional sheets, called *crossbands*, are located between, and placed perpendicular to, the core and the outside plies. There is generally an odd number

NOMINAL 1" × 12"

BOARD FOOT MEASURE

of plies (3, 5, or 7) that gives a balanced effect, so that the panel tends to remain flat with changes in moisture content. Some panels are made with cores of solid lumber or particle board instead of veneer.

Plywood veneers are produced by rotary cutting, as at the bottom of page 66. For hardwood face veneers where grain appearance is important, the veneers may be quarter sliced or plain sliced.

Plywood is produced in standard 4 by 8 foot sheets, with the grain of the face and back veneers parallel to the 8-foot dimension. Thicknesses range from 5/16 inch to 1-1/8 inches.

Plywood provides a strong backing for finish materials, and is widely used in construction as wall and roof sheathing, subflooring, underlayment, and formwork. Because of its great

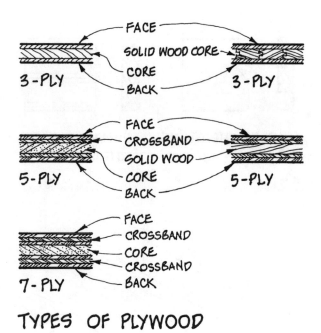

TYPES OF PLYWOOD

resistance to shrinking and splitting, and less warpage. In addition, a sheet of plywood covers a large surface area with relatively few pieces of material.

Classification

Plywood is classified as *interior* or *exterior*, depending on the type of adhesive used: moisture-resistant for interior use and water-proof for exterior use. Plywood is also classified as softwood or hardwood, depending on the species of the face veneers. Plywood used in construction is primarily softwood.

Plywood is graded according to the quality of the veneers, with A being the best and D the poorest. The grade of a plywood panel is desig-nated by two letters representing the veneer grade on the face and back; for example, an A-D panel has an A-grade face and a D-grade back. The grade is marked on each panel for easy identification. For exterior plywood, the inner plies must be grade C or better, while interior plywood may have D-grade inner plies.

strength and stiffness, plywood is particularly effective in resisting lateral loads from wind or earthquake, in the form of roof and floor dia-phragms and shear walls.

The advantages of plywood over sawn lumber are its great strength in both directions, greater

PLYWOOD VENEER CUTTING

The species of wood used for face and back veneers is identified on each panel by a group number, ranging from group 1 species (the strongest and stiffest) to group 5 species (the weakest).

Some unsanded plywood panels used for structural purposes, such as roof sheathing, subflooring, and wall sheathing, are not marked with the grade and species group. Instead, they are marked with a *span rating* consisting of two numbers; the first denotes the maximum recommended roof span in inches, and the second the maximum recommended span for subflooring. For example, a panel identified as 32/16 can be used as roof sheathing over rafters spaced 32 inches on center or as subflooring over joists spaced 16 inches on center. In addition to plywood, such panels may also be made of composites and oriented strand board.

Two typical grade marks used by mills belonging to the American Plywood Association (APA) are in the next column, by permission of the American Plywood Association.

Hardwood plywood is more expensive than softwood plywood, and is used primarily for decorative applications, such as paneling, cabinet work, face veneers on doors, etc. The grading and sizing of hardwood plywood is different from that of softwood plywood previously described.

The way in which hardwood plywood panels are matched affects the finish appearance. In *book matching*, also called *edge matching*, every other sheet is turned over. In *slip matching*, adjacent sheets are joined side by side without turning, thus repeating the grain pattern. Purposely unmatched veneers are called *random matching*.

Sanded Grades

(Also available in Groups 1, 3 and 4)

Unsanded Grades

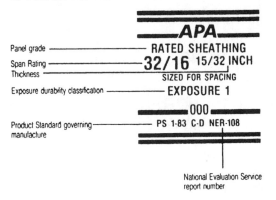

In addition to conventional construction plywood, other special types include overlay (covered with resin-fiber overlay); marine; prefinished (stained and ready to use); and patterned sheets (grooved, roughsawn, etc.). The major uses of these special plywoods are for furniture, cabinets, flooring, exterior siding, and interior wall finishes.

MISCELLANEOUS PANELS

Several types of pressed fiber boards are used in construction. In general, these consist of wood or other fiber mixed with a binder and pressed into a flat sheet. They are commonly used for non-

BOOK MATCH   **SLIP MATCH**   **RANDOM MATCH**

METAL FLASHING   **HORIZONTAL WOOD DRIP MOLDING**

HORIZONTAL PLYWOOD JOINTS

structural or semistructural purposes, such as concrete forms, cabinets, doors, wall paneling, partitions, decking, and insulation.

Hardboard is made from wood fibers that have been highly compressed under heat and pressure into dense, durable boards. It is available in two categories: basic and prefinished, and in three types: tempered, standard, and service standard. These are available in 4 by 8 foot sheets that are 1/8 inch to 3/8 inch thick.

Prefinished hardboard is available in a variety of patterns, textures, and finishes, such as baked enamels, plastic laminates, etc.

Prefinished hardboard is used for exterior siding, soffits, interior walls, ceilings, cabinet work, pegboards, and acoustical treatment.

Fiberboard is manufactured from waste paper, wood pulp, and fibers. It is used for acoustical tile, sheathing, and interior wall finishes. The standard size is 4 feet by 8 feet, in thicknesses from 1/2 inch to 1 inch. Fiberboard roof insulation and laminated fiberboard decking are manufactured in 2 by 4 foot sheets.

BUTT JOINT   **VEE JOINT**   **SHIPLAP JOINT**   **BATTEN JOINT**   **METAL TEE JOINT**

VERTICAL PLYWOOD JOINTS

Flakeboard is composed of large wood flakes bonded together with synthetic resins under pressure. Flakeboard is lightweight and has good insulation value and acoustical properties, but its surface is easily damaged. Its main use is as an insulating backup material or as an acoustical material on upper walls and ceilings.

Particleboard is dry-formed of wood particles bonded together with synthetic resin. It is used primarily as core stock for plastic laminate or hardwood veneers and used in the manufacture of furniture, cabinets, countertops, wall paneling, and doors of all types.

Beadboard is an insulating board consisting of a core of small, expanded polystyrene beads with heavy paper laminated to both sides. The major use of beadboard is as an insulating material, such as perimeter insulation on foundation walls. Its insulation value is less than that of extruded polystyrene insulation of the same thickness.

Plastic laminates consist of a base of phenolic-resin impregnated kraft paper over which a patterned sheet is applied. Over all this is laid a sheet of paper treated with melamine resin. These layers are then cured with intense heat and pressure to fuse the material into a thin sheet which can be applied to plywood or other backing with adhesive. Popularly known by trade names such as Formica, the material has found popular acceptance for countertops, wall coverings, and furniture.

GLUED LAMINATED LUMBER

Glued laminated (*glulam*) structural members are fabricated from layers of wood that are bonded with adhesives, in which the grain of all layers is approximately parallel longitudinally. The usual thickness of laminations is 1-1/2

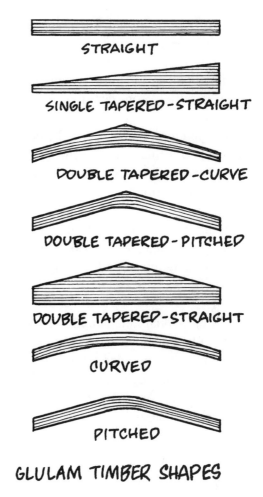

STRAIGHT

SINGLE TAPERED-STRAIGHT

DOUBLE TAPERED-CURVE

DOUBLE TAPERED-PITCHED

DOUBLE TAPERED-STRAIGHT

CURVED

PITCHED

GLULAM TIMBER SHAPES

inches, although 3/4-inch laminations are used to achieve small radius curves. Members are produced in several standard widths and a great range of depths, up to about 75 inches.

Glued laminated members are factory produced under rigidly controlled manufacturing conditions, resulting in members that are superior to sawn lumber in several ways. For the same size member, they can span greater distances and support heavier loads. Glulams are more weather-resistant; they are consistent in size, appearance, and strength; and they are more dimensionally stable than solid timber.

Glulam members are available in three appearance grades:

Industrial is the grade used where appearance is not a prime concern.

Architectural is the grade used where appearance is an important consideration.

Premium is the top grade, specified where appearance is of primary importance. It is the most expensive grade and arrives at the site fully wrapped for protection.

In specifying laminated timbers, one must designate the type of adhesive (interior or exterior), the stress grade required, and the appearance grade desired.

In general, individual laminations are not the full length of the member. Therefore, they must be joined end to end in order to produce a member of the required length. The two most common types of joints are *scarf joints* and *finger joints*, as shown below.

SCARF JOINT   FINGER JOINT

Laminated decking is manufactured from layers of kiln-dried lumber that are bonded with adhesives. It is available in 3- to 5-inch nominal thicknesses and in various standard lengths. The interior surface of the decking is intended to be exposed and is available smooth, grooved, prefinished, or stained.

LAMINATED WOOD DECKING

WOOD PRESERVATION

Insects, decay, and fire represent continual threats to wood. Proper seasoning may reduce some of these hazards, but for the most positive protection, other means must be employed.

Insects

The insects most destructive to wood construction are *termites*, which cause extensive damage, particularly in warm, humid climates. Termites eat wood from within, so that a wood member may appear sound, but may actually be eaten away inside.

Preventive measures include proper drainage to minimize moisture, good ventilation, and impervious concrete foundations. Wood members should be adequately separated from the ground or, if not, they should be pressure treated with a preservative.

Other measures include the use of termite shields, metal strips used to prevent the insects from reaching the wood and poisoning the ground adjacent to the building. Because termites attack from within, surface coatings are generally ineffective, and preservatives that completely penetrate the wood should be used instead.

Carpenter ants use wood for shelter rather than for food. Measures used to prevent termite

LAMINATED WOOD ARCH

FINISH FLOOR

ARCH FOUNDATION

TIE ROD

TWO-HINGED ARCH

HINGE

LAMINATED WOOD FRAME

FINISH FLOOR

TIE ROD

HINGE

THREE-HINGED FRAME

LAMINATED PARABOLIC ARCH

HINGE

FINISH FLOOR

HINGE

TIE ROD

THREE-HINGED ARCH

TYPES OF LAMINATED WOOD FRAMES & ARCHES

attack are usually effective against carpenter ants as well.

Marine boring organisms damage wood structures located in salt or brackish waters. The most effective protection is heavy treatment with creosote.

Decay

Decay in wood is caused by fungi that feed on the cell walls. The development of any fungus requires mild temperatures, moisture, and air. Without all three, decay cannot occur. Decay can be avoided if wood is kept dry and well ventilated, or if it is kept continually and completely submerged in water so that air is excluded. Intermittent wetting provides a favorable environment for decay. Where decay is possible, the wood should be a decay-resistant species, such as redwood, or be pressure treated with a preservative.

Preservatives

Chemical preservatives that protect wood from fungi, as well as insects and marine organisms, are of two types: oil-borne solutions, such as creosote; and waterborne solutions, such as chromated zinc chloride. Preservatives may be brushed, sprayed, or dipped, but for maximum effectiveness, they should be applied under pressure for deeper penetration. The oil-borne preservatives cause discoloration or an oily surface that is difficult to paint. Because of the toxicity of preservatives, their use is often restricted or controlled by regulations.

Fire

Fire is an ever-present danger to wood, with the exception of heavy timbers, which burn very slowly. Wood can be made fire resistant by either impregnation with a chemical solution, such as ammonium phosphate, or by the use of a surface treatment. Surface applications, such as intumescent paint, retard the increase of temperature and thereby reduce the rate of flame spread.

WOOD FRAMING

Years ago, when tall trees, and hence large timbers, were plentiful, a designer faced with a 50-foot span would call for 50-foot-long sawn girders to be placed at intervals across the structure. Here was roof framing at its simplest: little engineering, no fabrication, no assembly, and a minimum of small members to be concerned about.

Today, such large timbers are costly and difficult to obtain. Instead, long-span wood construction utilizes trusses, rigid frames, built-up

PITCHED

FLAT

SCISSORS

SAWTOOTH

WOOD TRUSSED RAFTER TYPES

3/4" INTERMEDIATE AND SIDE MEMBERS

DEPTH DEPENDS ON SPAN

SPAN

TWO LAYERS OF 4'-0" WIDE PLYWOOD LAMINATED WITH 4'-0" LAPS LENGTHWISE

2" THICK TO PROVIDE FOR T & G JOINTS

STRESSED SKIN PLYWOOD PANEL

girders, and glued laminated beams. Several types of trussed rafters (small, closely spaced wood trusses); plywood girders; and a stressed skin panel are shown on this and the next page.

Since the beginning of the 20th century, when grading rules and working stresses were established, wood framing has become relatively standardized. There are two wood wall framing systems commonly used for dwellings and other small structures: *platform framing* (also called western framing) and *balloon framing*. In platform framing, the studs are one story in height and the floor joists bear on the top plates of the wall below. In balloon framing, the wall studs are continuous for the full height of the building, usually two stories, from the foundation to the top plates under the roof rafters.

Wood post and beam systems employ beams, rather than joists and rafters, to support floors and roofs. The beams in turn rest on posts or columns, rather than studs, which transfer the building loads to the foundation. The resulting

VERTICAL MEMBERS 2'-0" O.C.

4⁹×8⁹ PLYWOOD LAYERS GLUED AND NAILED TO WOOD FRAME AND LAPPED 4'-0" HORIZONTALLY AND 2'-0" VERTICALLY

HORIZONTAL WOOD MEMBERS GLUED AND NAILED TO PLYWOOD

4'-0" TO 8'-0"

WOOD FRAME WITH DIAGONAL BRACING BETWEEN VERTICAL MEMBERS

4'-0" TO 8'-0"

4⁹×8⁹ PLYWOOD WITH TWO OUTSIDE LAYERS LAMINATED TO CENTER LAYER AND LAPPED 2'-0" VERTICALLY AND 4'-0" HORIZONTALLY

PLYWOOD GIRDERS

skeleton frame forms a three-dimensional modular grid, which is often left exposed.

Lateral stability is provided by rigid connecting joints, as well as by enclosing exterior walls.

The extensive subject of wood framing is covered in Chapter 23 of the International Building Code. Candidates are encouraged to review this chapter, with particular attention to nomenclature, stress grades, and common practices used in wood framed construction.

WOOD JOINING

In the days when lumber was plentiful and nails were scarce, it was customary to use large timbers for framing members, and to join them with mortise-and-tenon joints, fastened with

wooden pins. The mass production of nails and other fasteners in the 19th century brought about a complete change in all types of wood joining.

Wood joints are classified as exterior or interior, and for both types there is a wide choice of fasteners available, including nails, spikes, screws, bolts, pins, metal connectors, and adhesives. The method of joining is influenced by the species of wood, its characteristics, size, grain, moisture content, exposure, and appearance desired, as well as the necessary strength. Some examples of metal connections are shown on the following page.

The most common connections in wood structures are made by nails, which are driven into the wood with a hammer or a mechanical gun. *Common nails* are used for most structural connections, *box nails* are thinner than common

FRAMING ANCHOR   POST CAP   FRAMING ANCHOR

PLYWOOD SHEATHING CLIP   JOIST HANGER

METAL FRAMING CONNECTORS

nails and consequently have less holding power, and *finish nails* are thin nails with small heads used to attach finish wood elements.

Wood joining is done either at the site or at the mill or shop. Exterior joints must consider weathering, structural joints must meet structural requirements, and interior joints largely consider appearance. In general, the closer a joint approaches invisibility, the more difficult and costly it becomes. Some common wood joints are shown on the following page.

FINISH WOODWORK

Millwork consists of shop-fabricated items, such as door and window frames, stairways, paneling, etc., which are fabricated in a mill and delivered to the job, ready for installation. Millwork should always be protected by a primer or sealer coat before leaving the shop. Once on the job, it should be handled and stored with care to

prevent warping, opening of joints, or other damage. During installation of millwork, ventilation should be provided so that decay or dry rot will not develop where members trap moisture against an unfinished wall.

Wood trim, molding, and ornamental shapes are fabricated from the better grades of both softwood and hardwood. They may also be made from material composed of wood fibers or chips held together with plastic binders and then fused under heat and pressure. All of these shapes are used principally to cover joints where two elements meet and are likely to pull away from one another, or where joints would be unattractive if left exposed. Trim shapes are generally applied by finish carpenters using conventional tools and fasteners. Some common shapes are shown on the following page.

Wood siding and paneling are made from common dimension lumber, cut and dressed to

LAP   **SHOULDER**   **RABBET**   **MITER**   **SHOULDER MITER**

QUIRK MITER   **T&G MITER**   **BUTT**   **TONGUE & GROOVE**   **SHIPLAP**

SPLINE   **FILLET**   **V-JOINT**   **BATTEN**   **SQUARED SPLICE**

SPLICE   **SCARF**   **MORTISE & TENON**   **DADO**   **DOVETAIL**

TONGUE & GROOVE   **OPEN JOINT**   **METAL JOINT**   **METAL U INSERT**   **OPEN JOINT WITH FILLER**

WOOD JOINTS

¼ ROUND   **½ ROUND**   **COVE**   **BEAD**   **CROWN**   **CASING**   **BASE**

WOOD TRIM SHAPES

standard sizes, and available in a variety of shapes and species. Almost all siding is made from seasoned softwoods, while paneling may be manufactured from both softwoods and hardwoods. Only the better grades of wood are used for siding and paneling, which are stained, painted, or allowed to weather naturally. Exterior siding patterns should be selected for their

CHANNEL   BOARD & BATT   TONGUE & GROOVE   SHIPLAP

VERTICAL PATTERNS

BEVEL   RABBETED BEVEL   VEE JOINT T&G   DROP T&G

HORIZONTAL PATTERNS

WOOD SIDING PATTERNS

ability to withstand weather, and they should always be applied over lapped building paper. Shown above are some common wood siding patterns.

CONCLUSION

The future of wood in construction appears to be very promising for several reasons. First of all, reforestation has become widespread, assuring a continuous supply of the raw material. Second, engineered wood products continue to be developed through technology and the imaginative efforts of industry. Finally, we have yet to find another material for small structures that is as inexpensive, easily worked, and universally popular as wood.

Whether because of our tradition and heritage, or perhaps a powerful psychological attraction, wood will continue to play an important role in building construction, from rough framing to finishing, and from the roof that keeps us dry to the furniture we use daily.

LESSON 4 QUIZ

1. If the primary concern for a structure is fire resistance, one should use

   A. post and beam framing.

   B. heavy timber framing.

   C. platform framing.

   D. balloon framing.

2. Which of the following will help extend the life of wood?

   I. Keep all underfloor wood members dry and well ventilated.

   II. Keep subsurface wood supports totally submerged in water.

   III. Use hardwood members in areas close to the earth.

   IV. Use antitermite chemicals on the surface of wood members close to the earth.

   V. Apply intumescent paint on all exposed wood members.

   A. I and V

   B. II, III, and IV

   C. I, II, and V

   D. I, III, IV, and V

3. An architect discovers that the anticipated load of a proposed floor exceeds the safe carrying capacity of conventional wood joists spaced at 16 inches. Because the design is limited to a relatively shallow framing depth, the practical solution would be to use

   A. conventional joists more closely spaced.

   B. shallow wood trusses.

   C. glued laminated beams.

   D. plywood girders.

4. Mortise-and-tenon joints were used in most 18th century timber framing because

   A. it was the easiest type of joint to produce with the available tools.

   B. joint strength could not be achieved by any other method.

   C. metal fasteners were scarce.

   D. appearance was of primary importance.

5. The principal reason that lumber is graded is to establish

   A. uniform standards of quality.

   B. uniform standards of appearance.

   C. the strength of a particular member.

   D. the characteristics of a particular member.

6. Wood that has a moisture content of 30 percent is generally

   A. air dried.   C. dry.

   B. kiln dried.   D. green.

7. Which type of manufactured panel would be most appropriate to use for perimeter foundation wall insulation?

   A. Beadboard

   B. Fiberboard

   C. Flakeboard

   D. Hardboard

8. Which type of manufactured panel is generally used as core stock for hardwood wall paneling?

   A. Prefinished hardboard

   B. Tempered hardboard

   C. Particleboard

   D. Plywood

9. If you wanted to use wood siding with a highly figured grain pattern, you would specify

   A. rift cut lumber.

   B. plainsawed lumber.

   C. quartersawed lumber.

   D. factory and shop lumber.

10. The strength of a wood member is affected by which of the following?

   I.   The species of tree from which it is cut

   II.   The method used in its seasoning

   III. The way it is cut from the tree

   IV.   The number of defects it has

   V.   The direction of the applied loads

   A. I, IV, and V

   B. II, III, and IV

   C. I, II, III, and V

   D. All of the above

METALS

INTRODUCTION

All metals come from the earth, usually as metallic ores, which are metal-bearing minerals or rocks. There are a few metals, however, that are found in a purer state, such as gold, silver, and copper.

The knowledge of metals, as well as their earliest use, dates back to prehistoric times. The Bronze Age, in fact, was named after the bronze tools, art objects, and utensils made during that period. Metals were employed in early construction for a variety of purposes. In addition to purely decorative applications, lead was used for plumbing and bronze was used for concrete reinforcement in ancient Rome. Copper roofing covered Gothic cathedrals, and somewhat later, iron chains were used as tensile ties, as in the base of Michelangelo's dome for St. Peter's in Rome.

It was not until the Industrial Revolution of the mid-18th century, however, that the first metal members intended for construction were produced. Metal as a structural material, however, was neither easily available nor architecturally acceptable until the beginning of the 19th century. Thus, the use of metal to support building loads is a relatively modern development.

With the advent of cast iron girders, beams, and columns, metal bridges began to appear. Later, large halls and factory buildings were framed with these new cast iron sections. Pioneer designers, such as Labrouste with his libraries, Eiffel with his famous tower, and William Jenney with his multistory structures, paved the way for the acceptance of metal-framed construction.

The development of reinforced concrete was a further advance in the use of metal for construction. Here, steel with its tensile strength and concrete with its compressive strength were combined to form a new structural material, which was able to express completely new design concepts.

Today, the skyline of every major city in the world reflects our dependence on the use of metal for tall building construction. In addition, modern architects rely on a vast number of metal products developed through modern technology for the construction industry.

It is perhaps ironic that metals, which were formed when the earth was created, furnish many of the modern building products that are invaluable for today's architecture.

CHARACTERISTICS

Metals are substances that are characterized by their luster, opaqueness, hardness, ability to conduct heat and electricity, and by their superior ability to resist deformation.

Extracting a metal from its ore is called *smelting*, and invariably this involves some sort of heat treatment. Even after it is extracted, the metal still contains small amounts of impurities, which may be further removed by various refining processes. In some cases minor impurities may enhance the metal by forming an alloy that has special properties, such as increased strength, hardness, or corrosion resistance. Because some metals, such as lead, copper, and iron, are very soft in their pure form, they are often combined with controlled quantities of other substances to form *alloys* when used in building construction.

The physical, chemical, and mechanical properties of metals are so diverse that architects can know only some of the significant characteristics of the metals widely used in construction. This data may include strength, toughness, corrosion resistance, appearance, cost, and methods of forming, joining, and handling.

Metals are classified as either ferrous or non-ferrous. The *ferrous metals* are those containing a substantial proportion of iron, such as stainless steel and galvanized iron; while the *non-ferrous metals* are all the others, such as aluminum, copper, and zinc.

DETERIORATION

Almost all metals deteriorate as a result of exposure to air, water, soil, or other chemical agents. Surface discoloration, or tarnish, is merely unsightly; however, corrosion, such as the rusting of iron, can result in actual failure.

Galvanic action, or *electrolysis*, is a relatively common type of deterioration that occurs when different metals, or alloys, are in contact. If this contact takes place in the presence of an electrolyte, such as moisture, an electrical current will flow from one metal to the other, and in time, one metal will corrode while the other will remain intact. The degree and speed of deterioration depend on the amount of moisture present. Dry air will result in slow action, while an ocean atmosphere will produce intense and swift deterioration.

The following list of metals is arranged in order of galvanic activity. Each metal can be corroded by all that follow it; for example, lead is corroded by brass, and gold is virtually corrosion-proof. In general, metals far apart on the list should not be placed in contact with each other.

1. Aluminum
2. Zinc
3. Iron and Steel

4. Stainless Steel
5. Tin
6. Lead
7. Brass
8. Copper
9. Bronze
10. Gold

In order to prevent galvanic action, different metals should be isolated from one another, or compatible metals should be used. For example, if aluminum siding is applied with steel nails, the nails should insulated from the siding with neoprene washers, or—better yet—aluminum nails should be used in place of steel nails. If uninsulated steel nails are used, the aluminum around the nail will be gradually eaten away, and the siding may eventually fall off.

Other forms of corrosion may be prevented by changing the chemical composition of the metal or by applying a surface treatment. An example of the former is alloying, such as stainless steel, while an example of a surface treatment is the use of a protective coating, such as galvanizing or anodizing.

FORMING METAL

Forming is the process by which extracted metal is transformed into a useful product that has a finished shape. Products may be either cast or wrought.

Cast products are obtained by pouring molten metal into a mold of the required shape and allowing it to cool.

Wrought products are obtained by forcibly shaping solid metal to a required form by a variety of methods. These methods include hot

or cold rolling (bars, sheets, strips, angles, channels, etc.); forging (hammering hot metal); pressing (from sheets); drawing (into wires or tubes); and extruding (forcing a hot mass of metal through an opening that has the shape of the required section).

A particular metal or alloy may be more suited to one method of forming than another. In this regard, one should be familiar with the metal's mechanical properties, such as malleability (ease of hammering); ductility (ease of drawing); toughness (resistance to fracture); and hardness (resistance to abrasion).

FERROUS METALS

Iron

The principal constituent of all ferrous metals is iron, which is the second most abundant metal and fourth most abundant element on earth. All commercial ferrous metals contain some carbon, and small variations in carbon content have an important influence on their properties. Pure iron, which is difficult to obtain, is tough, malleable, easily magnetized, and quick to oxidize.

Iron is extracted from its ore by smelting, a process that goes back more than 5,000 years. Today, blast furnaces are used to reduce the ore to pig iron, the raw material from which all ferrous metals are made. Pig iron contains about 93 percent iron, 4 percent carbon, and small quantities of silicon, phosphorus, and sulfur.

Wrought iron is almost pure iron with a very low carbon content. It is soft but strong, extremely ductile, easily worked, and relatively resistant to corrosion. It can be forged, bent, or rolled into shape, but it cannot be cast, tempered, or easily welded. Historically, wrought iron was the prime metal used for

FERROUS METALS

tension members, such as chains, crane hooks, and anchors. In construction today, however, it is used mainly for ornamental ironwork, grilles, plumbing pipes, and outdoor furniture. Wrought iron is available in pipe, sheet, bar, and bent shapes.

Cast iron is produced by resmelting pig iron with steel scrap. It has a relatively high carbon content (2 percent or more) and is available in a variety of types, each with distinct characteristics (white cast iron, gray cast iron, malleable iron, etc.).

Cast iron has a high compressive but low tensile strength. It is easily cast into almost any shape, but it is generally too hard and brittle to be shaped by hammering, rolling, or pressing. Cast iron surfaces are somewhat rough and uneven, but they have good resistance to corrosion.

Historically, cast iron was used for compression members, such as the columns and arches of the Crystal Palace, which was built in 1851. Today, however, its use is limited to pipes, certain plumbing fixtures, ornamental iron work, hardware, and a multitude of special castings.

Steel

Steel is an alloy of iron that contains no more than 2 percent carbon. Structural steel contains about a quarter of 1 percent carbon, plus traces of various impurities.

There are three principal methods of making steel: the open hearth process, the basic oxygen process, and the electric furnace process. They all involve the removal of unwanted impurities and excess carbon from pig iron and the addition of other elements to produce the desired composition.

The large-scale use of steel dates from the latter part of the 19th century, nearly coinciding with the construction of the Eiffel Tower—the last great structure built of wrought iron.

Steel is a hard, strong material that is also tough and malleable. It is the most widely used structural metal in building construction, because it provides great strength at relatively low cost. Steel can be rolled, drawn, bent, cast, and joined by rivets, bolts, or welds. It is used for structural framing, concrete reinforcing bars, lathing, conduit, pipes, fixtures, miscellaneous and ornamental work, and for all kinds of connectors, such as nails, pins, and bolts.

Listed below are various types of steel together with some of their properties.

Structural steel. This is steel used for structural purposes, containing varying amounts of carbon and other elements. Included in this type are also a variety of high-strength steels.

Alloy steel. This is steel containing other elements that are added to provide special properties. For example, stainless steel, containing chromium and nickel, is strong, hard, and corrosion-resistant.

Weathering steel. This is steel containing up to one half of 1 percent copper, which develops a tightly-adherent oxide coating when exposed to the weather. It requires no finish.

Heat-treated steel. This is steel that is reheated and cooled slowly, or annealed, for improved workability.

Case-hardened steel. This is steel with a hard, high carbon surface produced by a special process.

NON-FERROUS METALS

Almost all non-ferrous metals share one desirable characteristic: they resist corrosion. In addition, they generally have excellent workability. On the other hand, the initial cost of non-ferrous metals is usually much greater than that of ordinary ferrous metals. As with iron and steel, almost all non-ferrous metals used in construction are alloys.

Aluminum

Aluminum is the most abundant element in the earth's crust. It is obtained from bauxite by the electrolytic method, which was developed less than 100 years ago. Before that time, aluminum was considered a precious metal.

The important properties of aluminum include its light weight (about one third that of steel); good thermal and electrical conductivity; and great resistance to corrosion (except for galvanic action and some oxidation). It is also highly reflective, making it useful as a barrier to radiant heat transmission.

Pure aluminum is soft, but as an alloy it can be as hard and strong as mild steel. It is available

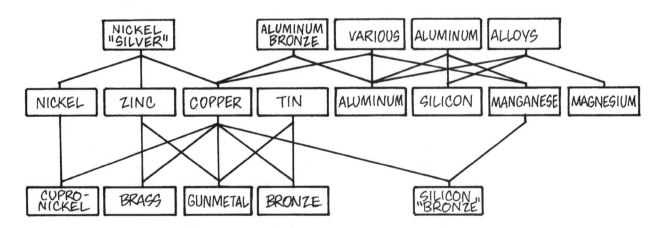

NON-FERROUS METALS AND ALLOYS

in nearly all fabricated forms, such as castings, extrusions, sheets, strips, bars, and rods. Aluminum may be joined by riveting, welding, soldering, or adhesive bonding. The material takes a great variety of finishes, including etching, embossing, anodizing, plating, baked enameling, and painting (although never with a lead-based paint).

Aluminum is used extensively in construction. Its many applications include framing of light-weight structures, railings and grilles, siding and curtain walls, windows, doors, flashing, insulation, roofing, screening, and hardware.

Copper

Copper is a useful metal that is malleable, ductile, and of fairly high mechanical strength. It is remarkably resistant to corrosive agents, particularly sea water, and it has extremely high electrical and thermal conductivity.

Copper is used in construction for electrical work, water distribution lines, roofing and flashing, and for screening mesh. When exposed to the elements, copper develops a distinctive green patina that makes any further finish unnecessary.

Other Metals

Brass is a common alloy of copper and zinc. In general, all brasses resist corrosion and are easily worked. They are used for precise castings, finish hardware, and for plumbing, heating, and air-conditioning components and fittings.

Bronzes are alloys of copper and tin, with small amounts of other metals. Their properties and uses are very similar to brass.

Lead is a heavy, soft, toxic metal of low strength. It is easily worked, corrosion-resistant,

and relatively impenetrable to radiation. It is used in construction for acid and radiation resistance, for vibration control under foundations and machinery, in rough hardware items, and for roofing and flashing (some examples of which are 2,000 years old). However, lead is rarely used these days for plumbing (a term derived from the Latin *plumbum*, or lead), because of the danger of lead poisoning.

Zinc is a relatively low-strength corrosion-resistant metal that is used in building construction for roof covering and flashing and for protective coatings on steel, such as galvanizing.

Monel is a nickel-copper alloy that is strong, bright, ductile, and corrosion-resistant. Its uses in construction include roofing, flashing, counter tops, sinks, and other commercial kitchen equipment.

METAL FINISHES

Finishes are applied to metals for appearance or for protection from corrosion. All metals can be mechanically finished by means of grinding, polishing, sandblasting, hammering, or otherwise treating the surface to obtain a special textural effect. In addition, metals may be treated with an applied coating, such as electroplating, enameling, spraying, dipping, or sherardizing (coating with zinc dust).

Most non-ferrous metals, as well as stainless steels, can be (and often are) left to weather with no additional treatment. Ferrous metals, however, require a protective coating to prevent corrosion. One exception, of course, is weathering steel, which acquires a brownish-colored protective oxide coating that deters further rust and corrosion.

Anodizing

Anodizing is a metal finish applied to aluminum, which begins by inserting the material into an electrolyte. When an electric current is applied, a coating is formed on the aluminum surface in a wide choice of hues.

Galvanizing

Galvanizing is, by far, the most popular method of protecting iron and steel against corrosion. In this process, a coating of zinc is applied by immersing the steel in a bath of molten zinc. The amount of coating is expressed in ounces per square foot of sheet. Even if the zinc coating is broken, because of wear or damage, galvanic action causes the zinc to corrode, thus protecting the iron or steel for as long as any zinc remains. Because of the effective protection it affords at a relatively low price, this use of zinc represents the largest consumption of the metal in the United States.

Galvanized sheets are available in plain flat, corrugated, and special shapes. They are commonly used in construction for roofing, siding, decking, flashing, and cladding, as in kalamein doors (galvanized metal-covered wood core doors used for high fire resistance).

Zinc corrodes to a self-protecting oxide, therefore making it more resistant to corrosive damage than steel. However, zinc is not immune to deterioration. Therefore, when zinc-coated products are exposed to corrosive conditions, they often require the additional protection of paint. Most paints will not adhere to galvanized metal unless the surface has been completely cleaned and prepared. For this purpose a phosphatizing solution may be used to provide the necessary paint bond. Among the available products, portland cement-based paint is an excellent primer for galvanized surfaces.

THE USE OF METALS IN CONSTRUCTION

The use of metals in construction can be classified into six major categories:

1. *Structural*—structural steel, reinforcing bars and mesh for concrete, and wire rope
2. *Hollow metalwork*—doors, bucks, partitions, panels, windows, mullions, curtain walls, and panel systems that incorporate other materials, such as glass, stone, plastic, and so on
3. *Miscellaneous metalwork*—stairs, railings, fencing, gratings, rough hardware, ladders, and so forth
4. *Ornamental metalwork*—plaques, letters, finish hardware, railings, screens, grilles, expansion joint covers, etc.
5. *Flashing*—base and cap flashing, gutters and leaders, spandrel and through-wall flashing, copings, termite shields, etc.; and all of these applications are covered further in Lesson Six
6. *Miscellaneous*—rough hardware, nuts and bolts, rivets, screws, nails, washers, inserts, hangers, anchors, wire, and so forth

STRUCTURAL STEEL CONSTRUCTION

Structural steel construction consists of the fabrication and erection of hot-rolled members manufactured from medium carbon steel (about one quarter of 1 percent carbon). Standard rolled sections are available in a vast selection of weights and sizes, and they include wide flange beams and columns (designated W); American Standard beams (S); American Standard channels (C); angles (L); tees (WT, cut from W shapes); and tubing; as well as bars and plates.

ROLLED STEEL SECTIONS

In addition to standard rolled sections, built-up shapes can be constructed from combinations of standard shapes. The resulting configurations, such as plate girders, built-up columns, truss chords, rigid bents, and so forth, are employed where standard rolled sections are not available or efficient.

Structural steel is most often used to construct a skeleton frame. Steel fabrication (cutting, shaping, drilling, welding, and so on) is generally performed in a fabricating shop, where costs and quality can be closely controlled. The work that must be done on the site, such as connecting members by bolting or welding, is kept to a minimum. Structural steel construction requires protection for fire resistance and/or corrosion.

CABLE AND TENT STRUCTURES

Suspension bridges, such as the Brooklyn Bridge, were the first modern cable structures,

BUILT-UP STEEL SECTIONS

and large circus tents were the first modern tent structures. Today, tented cable structures, which combine the characteristics of both, are used to cover very large areas with thin sheet material. In many cases these structures are pneumatic, in which the inside air is under greater pressure than the surrounding outside air.

SPACE FRAMES AND DOMES

Space frames are truss-type structural systems that span in two directions, thereby requiring a minimum of support. Large, lightweight domes were first developed by Buckminster Fuller, who created the geodesic dome. In these structures, small members are connected in triangular shapes to create vast, dome-shaped enclosures. Today, the special connectors for forming space frames and geodesic-type domes are readily available to construct a variety of large structures.

LIGHTWEIGHT METAL FRAMING

Lightweight, or light-gauge, metal framing is analogous to wood framing. Instead of wood studs, joists, and rafters, light-gauge steel members, made of cold-formed sheet steel, are used.

Instead of using nails, connections are made with screws, bolts, or welds.

Lightweight metal framing involves relatively short spans, up to 32 feet, and relatively light loads. The system has many advantages: it is lightweight, incombustible, and impervious to decay, warpage, shrinkage, and termites. In addition, the components are easily handled and speedily erected. However, lightweight metal framing is usually somewhat more expensive than comparable wood framing.

OPEN WEB JOISTS

Open web steel joists, sometimes called bar joists, are shop-fabricated, standardized lightweight trusses made from hot-rolled or cold-formed steel sections. They are used in a similar fashion to wood joist construction, and they are available in a variety of spans, depths, and load-carrying capacities.

Open web joists may be obtained with a camber, with pre-installed wood nailer strips, or with the top chord forming a conduit raceway. The open web has the advantage of permitting pipes, ducts, and conduits to pass through the joists within the floor construction depth.

MAY BE SOLID OR PUNCHED

"C" STUD   CHANNEL STUD   NAILABLE STUD

LIGHTWEIGHT METAL STUDS
(LIGHTWEIGHT STEEL JOISTS SIMILAR)

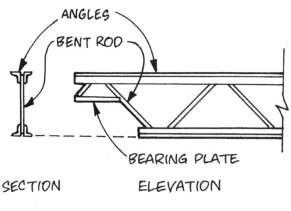

ANGLES
BENT ROD
BEARING PLATE
SECTION   ELEVATION

OPEN WEB STEEL JOIST

FLASH AND COUNTERFLASH

CANT STRIP

METAL DECKING

LIGHTWEIGHT INSULATING CONCRETE

SECTION THROUGH JOIST

4" MINIMUM BEARING

OPEN WEB STEEL JOIST

MECHANICAL LINES

MASONRY BEARING WALL

OPEN WEB JOIST CONSTRUCTION

Steel joists are light members and relatively weak in the flat direction. Therefore, they must be carefully handled and stored on the job site.

METAL DECKING

Metal decking is manufactured from sheet steel in a corrugated, ribbed, or cellular form. The edges overlap or interlock to form a working platform during construction and permanent formwork for a concrete floor slab.

The material is either plain or galvanized, with long, narrow sections having ribs about 6 inches on center and 1-1/2 to 4 inches or more in depth.

Cellular steel decking has the additional advantage of providing raceways to accommodate electrical lines.

Most floor decking now is *composite metal decking*, which has deformed or patterned ribs

RIBBED   CORRUGATED

CELLULAR   FLAT RIBBED

STEEL DECKING

that bond to the concrete so that the deck and concrete act together as a unit to support the loads.

MISCELLANEOUS AND ORNAMENTAL METAL

Ferrous metals are generally used for the multitude of metal items required for a project. These items are often made from conventional fabricated shapes, and they may include metal stairs, railings, fire escapes, gratings, and fences. For this work, shop drawings are usually furnished, in order to check sizes, details, and methods of anchorage.

Non-ferrous metals are used most frequently for ornamental metal work, but stainless steel may also be used. These items are fabricated from rolled, cast, or cold-formed shapes. Among these are decorative grilles and louvers, mesh and wire cloth, metal treillage, and flagpoles.

HOLLOW METAL DOOR BUCK

Ornamental expanded metal is made by slitting a sheet of soft metal and then expanding it in a direction normal to the slits.

CONCLUSION

The use of metals in contemporary construction has proliferated as technology has advanced. Today, there are literally thousands of metal items in every building project, regardless of its basic framing material or method. For example, lightweight metal door bucks and hollow metal doors are often used in masonry buildings.

Similarly, even in the simplest wood-framed structures one can find sheet metal ventilation louvers, aluminum windows, and brass fittings. From curtain walls to flashings to finish hardware, there are metal products used in construction that fulfill the required functions better than any other material is able to do. We can assume, therefore, that metals will continue to be widely used in the construction industry for a vast variety of applications.

LESSON 5 QUIZ

1. All of the following ferrous metals can resist tensile forces, *EXCEPT*

    A. alloy steel.

    B. heat-treated steel.

    C. cast iron.

    D. wrought iron.

2. Which of the following metals is most resistant to galvanic deterioration?

    A. Bronze

    B. Brass

    C. Copper

    D. Lead

3. Miscellaneous metalwork is most frequently fabricated from

    A. iron.

    B. aluminum.

    C. copper.

    D. steel.

4. Open web steel joists are

    I. small lightweight trusses.

    II. standardized.

    III. fabricated in a shop.

    IV. strong both vertically and horizontally.

    A. I and II

    C. I, II, and III

    B. II and III

    D. I, III, and IV

5. Steel is particularly well suited for structural framing because of its relative

    I. strength.

    II. ease of fabrication.

    III. low cost.

    IV. corrosion resistance.

    V. fire resistance.

    A. I and IV

    C. II, IV, and V

    B. I and III

    D. I, II, III, and V

6. Which of the following is *NOT* a property of aluminum components used in building construction?

    A. High resistance to galvanic activity

    B. Good electrical conductivity

    C. Light weight

    D. Considerable resistance to corrosion

7. Lightweight metal framing systems have all of the advantages below, *EXCEPT*

    A. dimensional stability.

    B. speed of construction.

    C. decay resistance.

    D. fire resistance.

8. The purpose of galvanizing iron and steel is to

    A. eliminate all corrosion.

    B. protect against deterioration.

    C. prevent galvanic action.

    D. provide a more attractive finish.

9. Which of the following features apply to metal decking?

I. It can support normal live and dead loads.

II. It may be nailed to underlying support members.

III. Its normal finish affords permanent weather protection.

IV. It can serve as permanent formwork for a concrete slab.

V. It is generally corrugated or ribbed.

A. I and V

B. I, IV, and V

C. II, III, and IV

D. I, II, IV, and V

10. Most fabricated aluminum window assemblies are produced by

A. casting.

B. pressing.

C. cold rolling.

D. extruding.

THERMAL AND MOISTURE PROTECTION

INTRODUCTION

The earliest building efforts were intended to provide protection and shelter—nothing more. Crude structures protected people from wild animals, unfriendly neighbors, and, not least of all, the weather.

Today, most of the wild animals have disappeared, and unfriendly neighbors are more of an annoyance than a physical threat. The weather, however, is another story; extremes of rain, wind, heat, and cold continue to create problems for architects and those who inhabit their buildings. Temperature extremes cause expansion and contraction of construction materials and, quite often, cracking and deterioration; and excessive heat loss or gain through a structure causes not only discomfort to the inhabitants, but also may require the use of expensive mechanical equipment and energy. Finally, leaks in buildings may range from an annoying, localized drip during a light rain to a damaging flow of water during a heavy storm. The results can be uncomfortable, costly, and—in some cases—actually hazardous.

In recent years, heat loss and gain in structures have become major concerns of building codes, mortgage lenders, and utility companies. The thermal conductivity of exterior walls, roofs, and windows is often regulated in order to minimize excessive heating and cooling equipment and the energy required to run it.

Building users have every right to expect moisture protection and thermal comfort, in much the same way that one assumes the roof will remain overhead. Nonetheless, complete protection of a structure from the elements is often difficult to achieve. It is also a matter that should concern all architects and the subject of this lesson.

Moisture problems in a structure derive from several sources and exist in various forms. Water is present below ground, at least to some extent, and it may leak into a building by capillary action or because of hydrostatic pressure. Another predictable source of moisture is precipitation in the form of fog, drizzle, hail, rain, sleet, or snow.

Water vapor is present in the air as humidity, and it also exists within a building due to equipment, activities, or simply, human habitation. Condensation of this vapor causes water to collect on interior surfaces or within concealed wall, floor, or roof spaces.

GROUND WATER CONTROL

Surface water consists of ponds and other surface accumulations of water, caused by rain, thawing ice, or snow. This water seeps into the ground to become ground water.

Ground water refers to the water contained in the voids and crevices under the earth's surface, which generally flows very slowly through a permeable material, called an *aquifer*. The level below which the earth is saturated with water is called the *ground water table*, which can be determined by test borings. Ground water may have to be controlled or diverted to prevent damage to building materials that it contacts, infiltration into the structure, or footing settlement.

Several terms are used in ground water control. These are listed below in ascending order of watertightness.

Permeable. Capable of being penetrated by water without causing rupture or displacement.

MOISTURE SOURCES

Pervious. Permitting leakage or flow of water through cracks, leaks, or other openings.

Water-resistant. Having no openings larger than capillary pores that permit leakage of water.

Water-repellent. Incapable of transmitting water by capillary action, but able to transmit water under pressure.

Waterproof. Completely impervious to water, whether under pressure or not.

DAMPPROOFING

Dampproofing consists of the materials and methods that prevent moisture from penetrating a building at or below grade. It is distinguished from waterproofing in that dampproofing cannot

DAMPPROOFED WALL

WATERPROOFED WALL

resist constant hydrostatic pressure. Most damp-proofing treatments are applied in liquid form, by brushing or spraying, to the earth-contacting surfaces of foundation or basement walls. These treatments include asphalt base coatings (usually in two coats); cement plaster (densely mixed and troweled or pneumatically applied); and liquid silicones or other plastics.

Dampproofing may also involve preventive measures, such as draining surface water away from a building; providing granular fill under a concrete slab on grade (to deter capillary action); installing a polyethylene film vapor seal over the granular fill; and employing footing drains (usually perforated clay drain tile) to carry ground water away from the structure.

WATERPROOFING

Waterproofing consists of the materials and methods that prevent water under hydrostatic pressure from penetrating those parts of a building in direct contact with the earth.

Membrane waterproofing is the most common method of waterproofing subsurface walls. The membrane normally consists of several layers of asphalt-saturated felt (specified as 2-ply or 3-ply) hot mopped together with tar or asphalt pitch. Membranes are applied on the earth-contacting side of walls so that water pressure will force the membrane against the water-proofed surface. Prior to backfilling, wall membranes should be protected from puncture by a coat of cement plaster, a sheet of fiberboard, or a wythe of masonry.

Waterstops are devices used to create water-proof construction joints in walls and floors below grade. Manufactured from noncorrosive metal or various plastics, waterstops permit movement without rupture.

PRECIPITATION CONTROL

Precipitation is the most common and predict-able source of moisture that can damage a structure, and its control depends on the form and type of roofing used.

Roofing describes the materials and methods used to weatherproof the exterior top surface of a structure. Several factors determine the selection of a roofing material, including climate, fire resistance, type and slope of roof, weight of roofing, durability, cost, appearance, and—not least of all—personal preference.

Climate affects the durability of roofing materials in numerous ways. For example, strong winds may damage slate or tile, and asphalt shingles may be blown right off the roof deck. Hail has been known to puncture roll roofing and even break thin tiles. Extreme temperatures may cause metal roofs to expand or contract, while asphalt products are adversely affected by high temperatures and ultraviolet radiation from sunlight. Finally, salt air, smoke, and industrial gases tend to corrode metal roofing, except for those materials resistant to atmospheric corrosion, such as copper, lead, or terne plate.

Fire resistance involves building code classifications A, B, and C, which refer to a roofing material's effectiveness in resisting severe, moderate, and light fire exposures, respectively. These classifications are based on Underwriters' Laboratories designations and have been adopted by most building codes throughout the country.

Type of roof and *slope of roof* are two related factors, as shown in the diagram in the right column. Roof slope is referred to as *incline* or *pitch* and expressed as the ratio between the vertical rise of the roof and its horizontal projection. For example, a 4:12 pitch is one in which the roof rises 4 inches for every 12 inches of horizontal projection. Roof pitches of 3:12 and greater have little problem in shedding water quickly, while flat or nearly flat roofs depend on a continuous waterproof membrane to contain the water until it drains or evaporates.

PITCHES FOR VARIOUS ROOFING MATERIALS

A *square* is the unit of measure used to express roof surface area and is equal to 100 square feet. For example, a gable roof 30 feet long by 10 feet wide measured along the slope would have an area of 30 feet × 10 feet × 2, or 600 square feet. This roof, then, would require six squares of roofing material (600 ÷ 100 = 6).

The *weight* of roofing materials varies considerably and can affect the design, structure, and cost of the roof. For example, copper roofing weighs about 100 pounds per square, while clay tile may weigh more than ten times as much.

The *durability* of a roofing material is a function not only of its inherent quality, but also the climatic conditions and the manner in which the material is installed. In general, the asphalt products are significantly less durable than the clay, stone, and metal materials.

The *cost* of roofing varies substantially and generally corresponds to its durability, as one might expect.

Personal preference in roofing materials usually relates to *appearance*, and generally speaking, those materials that are the most attractive and preferred also tend to be the most expensive.

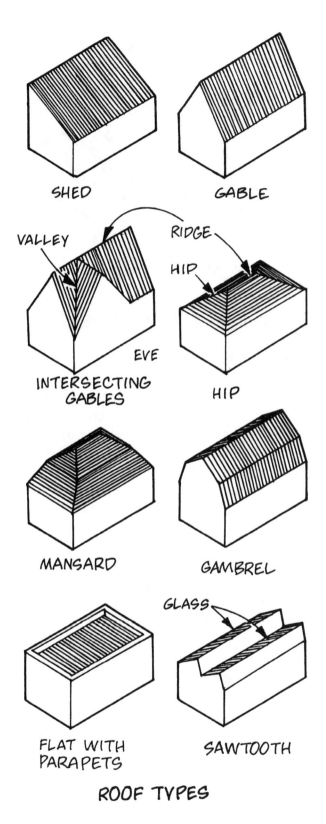

SHED

GABLE

VALLEY

RIDGE

HIP

EVE

INTERSECTING GABLES

HIP

MANSARD

GAMBREL

FLAT WITH PARAPETS

GLASS

SAWTOOTH

ROOF TYPES

ROOFING MATERIALS

There is a wide range of roof coverings available today, each of which may be appropriately used under specific circumstances. The most common roofing materials, and the forms in which they are available, are as follows:

1. *Asphalt*—built-up, shingles, and roll
2. *Wood*—shingles and shakes
3. *Metal*—sheet, corrugated, and strip
4. *Clay, cement, and slate*—tiles
5. *Glass and plastic*—sheets
6. *Plastic*—liquid coatings

Asphalt

Asphalt and coal-tar pitch are the bituminous materials used in built-up roofing. Asphalt is a by-product of crude oil refining, and coal-tar pitch, or tar, comes from coal. Both products are solid at normal temperatures and are heated to a liquid state before application. Asphalt is generally preferred for sloping roofs and coal-tar for flat roofs. These bituminous materials are used to saturate roofing felts, as an adhesive in built-up roofing, and as a final flood coat in which gravel is embedded.

Built-up roofs consist of alternate layers (or plies) of asphalt-saturated felts and hot asphalt cement. The roof is designated as 3-ply, 5-ply, etc., referring to the number of layers used over the unsaturated base layer nailed to the roof deck. The finish surface consists of slag or stone chips set in a final flood coat to protect the plies from the weather.

Asphalt strip shingles (composition shingles) are manufactured from asphalt-saturated felt, the top surface of which has an embedded, weather-resistant mineral surface. The material is cut into 36-inch-long strips that are slotted to

BUILT-UP COMPOSITION ROOF (4 PLY)

WOOD SHINGLE TERMINOLOGY

simulate individual shingles. Asphalt shingles are installed in a lapped fashion, with galvanized roofing nails, on roof decks having at least a 3:12 pitch. Nearly all asphalt strip shingles are manufactured with adhesive tabs along the underside. These tabs adhere to the shingle strip below, so that the shingles cannot be easily blown off in a high wind.

Asphalt roll roofing consists of material similar to that used in asphalt shingles, but it is manufactured in rolls that are 36 inches wide. It may be used on slightly to steeply pitched roofs, and it is installed by lapping and nailing.

Wood

Wood *shingles* are made from red cedar, cypress, and redwood, because of the decay resistance of these species. They are available in standard sizes, in a variety of grades, and either machine-sawn or hand-split, called *shakes*. Shingles are applied similarly on either roofs or walls in a lapped pattern over solid or spaced sheathing and fastened with aluminum or galvanized nails.

Wood shingles are tapered in thickness, with the thickness of the butt (the thick end) expressed as the number of shingles required to produce a total thickness. For example, 16-inch 5/2 random shingles means that the total thickness of the butt ends of five shingles, 16 inches long and of random width, is 2 inches. Random shingles (3 to 14 inches in width) are packed by the square, while dimension shingles (5 or 6 inches in width) are packed in 1,000-shingle bundles.

Wood shingles are installed on roofs with a slope of 4:12 or greater, and it is preferable to apply them in a way that will permit underside ventilation, in order to prevent cupping or rotting. The use of wood shingles or shakes involves the ever-present danger from fire; however, they may be pressure-treated with fire-retardant chemicals, or sprayed, brushed, or mopped with fire-retardant chemicals after installation. Wood shingle and shake roofs are relatively expensive.

Metal

Metal roofing materials include galvanized iron, copper, aluminum, and terne plate (steel coated

STANDING SEAM   BATTEN SEAM   FLAT-LOCKED SEAM

METAL ROOFING DETAILS

with lead and tin). Used to a lesser extent are lead, zinc, and stainless steel. The unique problems involved with metal roofing include corrosion, galvanic action, and movement caused by thermal expansion and contraction. To allow for thermal movement, several installation details are used, such as those shown above. Standing and batten seam roofs create a repetitive visual pattern, which is often used as a design feature.

Corrugated metal sheets, used for both roofing and siding, respond to thermal movement more satisfactorily than sheet metal because of their shape. Filler or closure strips are generally used at the open, corrugated ends.

Metals used on flat roofs are either soldered or welded, while on roofs with a pitch of 3:12 or greater, screws or nails made of a compatible metal are used.

Simulated metal roofing tiles consist of either galvanized steel or aluminum with a baked enamel colored finish. Both types of tile are installed over solid sheathing and roofing felt, using galvanized nails for the steel tiles and aluminum nails for the aluminum tiles.

One of the attractive features of metal roofing is the way it oxidizes when it weathers: lead oxidizes to white, copper turns blue-green, and terne plate weathers to a gray color.

Metal roofs, other than corrugated iron, are relatively expensive, but they are durable and can last for many years.

Clay, Cement, and Slate

Clay roofing tile is manufactured from the same clays that are used for bricks. They are available in a wide range of natural earth colors, as well as glazed finishes, and they are produced in several traditional patterns, as shown on the following page.

Cement roofing tiles are manufactured from portland cement and fine aggregate. They are generally less expensive than clay tiles, and are available in a variety of sizes, colors, and flat shapes that resemble clay tiles.

Slate roofing tiles (sometimes called shingles) are quarried from natural rock and split into thin rectangular slabs. Available in sizes around 12 inches by 16 inches and from 3/16 inch to 1/2 inch thick, slate is obtainable in a smooth or rough texture and in a variety of natural colors.

All tile roofs, regardless of material, have much in common: they are very heavy, unusually durable and permanent, and they are all fireproof.

GREEK   ROMAN   SPANISH

MISSION   SHINGLE   ENGLISH

ROOF TILE SHAPES

In addition, all tile roofs are relatively expensive. Tiles are always applied over sloping roof surfaces, lapped over the preceding courses, and fastened with nails applied through predrilled holes.

Glass and Plastic

Glass and translucent plastic sheets are used in skylights, clearstories, and broad roof areas that require light and weather protection, such as industrial structures and greenhouses. Small areas may employ flat sheets, but larger areas generally require corrugated sheets. Both glass and plastic have poor resistance to fire, and therefore wire-reinforced glass and fiberglass-reinforced acrylic sheets are commonly used. Glass used for roofing must be detailed with particular regard for thermal expansion and the low strength of the material.

Plastic Coatings

Plastic coatings are available as single-ply sheets, single-ply with foam insulation, and in a non-solid form ranging from a liquid to a viscous consistency, which can be sprayed, rolled, brushed, mopped, or troweled onto the roof. They are particularly well suited for use on curved, thin-shell concrete surfaces. With all plastic coatings, the substrate must be of a type to which the plastic will permanently bond. Some plastic roofing with thick foam insulation is installed and held in place with heavy gravel or crushed rock.

CONDENSATION CONTROL

Another source of moisture, in addition to ground water and precipitation, is the condensation of water vapor. Commonly known as humidity, water vapor is always present in the air, to one degree or another; and it is generated within a building by equipment, human breathing and perspiration, cooking and washing, and moisture in the ground that evaporates into crawl spaces.

The higher the air temperature, the more water vapor it can contain. At any given temperature, the ratio of the amount of water vapor the air contains to the maximum amount it could contain is called the *relative humidity*, which is expressed as a percentage. Thus, if air at 50 percent relative humidity is cooled, its relative humidity increases. At some temperature, called the *dew point*, it will reach 100 percent relative humidity and the water vapor will condense into liquid.

Water vapor always moves from high to low pressure areas, usually from inside to outside a building, and it can pass through most building materials. During summer, however, the outside air is often warmer than the air inside a building, and therefore, water vapor may penetrate to the inside of a building. Because condensation can damage almost any portion of a building, water vapor must be prevented from penetrating materials, by using vapor barriers, or be allowed to escape before condensing, through ventilation.

Vapor barriers are materials that prevent the passage of water vapor. They are made from aluminum foil, various types of sheet plastic, or asphalt-saturated felt. Because moisture forms on the cool side of material, *vapor barriers are installed on the warm side*, generally the room side of a wall, beneath the finish material. Surface condensation of glass can be controlled through the use of insulating glass, and condensation in attics and crawl spaces can be controlled through proper ventilation.

THERMAL CONTROL

Heat is transmitted in three ways: *conduction, convection*, and *radiation*. Conduction occurs when materials or objects are in direct contact. Convection is the process that occurs in a fluid medium, such as air or a liquid. Radiation takes place between two objects not in contact and not shielded from each other.

Heat is gained or lost by a building by these processes, and the purpose of thermal control is to slow down heat gain or loss in order to produce comfortable interior temperatures while conserving energy.

Each element of a building where heat is gained or lost requires a different method of thermal control: *caulking and weather-stripping* are used for cracks and openings; windows utilize *tinted, reflective*, or *insulating glass;* and *thermal insulation* is used in wall and roof assemblies.

Thermal insulation consists of materials that have high *thermal resistance* (R) or a high degree of reflectivity, such as aluminum foil. Some common types of thermal insulation are listed on the following page, along with their R values in square foot-hour-degree Fahrenheit per BTU. Enclosed air has excellent insulation properties, and so air enclosed in cells formed of foamed glass or plastic is often used as an insulator.

The choice of insulation material depends on its physical characteristics, resistance to the flow of heat, and cost. All materials have some resistance to heat flow, but an insulator is arbitrarily considered to be a material whose thermal conductivity (the reciprocal of R, and designated k) for a one-inch thickness is less than 0.5 BTU per hour per square foot per degree Fahrenheit.

Roof insulation can be placed in three different locations: above the roofing membrane, between the membrane and the roof deck, and below the roof deck. Each of these locations requires a different type of insulation, and each has its advantages and disadvantages. There are two advantages of placing the insulation above the membrane: the membrane is protected from temperature extremes and the membrane, being on the warm side of the insulation, acts as a vapor barrier.

ROOF INSULATION

PERIMETER INSULATION

Vapor barriers are often combined with insulation, and because condensation tends to form on the cool side of insulating material, aluminum foil-backed insulation should always be installed with the foil facing the warm side.

FLASHING

Wherever different building materials or different parts of a building intersect, there is a natural weakness or gap that may be penetrated by water.

Flashing is material used to provide a seal and prevent water penetration at joints exposed to

Type	Material	Uses	R Value
Loose fill	Glass or mineral wool*, vermiculite, perlite	Wall cavities and flat air spaces such as attics	4" thick = 3.90
Batt or Blanket	Glass or mineral wool* enclosed by paper or aluminum— vapor barriers available	Air spaces in framed walls, floors, and ceilings	3-1/2" thick = 11. 00
Board or Sheet	Cork, glass or mineral fibers, paper pulp	Wall sheathing and rigid roof insulation	1" thick = 2.75
Reflective	Aluminum foil often in combination with layers of paper and air spaces	Roof, wall, and floor insulation plus vapor barrier	1" air space with 2 reflective surfaces = 1.39
Foam	Plastics, spray type, or panels	Sheathing, irregular spaces	1" panel = 6.00
*Rock, slag, or glass, but not asbestos			

SLAB INSULATION

the weather, intersections of different materials, and expansion or contraction joints.

Flashing is either concealed or exposed. When concealed, flashing may be made from sheet metals, bituminous-coated fabrics, plastic, or other waterproof membrane materials. Exposed flashing is commonly made from aluminum, copper, galvanized steel, zinc, lead, or terne.

In selecting a flashing material one should consider durability, possible galvanic action, appearance, and expansion joints where necessary. Flashing is generally included in sheet metal specifications, which may also include scuppers, gutters, downspouts, skylights, and decorative items.

FLASHING DETAILS

MASONRY PARAPET

Labels: 12", COUNTER FLASHING, BASE FLASHING, BUILT-UP ROOFING, SPANDREL FLASHING, DOVETAIL ANCHORS, CANT STRIP

GRAVEL STOP

Labels: 4" MIN., ROOFING, METAL GRAVEL STOP, HOLD DOWN CLEAT

HEAD FLASHING OR WATER TABLE

Labels: DRIP

EXPANSION JOINTS

Temperature changes cause expansion and contraction in all building materials, which may produce cracking, distortion, or failure in portions of the structure. The purpose of expansion joints is to anticipate the amount of thermal movement likely to occur and to provide a complete separation that will allow movement, while maintaining the weathertightness and structural integrity of the structure.

Normally, expansion joints in masonry walls are provided every 125 feet or so, and in steel or concrete structures, as well as roofs, joints occur at about 200-foot intervals, depending on the temperature ranges expected. In any case, joints should be located at junctions in L, T, or U-shaped buildings, as well as in stairwells and elevator shafts.

Expansion joints vary from one-half to one inch in width; they provide a complete separation from the top of the footings to the roof, and they are made waterproof with waterstops, elastic joint sealants, metal flashing, or caulking.

METAL
EDGING

SYNTHETIC FLEXIBLE
FLASHING WITH
FOAM INSULATION

METAL
FLASHING

WOOD
BLOCKING

CANT STRIP

ROOFING

EXPANSION JOINT

CONCRETE ROOF

ROOF EXPANSION JOINT

PREMOLDED EXPANSION
JOINT FILLER

WALLS

EXTRUDED METAL
COVER

RETAINER CLIPS

PLAN SECTION AT WALL CORNER

FACE OF WALL

EXTRUDED METAL
COVER ASSEMBLY

COMPRESSIBLE MATERIAL

FINISH FLOOR

ANCHOR BOLT

EXPANSION
JOINT FILLER

SECTION AT FLOOR & WALL

EXPANSION JOINTS

LESSON 6 QUIZ

1. Which of the following characteristics are generally associated with tile roofs?

   I. Permanence

   II. Low initial cost

   III. Fire resistance

   IV. Considerable weight

   V. Suitability for low pitches

   A. III and IV

   B. II and V

   C. I, III, and IV

   D. I, III, IV, and V

2. The principal purpose of using granular fill beneath concrete slabs on grade is for the control of

   A. condensation.

   B. ground water.

   C. thermal loss or gain.

   D. expansion or contraction.

3. A sloping roof is framed with 2" × 10" rafters at 16 inches on center. The roof decking is 5/8-inch-thick plywood, and the finished ceiling is constructed with 1/2-inch-thick plasterboard attached to the bottom of the rafters. Which of the following would *NOT* be an appropriate system of thermal insulation?

   A. Mineral fiber rigid sheets

   B. Mineral wool batts

   C. Vermiculite loose fill

   D. Plastic foam panels

4. A polyethylene vapor barrier at roof level should be installed

   A. just above the finish ceiling.

   B. over the insulation on a roof deck.

   C. just beneath the roofing.

   D. between roof rafters.

5. Expansion joints are provided in a structure in order to

   A. reduce thermal movement.

   B. prevent thermal movement.

   C. permit thermal movement.

   D. produce thermal movement.

6. A square of roofing material refers to

   A. 100 square feet of roofing.

   B. the amount of the roof deck area.

   C. the amount of exposed roofing material.

   D. the amount of roofing material, including the necessary overlaps.

7. In which of the following ways can condensation normally be controlled in a structure?

   I. Employ insulating glass.

   II. Apply a vapor barrier in the walls.

   III. Use a loose-fill type of insulation in the attic.

   IV. Install perimeter drain tiles.

   V. Provide crawl space ventilation.

   A. II only

   B. III and IV

   C. I, III, and V

   D. I, II, and V

8. The preferred minimum roof pitch for the installation of asphalt roll roofing is

   A. dead level.   C. 3:12.
   B. 1:12.   D. 4:12.

9. Flashing is generally required to be installed in all of the following situations, *EXCEPT*

   A. at the juncture of a masonry parapet and the turned-up composition roofing material.

   B. at the standing seams of a sloping galvanized iron roof.

   C. at the penetration of a sloping asphalt sheet roof by a plumbing vent.

   D. at the head of a metal window frame in a masonry wall.

10. Which of the following insulation materials has the greatest resistance to heat flow per inch of thickness?

    A. Fiberglass batts

    B. Loose vermiculite fill

    C. Aluminum foil with air space

    D. Urethane panels

DOORS, WINDOWS, AND GLASS

INTRODUCTION

Wall openings in primitive structures served principally as the means of entering and leaving a building. They also provided light, air, and protection for early dwellers as they watched out for enemies. Holes in roofs were primarily intended for ventilation of open fires, which were used for heating and cooking, but they provided some light as well. No consideration was given to weather resistance, temperature control, or privacy. Thus, these crude openings fulfilled only the basic functional necessities.

In later times, solid doors were developed to provide privacy, weather protection, and defense against intruders, while openings in walls and roofs continued to furnish light and ventilation. In time, window openings were overlaid with frames, which could be opened and closed, and these frames were covered at first with an oiled paper and later with glass. Roof openings continued to be used, but only in warm and arid climates.

Today, doors, windows, and skylights serve a myriad of physical, visual, and psychological functions. Primarily, they allow free access of people, merchandise, light, and air; but in addition, they provide security, privacy, protection from the weather, and access to desirable views. Furthermore, building openings are an important part of the exterior composition; they confirm and often determine a building's scale, and they define the quality and mood of interior spaces.

There exists today a great variety of materials, systems, and products for building openings. Additionally, building codes specify standards for light and air, energy conservation, life safety, and security, to which building openings must conform. Therefore, what was once a relatively simple matter of design is now a complex and unique subject that requires careful study.

DOORS

Doors are the movable barriers that permit or prohibit access to a structure, as well as allow passage between interior spaces. They are held in position by door frames, composed of a *head*, or top piece, and two side pieces, or *jambs*. At the bottom of most exterior door openings are horizontal pieces called *thresholds, sills*, or *saddles*. Almost all doors are manufactured in a mill or factory and installed at the site, or sometimes preassembled, complete with frame and hardware, such as hinges, locksets, weatherstripping, and so on.

Doors are classified in a great variety of ways, such as by location (interior door, entrance doors) or by function (fire door, acoustical door). In addition, doors are classified by their method of operation (swinging door, revolving door); by physical type (paneled door, louvered door); by the material from which they are made (hollow metal door, screen door); and by door hand convention. Following is a description of various door types classified by their method of operation.

DOOR

HEAD
JAMB
DOOR STOP
TRIM
HINGE

THRESHOLD
OR SILL

DOOR ELEMENTS

Swinging doors are the most common type, and the most effective for weather protection and thermal and acoustical control. They are generally hung on butts or hinges that are attached to the jambs or bucks, but they may also be pivoted from the head and threshold. Swinging doors are most often used singly, but they may also be used in pairs to create a wider opening. When a door is permitted to swing to either side of a jamb, it is called double-acting.

Sliding doors refer to doors that move horizontally. They may roll on a track on the floor or be hung from rollers at the head. In either case, the end of the door opposite the rollers is normally held in place by guides. Sliding doors may operate along a wall surface or slide into a wall pocket.

Folding or *accordion* doors are composed of individual leaves that are hinged together in pairs. They slide along a single guide at the top and often the bottom, and in the closed position, they may form a wall.

For soundproof walls, special seals are used at the top and bottom to prevent sound transmission from one side to the other.

By-passing or *telescoping* doors consist of two or more leaves, each of which travels along its own channel or track. For very large openings, both folding and by-passing doors may be motor-operated.

Overhead doors operate in a variety of ways; they may slide vertically upward, roll up (much like a window shade), fold up in panels, or ride up and pivot inward on special hardware. Generally, all overhead door types are counterweighted for ease of operation. They may be motor-operated, and in the case of residential garages, they are often radio controlled from an individual car or from inside the house.

FLUSH SHUTTER FRENCH SASH PANELED

JALOUSIE GLASS DUTCH SCREEN LOUVER

SWINGING DOOR TYPES

Revolving doors usually consist of four leaves, at right angles to each other, that rotate about a vertical axis within a cylindrical enclosure. Their principal advantage is the ability to carry a continuous, two-way flow of pedestrian traffic, with a minimal interchange of air between inside and outside. For this reason, revolving doors are frequently used at entrances to large buildings. Where revolving doors are used for building entrances, swinging doors must also be provided nearby to permit the entrance of large objects, to allow for crowd control, and to provide for handicapped and other legal egress.

The classification of physical door types is based on the way in which door panels are made, such as paneled or louvered, and the material from which they are manufactured. Shown above are several door types frequently used in construction.

Materials commonly used in the manufacture of doors include wood, steel, aluminum, and glass. A discussion of each of these follows.

Wood doors are the most popular type used in construction. Frames are invariably made from softwoods such as pine, spruce, or fir; cores are constructed from softwood lumber, particle board, corrugated treated paper, plastic foam, or fiberboard; and face veneers may include softwood and hardwood plywoods, particleboard, and plastic laminates. Almost all wood doors are manufactured in mills under controlled conditions. Waterproof adhesives are used on exterior wood doors, while water-resistant adhesives are used for interior doors.

Flush doors may have a core of solid softwood (solid-core door), or a core made up of small pieces of wood arranged in a grid (hollow-core door).

REVOLVING   OVERHEAD COILING

SWINGING   SLIDING   FOLDING

DOOR TYPES BY OPERATION

HOLLOW CORE DOOR

RAIL
STILE
GRID CORE
LOCK BLOCK
LOCK RAIL
BACKING
CROSS-BANDING
FACE PANEL

SOLID CORE DOOR

RAIL
STILE
CORE BLOCKS GLUED TOGETHER
CROSS-BANDING
FACE PANEL

PANEL DOOR

TOP RAIL
STILE
BAR
MUNTIN
PANEL
CROSS RAIL
PANEL
BOTTOM RAIL

WOOD DOOR CONSTRUCTION

Panel doors consist of various sections held in place by solid wood stiles and rails (vertical and horizontal framework). Panels may be made from solid wood, plywood, glass sections, or fixed wood louvers.

Special-purpose doors are generally wood flush doors manufactured with a special core to resist fire (up to a 1-1/2-hour U.L. approved rating), sound, or radiation.

Steel doors are generally used for interior installations that require fire ratings and for exterior doors with or without fire ratings. They are available as swinging doors, and also as roll-up, fold-up, sliding, folding, bypassing, revolving, etc. Except for cast metal doors, which are used rarely and only for monumental purposes, steel doors are usually manufactured from 14 to 20-gauge cold-rolled steel, or in some cases, stainless steel, which requires little maintenance.

Hollow metal doors are constructed of a steel frame covered with sheet metal, and they are available either flush or paneled. The metal faces are stiffened by the use of steel reinforcing shapes or by solid core material, including particleboard, rigid foam, or other types of material. The resulting doors are rigid, permanent, and can be fabricated to meet any fire rating required by building codes.

Metal clad doors, commonly called *kalamein* doors, consist of a solid wood core covered with sheet metal. The core will ordinarily resist fire as long as the sheet metal cover prevents oxygen from reaching it. In recent years, kalamein doors have largely been replaced by fire-rated, solid-core doors.

Aluminum doors are normally fabricated from extrusions or rolled shapes. They are lightweight, corrosion-resistant, and dimensionally stable. However, aluminum doors must be protected from staining, scratching, and galvanic action. Aluminum doors are most commonly used as entrances, for storefront work, and in curtain wall construction. Aluminum doors are rarely used for fire doors because of their low melting point. However, there are special aluminum fire doors that are constructed with a fireproof core.

Metal security doors are composed of a steel frame covered by metal mesh or grilles. They operate in a variety of ways and serve to protect commercial and industrial buildings from unlawful entry.

Fire doors are used in fire-resistive construction and are U.L. rated and labeled, from class A to E, according to the door's location. The table on the following page describes the various classifications. In addition to the requirements in the table, fire door assemblies (frames, hardware, etc.) must have the same rating as the labeled door. The maximum fire door size is 4 feet by 10 feet, and all doors must be self-latching and equipped with automatic closing devices.

Glass doors are made of 1/2 to 3/4 inch thick transparent or obscure tempered glass and used for swinging or revolving doors. After tempering, the glass cannot be cut, drilled, or altered in any way. Glass doors are generally pivoted at the top and bottom, as it is difficult to support their great weight with conventional hinges.

DOOR HARDWARE

Door hardware comprises the largest portion of the finish hardware specifications. It includes all items that permit doors to operate properly, such as hinges, closers, locking devices, panic hardware, and weatherstripping. The selection of

Door Label	Fire Rating in Hours	Location in Structure	Glazing Permitted (1/4" wire glass)
A	3	Fire walls separating buildings or fire areas within a building	None
B	1-1/2	Vertical enclosures— fire stairs and elevators	100 sq. in./leaf (4" min. dimension)
C	3/4	Corridors and partitions	1296 sq. in./light (54" max. dimension)
D	1-1/2	Exterior walls— severe fire exposure	None
E	3/4	Exterior walls— moderate fire exposure	720 sq. in./light (54" max. dimension)

door hardware is governed by the required function, operating characteristics of the devices, durability, weather resistance, and appearance.

Originally, door hardware was always metallic, such as iron, steel, and stainless steel for heavy-duty installations, and aluminum, brass, and bronze for other uses. Now, however, ceramics and plastics are increasingly used. The location of door hardware has been established through years of usage and varies only slightly. Thus, door knobs are invariably located around 38 inches from the floor, and door pulls, as well as panic bolts, are placed around 42 inches from the floor.

Door hand convention is a standardized uniform reference method used by architects and hardware manufactures and suppliers. The hand of door is determined in the following way: Assume that you are standing outside the door and facing the door. In this case, the hinges are not visible to you, and the door swings *away* from you. If the hinges are on the left side, the door is left-hand; if the hinges are on the right side, the door is right-hand. If the hinges are visible and the door swings *toward* you, the door is either left-hand reverse or right-hand reverse, depending on whether the hinges are on the left or on the right. The illustration on the right should clarify door hand convention.

Hinges are the devices on which doors swing or pivot to open and close. They may be exposed, concealed, or invisible; but most commonly they are mortised into the door edge and jamb, so that only the knuckle is visible when the door is closed. Because only the butt end of the hinge is exposed, hinges applied to the edge of a door are known as *butts*, or *butt hinges*. Most hinges are made up of three parts: two leaves, one with an odd and the other with an even number of

DOOR HAND CONVENTION

knuckles, and a pin that joins the leaves. The pin may be removable (loose) or nonremovable (fixed or non-rising) for security situations. Pin tips are commonly oval or flat, but hospital tips are curved for ease of cleaning and to avoid catching articles of clothing. Hinges with a standardized screw hole size and pattern are called template hinges.

The size of butt hinges varies from 2-1/2 to 6 inches in length, which in general is the same dimension as the width. With a normal-height door, hinges are mounted approximately 8 inches from the head and 10 inches from the floor. When a third hinge is required, it is mounted midway between the top and bottom hinges. Illustrated below are several types of hinges commonly used in construction.

Closers are devices designed to automatically close doors quickly, quietly, and with no damage to the door or frame. In addition, they may also be used to hold a door open. They are either exposed or concealed, and generally consist of a spring (the closing element) and some type of

hydraulic mechanism. Closer installations may be of the parallel-arm type (minimum projection), or bracket-mounted type. Door closers are selected on the basis of door type and size, frequency of operation, exposure to weather, and appearance. A fusible link closer is used to close a door automatically in case of fire.

Locking devices are used to hold doors in a closed position and to provide security. When the locking mechanism is beveled, the device is referred to as a *latch*, and a latch automatically slides into position when the door is closed. When the locking mechanism is rectangular in shape and it must be projected manually, the device is referred to as a *dead bolt*. Such a bolt is often used in conjunction with a latch, in which case the unit is known as a *lock*.

Locksets are differentiated by the way they are installed. *Rim locks* are mounted on the interior surface of the door and have square or rectangular boxes. *Cylinder locks* are more or less concealed by fitting into holes drilled in the lock

MORTISED   BALL BEARING   T-STRAP   CABINET PIVOT HINGE   OLIVE KNUCKLED   INVISIBLE

FULL MORTISE   HALF SURFACE   FULL SURFACE

HINGE TYPES AND INSTALLATION

CYLINDRICAL LOCK UNIT LOCK

RIM LOCK MORTISE LOCK

LOCKSET TYPES

CYLINDRICAL LOCKSET

stile of the door. They are popular, inexpensive, and easy to install. *Mortise locks* fit completely into a rectangular cavity carved in the edge of the door. As they are almost entirely concealed, they are the most secure. *Unit locks* fit into a

door cutout and are therefore installed quickly and efficiently.

Panic hardware is used on exit doors of public buildings to quickly and easily open the doors in case of emergency. It is required by building codes, which specify that push bars to release the locking mechanisms must extend across at least three-fourths of the door width. Panic hardware may be of the vertical rod type, which exposes the latching at head and floor; or the mortise type device, which conceals the lateral latching.

Operating devices for doors include door lever handles, door pulls, push plates, kick plates, and escutcheons (decorative plates covering the locking mechanism). Door knobs should be avoided. Accessibility requirements for public spaces prohibit them, and while they are still allowed for private residences, homes too are better served by levers that provide greater access to the elderly and persons with disabilities.

Operating devices are available in a variety of shapes, designs, and materials. Finishes for door hardware should be selected on the basis of durability, weather exposure, corrosion resistance, and general appearance. Some common finish designations are listed below. The BHMA numbers listed are found in ANSI/BHMA A156.1, the standard for builder's hardware materials and finishes. The old US numbers are listed parenthetically.

BHMA 600 – Steel primed for painting (USP)
BHMA 605 – Bright brass, clear coated (US3)
BHMA 606 – Satin brass, clear coated (US4)
BHMA 611 – Bright bronze, clear coated (US9)
BHMA 612 – Satin bronze, clear coated (US10)
BHMA 613 – Dark oxidized satin bronze, oil rubbed (US10B)
BHMA 618 – Bright nickel plating on brass or bronze, clear coated (US14)

BHMA 619 – Satin nickel plating on brass or bronze, clear coated (US15)

BHMA 622 – Flat black coated brass or bronze (US19)

BHMA 625 – Bright chromium plated over nickel on brass or bronze (US26)

BHMA 626 – Satin chromium plated over nickel on brass or bronze (US26D)

BHMA 628 – Satin aluminum, clear anodized (US28)

BHMA 629 – Polished stainless steel, 300 Series (US32)

BHMA 630 – Satin stainless steel, 300 Series (US32D)

The BHMA numbers differ from the old US numbers in that they provide not just the visible finish but also the base metal. Thus, where US10B described an oil-rubbed bronze finish, the base metal could have been either solid bronze or bronze-plated steel. Although bronze-plated steel might be acceptable for decorative cabinetry, it would be inappropriate for heavily used exterior commercial building entry pulls.

Weatherstripping is the means employed to make exterior openings weather tight. It acts as a barrier to prevent wind and moisture from entering a building through cracks between doors or windows and their frames. This is accomplished by means of interlocking or friction devices which are manufactured from metals, such as aluminum, bronze, stainless steel, etc. or pliable materials, such as felt, rubber, and plastic. Some examples of weatherstripping are shown to the right.

WINDOWS

Windows are glazed openings constructed in a wall to admit light, air, and, in solar designed buildings, solar heat. The earliest windows were used to provide natural light only, but with the

FRICTION DEVICES

INTERLOCKING DEVICES

WEATHERSTRIPPING

development of hinges and fastening devices, the window also became a means for ventilation. For a number of years after the introduction of air conditioning, natural ventilation in large buildings became unnecessary, and the window returned to its original function of admitting daylight. Since the energy crisis, however, the ventilating window is once again reappearing in large commercial buildings.

Most windows today are standardized in size (stock windows) and manufactured as complete units, with operating hardware, glazing, weatherstripping, and—quite often—a factory-applied protective finish. Aside from admitting light, air, and desirable views, windows are selected for their ability to resist weather, open and close efficiently, provide thermal insulation, and admit solar heat. Windows also dominate the scale, proportions, and general design of the building in which they are installed.

Windows are manufactured in four basic types: residential, commercial, industrial, and monumental. Stock window units are manufactured from kiln-dried, straight-grain wood, which is treated with preservative, paint, or clad with vinyl, and also from extruded or rolled metal sections, such as aluminum, steel, stainless steel, and bronze. Operable windows function in a variety of ways, most of which are illustrated at the top of page 119.

Most operable windows consist of a frame, which is fixed to the surrounding wall or other supports, and a sash, which is the glazed panel fitting into the window frame. The various parts of a window are shown and identified below.

WINDOW ELEMENTS

Wood windows are manufactured according to well-established standards from woods that are able to resist shrinkage and warping due to weather exposure. The most common of these are ponderosa pine, white pine, sugar pine, fir, redwood, cedar, and cypress. Wood windows are fabricated in a mill from kiln-dried lumber (6 to 12 percent moisture content), and treated to resist moisture, mold, fungi, and insects. They are also available with a factory-applied plastic finish, or sheathed in aluminum. Both of these finishes eliminate the need for periodic painting or staining. Wood windows are relatively inexpensive, durable, and widely available in a variety of types and standard sizes; however, fire-resistive code requirements sometimes preclude their use.

Aluminum windows are made from extruded aluminum alloy sections that are strong, durable, and very light in weight. These aluminum extrusions are particularly well suited for windows, as the complex configurations, which are simple to extrude, can provide for glazing, weatherstripping, and condensation, all within one section. Aluminum windows are available either in a matte or highly polished metal finish, in various colored anodized finishes, and in plastic and baked enamel finishes, both of which protect the metal from oxidation. When installing aluminum windows, all trim, fasteners, etc., must be of a compatible metal or isolated from the aluminum in order to prevent galvanic action. A variety of sizes and types are standard and readily available.

Steel windows are manufactured from hot-rolled solid sections or from cold-rolled strip steel, which is more widely used. Standards have been established for types, sizes, hardware, and operating mechanisms, and most manufacturers conform to these standards. The durability of steel windows depends on their protection against

WINDOW TYPES VIEWED FROM OUTSIDE

corrosion, which is generally achieved by a factory-applied baked enamel finish or a plastic finish. Frequently, steel windows are glazed on the site.

Stainless steel windows are strong, corrosion-resistant, and usually manufactured from 16, 18, 20, or 22-gauge stainless steel sheet. All operating closers, fasteners, anchors, etc. must be compatible, so that no galvanic action can occur.

Replaceable windows supersede existing windows, or are applied over an existing window. They are available in a wide range of types, sizes, and materials, and are widely used in alteration and renovation work. They are also used to decrease heat loss and gain in existing buildings.

Screens consist of wire mesh supported by rigid frames placed over window and door openings to exclude insects. The mesh or wire cloth, sometimes called insect screening, is available

SKYLIGHT TYPES

in a variety of materials and finishes, such as steel, aluminum, copper, plastic, etc., which are painted, galvanized, or otherwise coated to improve durability. The most common insect screening is 22-gauge wire with 12 openings to the inch. Screen frames that support the mesh are fabricated from wood or metal and are available in stock or custom sizes.

A special type of screening is made of sheet aluminum that has been slit and formed into tiny louvers. This type of screening not only excludes insects, but it also controls the infiltration of light and heat.

DOOR AND WINDOW SYSTEMS

Door and window systems consist of large areas of a building's skin, most often prefabricated combinations of solid and glass panels. The most common material used in these systems is aluminum, available in a great variety of standard extruded shapes.

Storefront work comprises metal framework sections and glass panels designed as a unit. It includes the entrance door, frames, transoms, hardware, and fixed panels of glass. The advantage of this kind of system is the integration and standardization of all elements, that are related in design, function, and installation.

Curtain walls are exterior walls of a building that support no weight other than their own, and function solely as an enclosing skin. They usually consist of metal framework in combination with glass, plastic, metal, or other surfacing panels. The essential functions of a curtain wall are much the same as any other building wall: it must be weatherproof, it must provide some degree of thermal and sound control, and it must

be safe and secure. Curtain walls are also considered for their durability, ease of maintenance, and aesthetic suitability.

Skylights are overhead sources of natural light generally installed on a roof. They may be flat, pitched, vaulted (curved), or dome-shaped. Skylight frames are usually fabricated from metals such as aluminum, galvanized steel, or copper. They are glazed with glass block; flat or corrugated wire glass; or clear, tinted, or translucent sheet, corrugated, or sandwich-panel plastics. Prefabricated stock units, glazed with acrylic, are particularly popular in construction.

All skylights must be installed in a weather-tight fashion, they must be safe from breaking and falling, and they must be provided with condensation drains to conduct interior moisture to the outside through weep holes in the curb frame. Fire safety is also a concern with the use of skylights, and therefore, their size, position, and spacing are often regulated by building codes.

SKYLIGHT CURB DETAIL

GLASS

Glass is one of the oldest building materials still used. Some 3,000 years ago it was utilized for decorative purposes in Western Asia, and in ancient Rome glass was first employed in windows. Until relatively modern times, glass was difficult to make and therefore very costly. In fact, during the 18th century, individual glass windows served as a basis for taxation. Today's glass, however, is widely available, inexpensive, and vastly improved over earlier products. Float glass, for example, which was first developed about 40 years ago and is made by pouring molten glass onto the surface of molten tin, produces a glass that is perfectly flat and brilliantly clear. The widespread use of glass has become closely identified with modern architecture, and we can expect that glass of all types will continue to be developed and used.

Glass is a solid, supercooled, ceramic material made from sand, soda, and lime. It is a chemically inert, generally transparent, hard, brittle material that—unlike other ceramics—is shaped in a liquid state, at high temperatures, and then allowed to cool. If necessary, glass can be reheated and shaped again.

Glass is easily worked and can be fabricated in a wide variety of shapes. It can be cast, pressed, rolled, blown, extruded, spun, and ground. Spun glass fibers (glass wool) are used for acoustical and thermal insulation. Glass fibers are also used in textile manufacturing, and alkali resistant (AR) glass fibers can be used as reinforcing in concrete and plaster.

The glass industry still uses terms from the more archaic glass processes, such as *plate glass* and *annealed glass*. Presently there are no major plate manufacturers in the United States, and the only true plate glass still used is either recycled (reclaimed from existing applications) or wired glass imported from Japan or Europe. The term

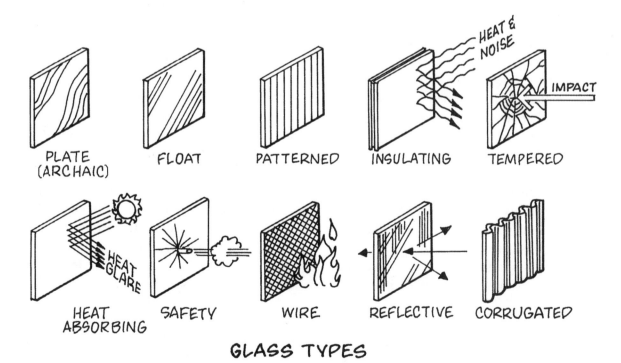

GLASS TYPES

double-strength glass (DS) might still be used by some to refer to ⅛-inch thick float glass, but like the old *single-strength* (SS) ³⁄₃₂-inch glass, it should be considered archaic as well—unless specifically referred to by the manufacturer.

Float glass, the typical glass used today, is annealed in the manufacturing process, so there is no need to refer to *annealed glass,* as all float glass manufactured in the United States is annealed. In general, float glass is available from ⅛-inch thick (3mm) to ⅞-inch (22mm) thick. Most glass, even in the United States, is manufactured in metric thicknesses, so the thicknesses should be considered nominal, with standard nominal ¼-inch-thick glass being 6mm.

Patterned glass is manufactured in a great variety of patterns, textures, and designs, all of which obscure vision and reduce light transmission. Among the popular patterns are ribbed, frosted, hammered, and fluted; it is also available tempered.

Tempered glass is heat treated for increased resistance to impact stresses. It is three to five times stronger than plate glass, much more costly, and pulverizes into small granules when broken. Tempered glass is used in doors, store fronts, and other areas accessible to the public. It may not be cut, drilled, or otherwise altered after manufacture.

Insulating glass (multi-glazing) consists of two or more sheets of glass separated by a hermetically sealed air space to provide thermal insulation, acoustical control, and an absence of condensation. Insulating glass can be manufactured from almost any type of glass, in exact sizes, and it may not be altered after it is manufactured. The seals may be glass-to-glass or metal-to-glass, and a reflective surface can be located on various faces of the insulating glass.

METAL-TO-GLASS SEAL   GLASS-TO-GLASS SEAL

INSULATING GLASS

Heat-absorbing glass (actinic glass) is tinted to absorb a high degree of solar radiation, and thus, it transmits less solar heat and glare into a building. It is usually bronze, gray, or blue-green in color.

Reflective glass consists of a reflective film laminated between two sheets of clear glass, or a thin film of metal oxide on the surface of the glass. It behaves somewhat like a mirror reflecting heat and glare, and thus, its performance is similar to that of heat-absorbing glass.

Laminated glass is composed of a plastic sheet sandwiched between two glass layers, all bonded under heat and pressure. When laminated glass breaks, the plastic sheet holds the broken glass in place, thus reducing the risk of injury in case of breakage. Laminated glass is also a better acoustic insulator than solid glass. There are two types: *safety glass,* which is used in automobiles and skylights; and *bulletproof glass,* which has four or more layers of glass laminated to three or more layers of plastic. This type is used where strong impacts may occur, as in banks and prisons.

Wired glass is made by placing wire mesh in the middle of glass during the manufacturing process. It has a high resistance to impact and

GLASS-TO-GLASS JOINTS

remains intact after breakage. Wired glass is used where fire resistance is required and in skylights or other overhead glazing. It is available with a variety of different wire patterns.

There are several modern glazing systems that render the metal framing members less visible. *Butt-joint glazing* consist of glass sheets with conventional head and sill frames, but no vertical mullions. A clear silicone sealant forms the vertical joint between adjacent glass sheets. In another system, the mullions are placed completely inside the glass, so that the windows appear flush and mullionless from the exterior. The glass is joined to the mullions with silicone sealant.

In addition to the glass types described above, there are several others that bear mention. *Mirrored glass* is glass with a metallic reflective coating applied to one surface. *Psychiatric glass* (one-way glass) is seen as a mirror on one side and is transparent on the other side, as long as the light intensity on the mirrored side is greater

than that on the other side. *Structural glass* is opaque and used for exterior building panels. *Corrugated glass* is used for decorative partitions, or in its wired form, for skylights and roof panels. *Glass block* is discussed in Lesson Three.

GLAZING PLASTICS

The term *plastic* refers to a vast range of synthetic materials. In this lesson, we are concerned only with those plastics that have, in recent years, replaced glass in applications such as skylights, translucent roof areas, fixed windows, interior partitions, luminous ceilings, and so on. For these purposes, acrylics, polycarbonates, polyesters, and polystyrenes are used. All of these materials are available in transparent, translucent, and opaque sheets, and all are either fire-resistant or classified as slow-burning.

Plastic, in flat sheets or corrugated form, can generally replace glass in most windows, skylights, shower enclosures, roof panels, or interior screens, where various transparent, obscure, or colored panels may be desired. However, plastic is not as hard as glass, it scratches far more easily, and thus, it is not as durable when exposed to normal use or weather. Plastic has a high coefficient of thermal expansion, and so the details must allow for a substantial amount of expansion and contraction due to temperature change. Plastic is normally more expensive than glass, but more resistant to fire and breakage. Another advantage of plastic is that it can easily be cut, bent, and formed.

GLAZING

Glazing is the process of placing glass or glazing plastics in windows and making a weather tight joint between the glass and its frame using various materials. Glass panels are set in the

GLAZING DETAILS

grooves designed to receive them, held in place with glazing beads, points, or clips, and sealed in place with various glazing compounds.

The various types of glazing compounds in general use are putties, elastic compounds, polybutene tape, polysulfide elastomer compounds, and structural glazing gaskets (compression or zipper types), which are molded or extruded shapes made from rubber, neoprene, vinyl, or other synthetics. These synthetics are particu-

larly effective in allowing for the thermal expansion and contraction of glass.

Clearance must always be allowed between glass and frame so that the glass is surrounded by a watertight seal of glazing compound. In addition, glass must never be placed in tension, by exposing it to greater forces than it can safely withstand, nor should glazing take place when moisture might be trapped, which could cause the watertight seal to fail.

LESSON 7 QUIZ

1. Which of the following glass types would one select in order to reduce light transmission?

   A. Insulating

   B. Patterned

   C. Reflective

   D. Laminated

2. Which of the following glass types are appropriate for skylight glazing?

   I. Laminated

   II. Tempered

   III. Wired

   IV. Heavy sheet

   A. I and III   **C.** I, II, and III

   B. II and III   **D.** I, II, and IV

3. Tactile finishes are generally applied to operating hardware in order to provide

   A. improved corrosion resistance.

   B. a more decorative finish.

   C. greater handling control.

   D. warnings to the handicapped.

4. The principal disadvantage of aluminum door and window sections is their

   A. high initial expense.

   B. lack of durability.

   C. poor resistance to galvanic action.

   D. poor resistance to building stresses.

5. What is the maximum height of a four-inch-wide wire-glass glazing strip located in a Class B labeled fire door?

   A. 13.5 inches

   B. 25 inches

   C. Full height of a 10-foot-high door

   D. No glazing is permitted

6. Which of the following are advantages of revolving doors?

   I. Emergency exiting

   II. Handicapped access

   III. Temperature control

   IV. One-way traffic flow

   V. Continuous pedestrian flow

   A. I and V   **C.** I, II, and IV

   B. III and V   **D.** III, IV, and V

7. A latching device that is completely concealed within a rectangular cavity carved in the edge of a door stile is commonly known as a

   A. mortise lock.   **C.** rim lock.

   B. unit lock.   **D.** cylinder lock.

8. Compared to glass, plastic sheet substitutes are generally less

   A. durable.   **C.** transparent.

   B. fire-resistant.   **D.** expensive.

9. Emergency exits in buildings often require the use of

   A. knurled knobs.

   B. lever handles.

   C. panic hardware.

   D. fusible links.

10. Which of the following qualities generally apply to wood windows?

I.   Low maintenance

II. Low initial expense

III. High resistance to fire

IV. High durability

V.   Wide availability

A. I and III

B. I, II, and IV

C. II, III, and V

D. II, IV, and V

FINISH WORK

8

INTRODUCTION

Finish work refers to the methods, materials, and treatments that comprise the interior and exterior finished surfaces of a building. Finishes are all visible as an integral element of the completed structure; in fact, most of what one sees in a completed building is finish work that is superimposed over the building's structural framework. Interior finishes include floor finishes, such as paving, planking, and carpeting; wall finishes, including paneling, veneering, and tiling; and ceiling finishes, such as plastering, painting, and acoustical treatment. Exterior finishes consist of the entire outside surface of a building, including wall coverings, ornamentation, and protective coatings, such as paint.

The selection of a finish material is determined by its characteristics, cost, and aesthetic effect. Exterior surfaces must be weather resistant, durable, relatively free of maintenance, and architecturally appropriate in scale, texture, pattern, color, and so on. Interior surfaces must also be durable; easy to maintain; functional (considering fire, thermal, and acoustical qualities where appropriate); and aesthetically suitable. As most of what is visible in a finished building is finish work, it is obvious that architects must give serious consideration to the design, detailing, and execution of a structure's finish work.

Finish work has always been the element that has differentiated the refined from the crude. For example, in 17th century New England, the original settlers constructed primitive shelters, which were nevertheless successful in keeping the colonists relatively warm and dry through the first few harsh winters. Within a short time, having solved the basic functional problems, the early Americans demanded greater comfort and elegance in their shelters. Packed dirt floors gave way to wood planks, rough walls were paneled with finished wood boards, and eventually, building exteriors were covered with smooth boards or masonry, embellished with decorative details, and painted. It was this finish work that gave to early American architecture the distinctive look that has been so appealing for more than 200 years.

Many exterior materials were discussed in previous lessons; some of these will be reconsidered in this lesson as finish materials.

PLASTER WORK

Plaster is one of the oldest finish materials still used in construction today; more than 4,000 years ago it was employed by the ancient Egyptians. Greek and Roman builders also used plaster extensively; in fact, our word *plaster* comes from ancient Greece, where it originally meant "to mold." Even with the introduction of countless new materials, plaster remains one of the most popular surface finishes in almost every part of the world.

Plaster is a cementitious material that is applied in layers on both interior and exterior surfaces. It is composed of portland cement (for exterior plaster or stucco), or gypsum and lime (for interior plaster); an aggregate such as sand, vermiculite, or perlite; and enough water to form a workable paste. In some cases, hair, fibers, or mineral aggregates are added to impart some desirable quality. Plaster mixtures are applied in two or three coats over a base of concrete or masonry, metal lath, or various types of lathing board.

In addition to portland cement plaster, which is used on the exterior, and gypsum plaster, which is used on the interior, several other types of plaster are available as follows:

Acoustic plaster—provides acoustical treatment for walls and ceilings

Bonding plaster—used on interior concrete walls and ceilings

Fire-resistant plaster—provides fire resistance for steel and other materials

Keene's cement plaster—contains lime putty for hard, water-resistant finish

Lightweight plaster—contains vermiculite or perlite aggregates for fire resistance

Bases for plaster include concrete, masonry, and lath. Concrete and masonry surfaces must be sufficiently rough and porous to provide a good bond; in lieu of such a base, lath should be spread over the surface, on furring channels, prior to plastering.

DIAMOND EXPANDED MESH

FLAT RIB LATH

HIGH RIB LATH

SELF FURRING PAPER BACKED LATH

METAL LATH TYPES

SQUARE END CASING BEAD   QUARTER ROUND CASING BEAD   CORNER BEAD   BULLNOSE CORNER BEAD

WINDOW STOOL   CONTROL JOINT   BASE   BASE SCREED

METAL TRIM SHAPES FOR PLASTER

Metal lath is a sheet metal or wire fabric into which a base coat of plaster is keyed. It is fabricated from copper alloy steel coated with a rust-inhibiting paint or from galvanized steel, and it is specified in pounds per square yard. Metal lath is available in several types, the most common of which are flat expanded (diamond mesh); rib lath (flat rib or high rib); and woven wire mesh or lath. When plastered, the metal lath is completely embedded, which creates a mechanical bond between plaster and metal.

Lathing board, sometimes referred to as plasterboard, gypsum lath, or gyplath, is composed of gypsum that has been mixed with water, hardened and dried, and sandwiched between two sheets of heavy, porous paper, which provides adhesion for the plaster. The standard size of lathing board is 16" × 48", and it is either 3/8 or 1/2 inch thick. Lathing board is available in solid sheets; perforated sheets (for better mechanical keying); in solid sheets with reflective aluminum foil on one side (for vapor and thermal control); and in Type X, which provides a fire-resistive rating.

Lathing board is generally nailed in a horizontal position to wall framing members that are spaced 16 inches on center. Vertical joints should be staggered and arranged to coincide with studs, blocking, and so forth, to which the board is solidly nailed.

Before plaster is applied, a variety of trim shapes are set, such as metal corner beads and casing beads for the protection of corners and edges, and plaster grounds and screeds, which ensure level and plumb surfaces, as well as a consistent thickness throughout. Interior plaster over metal lath should be a minimum of 5/8 inch thick, and over gypsum lath, 1/2 inch thick. Exterior plaster varies from 3/4 to 7/8 inch thick, depending on the base.

Plaster is generally mixed mechanically and applied in three coats, referred to as *scratch, brown,* and *finish* coats. In two-coat work, the scratch and brown coats are combined in a base coat. The proportions of a conventional gypsum plaster, applied over metal lath, are shown on the following page.

Coat	Sand/Plaster	Thickness
1st - Scratch	2 parts to 1	1/4 inch
2nd - Brown	3 parts to 1	1/4 inch
3rd - Finish	1-1/2 parts to 1	1/8 inch

Plaster is applied by hand in a variety of textures, or it may be machine applied to create a mechanically textured finish. Plaster must be cured, very much like newly poured concrete. It should never be applied when the temperature falls below 40° F, and in the summer, rapid evaporation must be avoided.

Veneer plaster is a specially formulated dense plaster that is applied in a thin coat over gypsum lath. It may have a smooth or textured finish and can usually be painted within 24 hours after plastering.

GYPSUM BOARD

Gypsum board is a prefabricated form of plaster used in place of conventional three-coat interior plaster. Because it is usually applied in large, single-thickness sheets, its application is much faster than using several coats of wet plaster. In addition, it is generally cleaner to use, requiring less protection of other work and less final cleanup.

Gypsum board consists of a gypsum plaster core reinforced with paper or other materials laminated to both sides. It is commonly referred to by the popular trade name *sheetrock*, or by the term *drywall*, because—unlike plaster—it is applied in dry sheets. Gypsum board is manufactured in 4-foot widths, from 6 to 12 feet in length, and from 1/4 to 5/8 inch in thickness (thin sheets may be used on curved surfaces).

GYPSUM BOARD EDGES AND JOINTS

Gypsum board is applied directly to wood or metal framework or to concrete or masonry walls above grade with nails, screws, or adhesives. Exposed corners and edges are protected with metal trim, and all joints, nailhead depressions, and other dents are covered with a perforated tape embedded in joint compound. When the compound has hardened, the surface is sanded smooth and painted or overlaid with a wall covering. A prime coat is often applied to gypsum board in order to prevent raising a nap on the paper surface.

Following is a list of some common types of gypsum board with a description of their uses:

Regular board. Surfacing for walls and ceilings.

Backing board. Backing for other materials, such as acoustical tile.

Insulating board. Aluminum foil laminated to one side, which serves as reflective insulation and vapor barrier.

Type X board. For fire-resistive rating.

Moisture-resistant board. Backing for ceramic tile in high moisture areas.

Decorative board. Prefinished with decorative paper or vinyl in various textures, patterns, and colors.

CERAMIC TILE WORK

Ceramic tiles are small, flat units composed of clay or clay mixtures fired in kilns at high temperatures. They are set on floor, wall, or ceiling areas to provide permanent, waterproof, durable, and easily maintained finish surfaces. Ceramic tile may be installed on the interior or exterior of a building, depending on the density of the tile, its finish, and its method of installation. Ceramic tile is commonly available in square, rectangular, hexagonal, and numerous other shapes; and its size varies from about 1 to 9 inches in length and width, and from 1/4 to 1 inch in thickness. Trim tiles are available in various shapes for use as corners, bases, coves, caps, and other such mouldings.

Ceramic tiles are manufactured by burning clays that have been pressed into the desired shape through either the dust-pressed process or the plastic process. Vitrification, or the fusion of the tile after firing, is a measure of tile density, and the common classifications are listed below:

Non-vitreous tile has a moisture absorption rate between 7 and 15 percent.

Semi-vitreous tile has a moisture absorption rate between 3 and 7 percent.

Vitreous tile absorbs less than 3 percent of its weight in moisture and has a density such that it cannot be penetrated by dirt.

Impervious tile repels almost all moisture and dirt. It is extremely hard and generally available only by special order.

CERAMIC TILE SHAPES

Finishes for ceramic tiles vary greatly, but essentially, they are either glazed or unglazed. Glazed tiles have a glassy, waterproof surface produced by ceramic material that is fused on their faces. The glazes may have several different textures, or degrees of matte finish, and they normally range from pure white to jet black and every hue in between. Unglazed tiles derive their color and texture from the clays used in their manufacture, or from minerals that are added prior to firing.

Some common types of ceramic tile are listed below:

Glazed interior tile. Non-vitreous, made by the dust-pressed process and used for interior surface applications.

Glazed weatherproof tile. Semi-vitreous or vitreous, may be used for moderate wear on the exterior.

Ceramic mosaic tile. Generally unglazed, semi-vitreous, and less than six square inches in area. (When larger, they are called pavers.) Often factory-mounted on large paper sheets for ease of installation, and used on both interior and exterior.

Quarry tile. Unglazed units, made by the plastic process, and nearly impervious to moisture, dirt, and stains. Weatherproof, durable, and suitable for heavy duty wear.

Inlaid, Faience, and Handmade tiles. Varieties of special, colorful tiles.

Other types of tile. The tile industry is rapidly expanding to include a wide variety of tile types, including porcelain, glass, terrazzo, and stone. Porcelain tile is an impervious tile without a clay backing and is suitable for exterior applications. The color is throughout the tile although the glaze can be different on the top and bottom of the tile. Glass tile is made from glass that can be "tumbled" to ease the edges and sometimes has color coatings, such as gold foil, on the back. Terrazzo tile is a manufactured tile consisting of an aggregate and cement matrix similar to terrazzo. Lastly, stone less than ¾-inch thick is generally referred to as stone tile and is usually installed in the same manner as ceramic tile, including thin bed methods not typical for dimensional stone.

Setting tile requires great care; backing surfaces must be rigid, water-resistant, and level or plumb. Poorly prepared surfaces or any subsequent structural movement can lead to cracking at the grouted joints and possible leakage. Ceramic tile is frequently set in a cement mortar bed about one inch thick and composed of one part portland cement, half part hydrated lime, and five parts sand. Tile may also be set with the use of adhesives (thinset), such as latex-portland cement mortar, epoxy mortar, or a mastic called organic mortar.

After tiles are cemented in place, they are grouted and pointed (to shape and compress the joint) with a rich mixture of cement and hydrated lime. The grout is worked into the joints, which range from 1/16 to 1/2 inch wide, and the entire surface is wiped clean after completion.

Ceramic tile is also available in prefabricated panels that fit standard tub and shower base dimensions. These prefabricated units use a plastic adhesive as the joint filler.

PLASTICS

In recent years, a great many plastic products have replaced building elements formerly made from other materials, such as flashing, flooring, countertops, etc. One such substitute material is *plastic siding*. It is made from a vinyl plastic and is available in various colors, textures, with or without insulation backing. Other items include *plastic countertops* with a molded-in lavatory, in a wide range of colors and marbleized designs; *plastic bath tubs* that include full-height enclosures; and *plastic shower stalls* consisting of integral base and walls. All of these are manufactured from various acrylics or fiberglass.

FLOORING

Finish flooring is the surface on which people or equipment move within a building. It covers a vast range of treatments, and it includes virtually every material that can be walked on, from a painted concrete slab to a custom-designed wood parquet floor.

Finish flooring in a building involves more than just covering up the rough construction. Materials such as ceramic tile, terrazzo, and concrete produce highly durable finishes that are capable of withstanding constant, heavy traffic. Cork, rubber, and carpet control the noise level in a room, vinyl is grease-resistant, brick is fire-resistant, and synthetic resin surfaces require very little maintenance. It should be apparent, therefore, that the selection of a finish flooring material is not a haphazard choice; rather it is based on occupancy, location, anticipated use, initial cost, resistance to fire, noise, and dirt, frequency and cost of maintenance, comfort, and finally, appearance and personal preference. Several common flooring materials are discussed below.

Wood Flooring

Wood flooring is a popular finish suitable for a wide range of uses. It is durable, comfortable, attractive, and easily maintained. Wood flooring is manufactured under strict rules that control the grade and moisture content of the wood. Close-grained, hard, and durable species of both hardwood (oak, maple, birch, beech, pecan) and softwood (pine, fir, spruce, hemlock, redwood) are used for flooring. Flooring may be plain-sawed or quarter-sawed, but vertical grain boards are preferred for the best installations. The basic types of wood flooring are strip, plank, and block, which are usually fastened to the subfloor by means of nails, screws, or mastic cements; all are available prefinished or unfinished.

All wood is susceptible to swelling and shrinkage caused by changes in humidity, and therefore, sufficient expansion space must be provided at a floor's perimeter. In addition, wood flooring used in humid climates should be treated against decay, mold, and insects.

Strip flooring is available in various thicknesses ranging from 5/16 to 25/32 inch, in widths ranging from 1-1/2 to 3-1/2 inches, and in random lengths. The strips most often have tongue-and-groove sides and ends. Strip flooring is applied

WOOD STRIP FLOOR @ BASE

over a wood subfloor or on spaced wood sleepers (horizontal members that elevate the finish floor above the subfloor below), and is generally fastened by blind nailing. It may also be applied directly to a concrete slab using waterproof adhesives. Strips are laid in conventional parallel lines, in various simple patterns, or in intricate parquet designs.

Plank flooring is available in the same thicknesses as strip flooring, but in widths between 3-1/4 and 8 inches. It is frequently laid in random widths with a V-groove where the board edges meet. Wide planks are susceptible to warpage, and therefore, they are often screwed to the subfloor through the face of the plank, which is then plugged and finished smooth. The wood plugs result in a distinctive appearance that has become the distinguishing mark of wood plank floors.

Parquet flooring consists of prefabricated squares measuring about 9 to 12 inches square and between 1/2 and 25/32 inch thick. They may be either solid strips held together with splines or plywood veneers, and they are available

TYPES OF WOOD FLOORING

WOOD FLOORING PATTERNS

unfinished or prefinished, with square or tongue-and-groove edges. Thin block flooring is fastened by nailing or by adhesives.

Solid block flooring consists of end-grained blocks that have been treated with creosote against moisture and decay. The blocks are usually set in a coating of bituminous material, and they are used in workshops and industrial buildings where a durable, heavy-duty floor is required. This type of flooring is very resistant to oil, grease, and mild chemicals.

Mortar-Set Flooring

Mortar-set flooring includes any masonry material that is set and utilized as a finish floor surface. Examples are tile, brick, slate, and other types of natural stone.

Brick of almost any type can be used as finish flooring, depending on the desired result. Acid-resistant brick is dense, hard, and often used for industrial flooring. Paving brick is also dense and hard, and it provides an attractive finish in a variety of natural colors. Building brick is warm and attractive, in a rustic way, but it is generally too porous and uneven for most interior floors. Brick is normally laid in a mortar setting bed over the subfloor; however, it may be laid with thinset mortar or adhesives. On the exterior, brick is often set in sand with tight joints.

Slate is very durable, attractive, and expensive. It may be slightly rough or relatively smooth, rigidly rectangular or completely irregular, and it is available in a rich range of natural colors. Slate paving is about one inch thick and generally laid in a mortar setting bed, in which case the joints are grouted and finished flush. However, it can also be laid with adhesives or set in sand on the exterior.

Stone flooring, other than slate, includes limestone and sandstone (flagstone) as well as granite and marble. All stone used for flooring is about one inch thick and has a relatively smooth surface. Stone is hard, durable, and heavy, and regardless of type, it is easily stained.

Poured-in-Place Flooring

In addition to concrete, which can be finished with stain or paint, poured-in-place flooring includes terrazzo, magnesite, and a variety of synthetic seamless floors.

Terrazzo is a concrete topping consisting of marble chips in a cement or synthetic resin binder, ground and polished to a smooth finish. Terrazzo is dense, permanent, hard-wearing, and relatively expensive. The topping is about 5/8 inch thick and generally laid over a 2-1/2-inch thick concrete setting bed; this, in turn, may be applied over rough concrete, wood, or steel decking.

A disadvantage to terrazzo flooring is its tendency to crack, but this may be alleviated by the use of regularly-spaced divider strips. These are available in plastic or a variety of metals that are partially embedded in the concrete setting bed. The crushed marble mixture is then poured between the divider strips, compacted, troweled smooth, and machine-ground to a smooth finish. When using a synthetic resin binder, dividers are unnecessary and often omitted.

Terrazzo floors are available in a wide variety of colors, depending on the color of the cement and marble chips used. It may also be produced with an abrasive finish, as a conductive floor (for hospitals), and in several prefabricated shapes, such as tiles, stair treads, and coved bases.

Magnesite seamless floors (magnesium oxychloride) are made from a composition of magnesium oxide, sand, and magnesium chloride, which forms a plastic material that is troweled to a smooth finish. The finished surface, ranging in thickness from 1/2 to 1 inch, may be applied directly over wood, concrete, or flat steel decking. Magnesite composition flooring is resistant to stains and fire, somewhat resilient,

TERRAZZO FLOORING

and relatively inexpensive. It is appropriate for use in schools, offices, and industrial buildings.

Elastomeric floors are composed of clear urethane resins applied as a liquid over an elastomer underlayment. They are generally hard, durable, and relatively easy to maintain. Colored vinyl chips are often embedded in the urethane for their decorative effect.

Rubberized plastic floors consist of several layers of various neoprene compositions troweled over a waterproof latex membrane. The finish is smooth, durable, and completely waterproof. This type of flooring may be used on the interior or exterior of a building.

Paint-type floor finishes consist of a synthetic resin (epoxy, urethane, polyester, etc.) and an activator. These, when mixed, are applied directly to concrete, wood, or metal to produce an exceptionally hard, durable, wear-resistant, easily-maintained, greaseproof floor finish.

Resilient Flooring

Resilient flooring materials are durable, non-absorbent, comfortable, and easily maintained. They are thin (1/16 to 3/16 inch thick) and available in tiles (generally 9 or 12 inches square) or in six-foot-wide rolls. These materials are laid over smooth wood or concrete subfloors and cemented in place with mastic cements. Trim shapes such as topset wall bases, stair nosings, and edging strips are generally available. Some common types of resilient flooring material are described in the following paragraphs.

Vinyl is available in sheet or tiles and may be used above or below grade. It is very resilient, durable, resistant to indentations, oil, and water, and easy to maintain, and therefore particularly appropriate for kitchens. Available in a large assortment of colors and patterns, it is moderately expensive.

Asphalt tile is relatively inexpensive and very durable, but it lacks resilience. Asphalt tiles are easily installed above or below grade in areas of heavy traffic, such as in schools, hospitals, and offices.

Linoleum is durable, resilient, easily maintained, and relatively inexpensive, considering its long life. It is available in printed patterns, inlaid designs, or solid colors throughout its thickness. However, it is unsuitable below grade or in the presence of subsurface moisture.

Rubber flooring is now made of synthetic rubber. It is durable, elastic, quiet underfoot, easily cleaned, and moderately expensive. While it is attractive and comfortable, it cannot resist oils or greases.

Cork flooring is available in sheet or tiles with a synthetic resin binder and surface. It is highly resilient, resistant to staining, durable, and easily maintained. It also has excellent acoustical properties.

Carpeting

Carpeting, once used almost exclusively as area rugs in homes, now includes carpet tiles and wall-to-wall carpeting, which are commonly installed in many commercial and institutional buildings. They add warmth, resilience, texture, and effective control of noise. Carpeting eliminates the need for a finish flooring material, as it can be installed directly over a plywood subfloor or a concrete slab. It may also be used on wall surfaces to improve the acoustical quality of a space, and also to prevent accidents in institutional buildings, such as nursing homes.

Carpeting is classified by material (acrylic fibers, nylon, polyester, wool); by method of manufacture (tufting, weaving, needle punching); and by texture (low pile, high pile). Most commercial grades of carpeting are durable, soil-resistant, and relatively inexpensive to maintain; however, their ultimate durability depends on several factors. With pile carpets, density of pile (tufts per square inch) is of primary importance; the longer and denser the pile, the longer the life of the carpet. Cushions or padding installed beneath the floor covering will also add years of life to carpeting. However, both carpet tiles and wall-to-wall carpeting are available with an integral foam backing, which eliminates the necessity for padding.

All carpeting requires maintenance, although, in general, it needs less care than resilient flooring. Embedded dirt can harm carpeting and it should therefore be shampooed periodically. Depending on the fibers and treatments used in their manufacture, carpets can be made moth-proof, mildew-resistant, flame-resistant, stain-resistant, and antistatic.

WOOD IN MASTIC ON CEMENT TOPPING

WOOD WITH VAPOR BARRIER OVER SLAB ON GRADE

WOOD ON BEVELED SLEEPERS ANCHORED IN MORTAR

RESILIENT FLOORING ON PLYWOOD OVER JOISTS

CERAMIC TILE IN SETTING BED OVER PLYWOOD

CERAMIC TILE IN SETTING BED OVER SLAB

BRICK IN MORTAR SETTING BED OVER SLAB

MARBLE ON PLYWOOD WITH WATERPROOF ADHESIVE

MARBLE IN MORTAR SETTING BED OVER CONCRETE SLAB

OXYCHLORIDE ON PLYWOOD SUBFLOOR

TERRAZZO OVER WOOD SUBFLOOR

CUT STONE IN SETTING BED OVER CONCRETE SLAB

FINISH FLOORING SYSTEMS

The initial cost of carpeting is relatively high. However, due to its moderate cost of maintenance, it is often the most economical floor covering to use, when considered over its entire life cycle.

ACOUSTICAL WORK

Acoustics, the science of sound and its control, is beyond the scope of this lesson; however, as materials and systems used for sound control are increasingly used for interior finishes as well, we shall consider their use as another aspect of finish work.

A wide range of acoustical materials are used to control or minimize sounds. The criteria in their choice include not only acoustical efficiency, but also fire resistance, method of application, ease of maintenance, and appearance. Almost all acoustical materials control sound by absorption, and they may be classified as follows:

Acoustical tiles are manufactured from wood, mineral, or glass fibers with perforated, textured, or patterned surfaces that allow sound to penetrate. They are lightweight, fragile, and most often factory finished. Available in one, two, and four-foot modules, they have square, beveled, rabbeted, or tongue-and-groove edges.

Acoustical panels are made of perforated steel, aluminum, fiberboard, or hardboard, which is backed with a soft, sound-absorbing batt or blanket. They are permanent, far more durable than tiles, and have acoustical properties that depend on the quantity and size of the perforations and the sound absorption value of the pads used behind the panels.

Prefabricated tiles and panels are often nailed or cemented to a solid backing surface. Because tiles are so fragile, they are almost always used for ceilings, and frequently, acoustical tile ceiling systems are suspended from the structure above. This creates a plenum for mechanical conduits and recessed lighting fixtures. When a fire-rated ceiling is required, acoustical tile supporting systems must have an approval from the Underwriters' Laboratories.

Wet materials include acoustical plaster and mineral-fiber products to which a binding agent is added. These may be hand troweled or machine sprayed to produce an incombustible surface, usually with both acoustical and thermal insulation values. Especially suited for

ACOUSTIC TILE INSTALLATION

irregular or curved surfaces, these materials are quickly installed and very effective.

Vibration control consists of isolating or reducing mechanical vibrations in or near a building. To control vibration, dense materials such as lead, solid concrete block, or concrete must be used to isolate the vibration source from the building spaces.

Several methods are used to reduce sound transmission through walls. These include staggering wall studs or using two separate sets of studs, mounting the finish material on resilient furring channels, and using fiberglass or other acoustical insulation.

PAINTING

The use of paint goes back to prehistoric times. It was used some 25,000 years ago in the famous cave paintings at Lascaux, and perhaps even earlier to decorate earthenware pots. Throughout prehistory, paint served to ornament various elements used for ceremonial or religious rites, and until comparatively recently, in fact, paint was used almost exclusively to embellish or beautify buildings.

Today, the principal purpose of paint is to protect and preserve the material being painted and secondarily, for aesthetics. Originally, paint consisted of a simple mixture of white lead and linseed oil that was applied in three to six coats over a long period of time. Modern technology, however, has changed all that; some synthetics are capable of covering in one coat and drying in only a half-hour. Additionally, because of the danger of lead poisoning, titanium dioxide and other "safe" pigments have completely replaced white lead.

An incredibly vast range of materials is now available to treat finish surfaces; paint can resist the damaging action of weather, moisture, mildew and decay, it can make surfaces more sanitary, it can modify the light in a space, and it can produce a myriad of psychological effects through the use of color and texture. Paint, incidentally, is only one of many organic coatings, which is the proper term applied to all types of protective liquid coverings.

Paint is a protective coating that combines a pigment and a vehicle. When applied to a prepared surface, this mixture forms a solid film that acts as a barrier between the material painted and those elements that may adversely affect it.

Pigments are finely ground solids that are held in suspension by the vehicle. They provide the paint's color, as well as its *hiding power,* or opacity. Hiding power is a function of the difference in indices of refraction of the pigment and the vehicle. A large difference produces good hiding power and also minimizes the damaging effect of sunlight, as much of it is reflected. Colored pigments are finely ground solid particles made up largely from inorganic materials, such as iron oxide that produces yellows and sodium silicate that produces blues. Synthetic color pigments are also available that widen the range to include the total color spectrum. Colored pigments differ from white pigments in that light is selectively absorbed. Extender pigments are additives used in a paint mixture to control gloss, increase durability, improve workability, and reduce cost.

Vehicles, which constitute the liquid portion of a paint mixture, consist of a binder that forms the paint film, driers to speed up formation of the film, and solvents or thinners that control consistency and aid in drying. Depending on the type of solvent used, a paint will form a solid film by oxidation, evaporation, or by thermosetting action caused by applied heat. Vehicles contain drying oils or resins, alone or in combination. Driers, such as linseed oil, have the ability to absorb oxygen and change into a solid state. Resins that are natural (varnish) or synthetic (phenolics, epoxides, alkyds, latexes, urethanes, polyvinyls) all add to a paint's durability and protective quality.

Paint types are numerous and widely varied. They may be classified by location (exterior enamel); by the material on which they are applied (wood stain); by their finish (semigloss enamel); or by their unique characteristics (lacquer). Following is a brief review of several types of coatings.

Pigmented Coatings

Pigmented coatings consist of white pigment, to which color may be added, and a vehicle. They include house paints, metallic paints, colored lacquers, water-based paints, and synthetic resin paints. These are generally available ready-mixed for immediate use.

1. *Enamels* are pigmented paints that use varnish as the vehicle. They form a hard, tough film that is durable and resistant to weathering. Enamels are available in a gloss or matte finish.

2. *Baked enamels* are always factory-applied, as they require a controlled temperature of between 200 and 300° F to harden. A baked enamel finish is hard, durable, washable, and resistant to most mild chemicals.

Clear Coatings

Clear coatings protect and beautify surfaces without obscuring their natural appearance. Although preferences still vary, environmental concerns have resulted in major changes as the coating industry attempts to reduce volatile organic compound (VOC) emissions.

Varnishes using volatile solvents such as turpentine and mineral spirits have been replaced by polyurethanes and acrylic modified urethane coatings. Lacquers made from a highly flammable nitrocellulose base have been replaced by acrylic lacquers. And shellac, an alcohol-soluble resin formerly used as a sealer or prime coat, has been replaced by water-based primer-sealers that are more durable and less susceptible to water spots. Shellac as a floor finish has been replaced by acrylic modified urethanes.

Clear sealers include a variety of systems that prepare surfaces for another finish. Water-borne sealers and water-repellant compounds are now readily available using acrylic, urethane, and other binders, often with better results than the less environmentally gentle sealers they replace.

Stains, although not strictly clear coatings, have a pigment content that is lower than opaque paints. They do not obscure the natural grain of wood or substrate. They also have low viscosity and deep penetration; because the stain is absorbed by the substrate rather than forming a film on its surface, the substrate and its grain remain visible.

Bituminous Coatings

Bituminous coatings are made from coal tar and asphalt, and are used as a protective coating for submerged ferrous metal and for waterproofing masonry materials.

1. *Coal tar pitch* must be melted to a fluid for application. It is used to protect metal and is applied by dipping. Coal tar mixtures may be applied hot or cold and are used as waterproofing agents.

2. *Asphalt* coatings are available as paints, enamels, and emulsions. In comparison to coal tar products, they are more weather resistant and less affected by temperature

extremes. They are commonly used for dampproofing and waterproofing work.

Miscellaneous Coatings

Beyond the coatings discussed elsewhere in this lesson, numerous products exist for more specific applications. Care should be taken to establish the suitability of the coating for both the substrate and the application.

1. *Cement* coatings consist of Portland cement and, occasionally, lime (with water as the vehicle). They may also contain pigments, water repellents, or fillers. Cement coatings are used for damp-proofing masonry and concrete surfaces, and for steel protection.

2. *Fire-resistant* and flameproof paints (intumescent paints) do not support combustion and have developed to the point where they have fire ratings that can be used to protect structural steel in fire-rated construction. They can also be used to improve flame-spread ratings and stop heat transfer to combustible materials.

3. *Rust-preventive paints and primers* are characterized by their rust-inhibitive qualities, low permeability to corrosive elements, and low water absorption. They are available as primers and as finish paints, and typically include zinc or (in some cases) Portland cement as the principal ingredient.

4. *Antibacterial* and insecticidal paints are produced by adding counteracting ingredients to the paint. Some ingredients lose effectiveness over time and some may have toxic effects harmful to plants and animals.

5. *Epoxy coatings* resist chemicals, moisture, or stains. Both one-part and two-part coatings are available.

6. *Specialty coatings* are being promoted by paint manufacturers for a wide variety of purposes and can provide the design team with options not previously available. Care should be exercised, however, to verify manufacturers' claims, preferably by visiting local applications of the product to judge its success. Where no local application is available, another option might be a better choice.

Paint Application

Paint application requires knowledge, skill, and understanding of painting materials and methods. Paint is applied with brushes, spray guns, rollers, trowels, or rags at the job site, or by dipping, tumbling, or spraying at the mill, shop, or factory. Frequently, materials receive a prime coat at the shop and are finish painted at the job site.

All materials receiving paint must be properly prepared to insure adhesion of the film coating and maximize the life of the coating. Surfaces must be clean, dry, and free of all corrosion, grease, or surface defects that will prevent adhesion. Paint should be applied at temperatures between 55 and 85° F, for best results.

In addition to selecting the paint, architects must specify the surface preparation (such as sealing knots in wood); the method of application (brush, rollers); and the number of coats desired (prime coat, finish coat, and so on).

All painted surfaces must eventually be maintained or refinished, but paint failures, such as blistering, scaling, and peeling, will be minimized if surfaces are free of all moisture, well prepared, and finished with the appropriate coating.

LESSON 8 QUIZ

1. Which of the following finish floorings would one choose if the most important criterion was resilience?

   A. Elastomeric-type flooring

   B. Asphalt tile flooring

   C. Cork sheet flooring

   D. Terrazzo with synthetic resin binder

2. Vermiculite is sometimes added to a plaster mix in order to enhance the mixture's

   A. durability.

   B. workability.

   C. water resistance.

   D. fire resistance.

3. Which of the following are advantages of using a suspended acoustical tile ceiling system?

   I. Light fixtures may be recessed.

   II. Mechanical conduits may run above the ceiling.

   III. Enclosure provides a one-hour fire rating.

   IV. Acoustical tiles provide a tough, durable ceiling.

   V. Almost all systems are conveniently modular.

   A. I and IV   C. II, III, and IV

   B. I, II, and V   D. I, II, III, and V

4. In a remodeling project, there are several rough concrete basement walls that require a smooth plastered finish. Before plastering, a plumb surface should be created using

   A. gypsum lath.

   B. gypsum board.

   C. plywood.

   D. metal furring channels.

5. All the following are advantages of using gypsum board in place of wet plaster, *EXCEPT*

   A. it is generally less expensive.

   B. it is generally more durable.

   C. it is cleaner to use.

   D. it is faster to use.

6. Painting failures are most often caused by

   A. poor quality paint materials.

   B. faulty application methods.

   C. surfaces that are not clean and dry.

   D. painting when the weather is hot and humid.

7. Both Keene's cement plaster and ceramic tiles are suitable to use on the walls of an institutional shower room. One might select the plaster rather than tiles because it is

   A. more water-resistant.

   B. more durable.

   C. less expensive.

   D. less difficult to maintain.

8. Which of the following apply to the scratch coat of plaster?

   I. It is generally the first plaster coat.

   II. It consists of a mixture of portland cement, or gypsum and lime, with water and sand.

   III. It is generally applied over gypsum lath.

   IV. It is always applied by hand.

   V. It is rarely less than 3/4 inch thick.

  A. I and II   **C.** III, IV, and V

  B. I, II, and III   **D.** I, II, III, and IV

9. The major disadvantage of wood flooring is its susceptibility to

  A. weather-related swelling and shrinking.

  B. indentations from heavy traffic.

  C. damage from fire.

  D. stains from oil, grease, and chemicals.

10. For which of the following reasons would a urethane coating be preferred?

  A. It dries quickly.

  B. It affords a high degree of protection.

  C. It prevents rust.

  D. It provides resistance to fire.

VERTICAL TRANSPORTATION

INTRODUCTION

The first architect who decided to build up, rather than out, might have made that decision more than 5,000 years ago. Regardless of the precise moment in history, from the time that multistoried structures first appeared on the architectural scene, builders have had to consider how to get people from one level to another.

The earliest forms of vertical transportation were fairly primitive ramps, ladders, and stairs.

In those isolated cases that involved mechanical ingenuity, the device was generally intended to move materials, rather than people. As an example, the ancient Romans used a movable platform hoist that operated in a shaftway containing guides. Some of these hoists were powered by hand-driven windlasses, and others used animal power; but in either case, the hoist was used to lift materials during construction or to transport products to elevated stories or even over steep mountain cliffs.

During the early 19th century, steam-driven hoists replaced human and animal labor, but they did little more than their ancient counterparts. These early hoists were rarely used to transport people, principally because they lacked any kind of safety device, and as a result, they were extremely hazardous. Hoisting ropes were made of fiber, and if the rope failed, as it often did, there was no way to stop the hoist from crashing to the ground.

In 1853, Elisha Graves Otis developed an elevator safety device that ultimately altered the shape of cities throughout the world. The device consisted of a pair of spring-loaded elements that meshed with ratchets in the guide rails when the tension of the hoisting rope was released. Otis demonstrated his safety device by ascending in a hoist that was part of an exhibit at the New York Exposition of 1853. Halfway up in the open-sided shaft, an assistant suddenly and dramatically sliced the hoisting rope with an axe, but the platform held steady. The gathered crowd stood astonished as it witnessed the birth of the safety elevator. By the early 1900s, elevators served practically every new multistoried commercial structure, and in subsequent years, improvements in elevatoring made possible the 100-story structures of today.

Other forms of vertical transportation widely used in contemporary construction are the moving inclined ramp and the moving stairway. The moving stairway was developed by Otis' company and first introduced to the world at the Paris Exhibition of 1900. Although it caused quite a sensation, it was a far cry from the sophisticated escalators that are found in most of today's department stores.

Vertical transportation refers to all the systems used to move people and materials vertically. These can be divided into two categories: those that require human effort, such as stairs, ramps, and ladders; and those that are mechanically powered, such as elevators, escalators, moving ramps, dumbwaiters, and vertical conveyors. This lesson begins with stairs, ramps, and ladders, and then examines mechanically powered devices.

STAIRS

Stairs are the most common means of vertical circulation between floors of a building, and their design is dictated by considerations of safety and convenience. Stairways may be as narrow as 36 inches, but when serving an occupant load of 50 or more, they must be no less than 44 inches wide. The rise of a step should not exceed 7 inches, and the run of a tread should not be less than 11 inches. In addition, safe practice dictates maintaining one of the

following conventional relationships between riser and tread:

Riser + Tread   = 17 to 17.5 inches
Riser × Tread   = 70 to 75 inches
2 Risers + Tread = 24 to 25 inches

Stair landings should be as long as the stairway width (up to 44 inches maximum), the vertical distance between landings may not exceed 12 feet, and headroom clearance should never be less than 6'-8".

Fire stairs are required for emergency exiting, and their number is controlled by the occupancy of the building and the occupant load of each floor, as specified in the building code. In general, all such stairways must be enclosed with fire-resistive walls and be equipped with complete fire assemblies, including fire doors that open in the direction of emergency travel.

Monumental stairs, often referred to as decorative stairways, are often used in larger buildings to connect the main floor to a mezzanine or

CRITICAL STAIR DIMENSIONS

second floor. Stairways more than 88 inches in width require intermediate handrails, but in any event, monumental stairs are rarely permitted to be used as legal fire stairs.

Residential stairs are governed by more lenient regulations than are fire stairs in public buildings. Because of their considerably smaller occupant load, residential stairs may be narrower, only one handrail is required, fire-resistive construction is not mandatory, and winders and spiral stairs are sometimes acceptable.

RAMPS

Ramps are inclined walkways that allow easy vertical transition between different levels. The slope of ramps may be summarized as follows:

1:20 (5.0 percent) or less, not considered to be a ramp

1:15 (6.7 percent) or more, requires handrails

1:12 (8.3 percent) maximum slope permitted for access for persons with disabilities

1:8 (12.5 percent) maximum slope permitted by building code (typically in theater aisles)

Ramps are usually as wide as the corridors leading to them, except for handicapped ramps, which must be a minimum of 36 inches wide.

HANDICAPPED RAMP DIMENSIONS

In addition, handicapped ramps have a maximum rise of 30 inches, and landings must be at least five feet long. Handrails are required on handicapped ramps if the ramp is more than six feet long or has a rise greater than six inches.

LADDERS

Ladders are generally used for access to roofs or in utility and service areas where space is tight and traffic is minimal. Although occasionally made of wood, most permanent ladders in buildings are fabricated from metal. Vertical ladders should be a minimum of 18 inches wide, have rungs spaced 12 inches apart, and be installed at least 6 inches from walls to allow for adequate toe space.

ELEVATORS

Elevators are movable enclosures that provide vertical transportation for people and freight. They generally consist of an enclosed platform, or car, which is raised or lowered along rails within a vertical shaft, and the mechanical equipment that provides power, control, and safety for the operation.

The two major types of elevators in common use are *hydraulic* and *electric*. Each type has distinctly different characteristics and uses. Hydraulic elevators are directly ram-driven from below, while electric elevators employ steel cables with counterweights and operate on the traction principle. In other words, the hydraulic elevator platform is *pushed* up by a rod, whereas the electric elevator platform is *pulled* up by cables.

Hydraulic Elevators

Hydraulic elevators are commonly used for low-rise buildings (about 50 feet or five stories

ELECTRIC ELEVATOR

HYDRAULIC ELEVATOR

maximum), and have speeds that vary between 25 and 150 feet per minute (fpm). Because of their short travel distance at relatively low speeds, hydraulic elevators are commonly used for freight in industrial and low-rise commercial buildings; for passengers in garden apartments and motels; and occasionally in single-family residences.

Hydraulic elevator platforms sit over a plunger, or ram, which operates in a cylinder that usually extends as far into the ground as the elevator rises. Oil serves as the pressure fluid, the supply of which is controlled by high-speed pumps.

Because of their simplicity of operation, hydraulic elevators cost less than electric elevators. In addition, they have no wire cables or overhead machinery, and consequently, they do not require a penthouse. Hydraulic elevators are especially suited to carry freight; single ram capacities are available up to 10 tons, and multiple rams have been used to carry up to 50 tons.

Electric Elevators

Electric elevators are generally used in commercial and institutional buildings greater than 50 feet in height. They have capacities up to 10,000 pounds and may attain speeds, in buildings over 50 stories, of up to 1,800 fpm.

Traction is used to transmit lifting power to the hoisting cables of an electric elevator. This is achieved by means of the friction that develops when the cables run over grooves in the machine-driven sheave. On one end of the cables is the elevator car, and on the other end are counter-weights, weighing about 40 percent of the load capacity, which are used to reduce power requirements.

The motor and drum assembly that moves the elevator car is called a traction machine, and it may be gearless or geared. The gearless machine has the motor, sheave, and brake all mounted on a common shaft; thus one revolution of the motor turns the main sheave one revolution. Geared machines, on the other hand, have the motor and brake on one shaft, which in turn drives a second main shaft. The two shafts are connected by means of gears, so that the motor shaft may make several revolutions for each turn of the main shaft. Gearless machines are used for high-speed installations, while geared machines, with their greater flexibility, are preferred for low-speed applications.

Roping

Roping for elevators has a considerable effect on the loading and stress of the cables, machine bearings, and building members. Traction-type machines are classified as either single-wrap or double-wrap. In the single-wrap design, the cables pass only once over the elevator machine sheave. For high-speed service, additional traction may be required, and this is obtained by using the double-wrap design. In this case, cable life is usually shorter, since there are more bends in the cable. Elevators are roped either 1:1 or 2:1, referring to the distance the cable moves in relation to the distance the car moves. In 2:1 roping, the car speed is one-half that of the cable; however, 2:1 roping requires that only half the weight be lifted by the motor, therefore

allowing a smaller elevator motor to be used. Illustrated on the following page are several elevator roping arrangements.

Safety Features

Safety features on elevators are numerous and highly refined, since the potential hazards associated with elevator use can be critical. The main brake is mounted on the motor shaft of the elevator machine and operated automatically by the control panel. The brake is self-applying, so that the car will be stopped in the event of a power failure.

The *governor* measures and limits the elevator speed by means of the control panel. In case of excess speed, it actuates the safety rail clamp. Top and bottom limit switches will also actuate the safety rail clamp if the elevator attempts to exceed its proper range of travel. The safety rail clamp is, in effect, another type of brake. It consists of metal jaws on the car that, in case of emergency, clamp the guide rails and hold the car in a fixed position. If a car is disabled between floors, an emergency exit hatch in the roof of the car permits access or egress.

Car bumpers are located at the bottom of the shaft to stop the car if it should overtravel at low speed. Their purpose is to arrest the car's motion more gently than a solid stop; however, they are not designed to stop a free-falling car.

The doors of an elevator car have safety edges consisting of a spring-loaded lip. If this lip encounters a person, package, and so forth, the door will reopen and prevent the elevator from moving. In addition, automatic (unattended) elevators have an electric eye system that prevents the door from pinching passengers or objects. Car and door interlocks are provided at each floor to prevent the possibility of a lobby door opening when the elevator is elsewhere. Cars are also

DRIVE SHEAVE

SECONDARY SHEAVE

TO CAR

SINGLE WRAP

TO COUNTERWEIGHT

DRIVE SHEAVE

SECONDARY SHEAVE

TO CAR

DOUBLE WRAP TO COUNTERWEIGHT

ELEVATOR MACHINE

IDLER

COUNTERWEIGHT

ELEVATOR CAR

SINGLE WRAP TRACTION
ONE-TO-ONE ROPING

DOUBLE WRAP TRACTION
ONE-TO-ONE ROPING

ELEVATOR MACHINE

IDLER

COUNTERWEIGHT

IDLERS

ELEVATOR CAR

DOUBLE WRAP TRACTION
TWO-TO-ONE ROPING

IDLERS

COUNTER-WEIGHT

ELEVATOR MACHINE

SINGLE WRAP TRACTION

ELEVATOR MACHINE

IDLERS

UNDERSLUNG TRACTION

ELEVATOR ROPING ARRANGEMENTS

equipped with automatic leveling devices to reduce the hazard of passengers tripping at lobby thresholds.

Elevators are not considered legal exits. In case of fire, automatic controls generally close the elevator doors and return the cars to the lower terminal, where the doors open and the elevators become manually operable only by a key.

Capacity and Speed

The capacity and speed of elevators vary considerably, depending on their use and the height and overall quality of the project. Normally, a small office building requires a minimum-size elevator that is rated at 2,500 pounds capacity and has a car 5 by 7 feet in size. This allows the use of a 3'-6" wide center-opening door. Passenger elevators, even in heavily-traveled prestige office buildings or monumental institutional buildings, rarely exceed 4,000 pounds capacity.

Elevator speeds should be adequate to provide prompt, efficient service. The maximum usable speed is limited by the building height, since acceleration and deceleration require a substantial distance. In other words, elevator cars, without using "jack-rabbit" starts or abrupt stops, are unable to attain or reduce a high speed in a short travel span. As an approximate rule of thumb, the rated elevator speed may be figured as 1.6 times the rise in feet, plus 350. Thus, with a 300-foot-high building, a speed of about 800 fpm would be called for $(1.6 \times 300 + 350)$. Listed below are recommended elevator speeds for office or general purpose buildings.

Operating Systems

Operating systems used in elevators today are almost all automatic types, replacing the older, operator-controlled car switch type. In the single automatic operation, the car responds to the first button pressed, ignoring all other calls until the car reaches its first destination. Elevators using this operating system are unable to store calls, but their use in apartments and hospitals is quite acceptable.

With the collective operating system, calls may be stored. Selective-collective systems answer all calls in the direction of a car's travel; that is, when traveling up, the car will not stop at a floor where a down button has been pressed. Fully automatic systems are generally used for tall office buildings. They have all the advantages of the selective-collective system, but in addition, service can be adjusted for varying traffic conditions. For example, during early morning hours, cars can be regulated to operate at fixed

	Recommended Speeds in Feet per Minute			
Height in Floors	**Small**	**Average**	**Prestige**	**Service**
2–5	200–250	300–350	350-400	200
5–10	300–350	350–500	500	300
10–15	500	500–700	700	350–500
15–25	700	800	800	500
25–35	–	1000	1,000	500
35–45	–	1,000–1,200	1,200	700–800
45–60	–	1,200–1,400	1,400–1,600	800–1,000
over 60	–	–	1,800	1,000

intervals, or when loaded; and after reaching the highest floor, the car returns to the entrance lobby. In tall buildings, elevators may be zoned, with each car serving only a specified group of floors. This permits high-speed operation for a portion of the trip and generally results in more efficient use of elevator equipment.

Architectural Considerations

Architectural considerations in the use of elevators include the determination of elevator size, number, and location for efficient traffic. These requirements depend on building population and function, building height and number of floors, volume of traffic, car capacity, and speed of elevator operation.

Elevator traffic is generally computed for peak or critical traffic periods, which vary with the type of building. Office buildings might reach their peak period during lunch time, whereas the peak period in hospitals might occur during visiting hours. Traffic is measured by the number of persons handled during a five-minute peak interval. When this figure is divided by the five-minute handling capacity of an elevator, the minimum number of elevators can be determined.

The handling capacity of an elevator is computed on the basis of both its car size (the number of people carried) and its round-trip time. Normally, an average person requires two square feet of space in order to feel comfortable in an elevator car. During rush hours, however, this may be reduced to as little as 1.3 square feet.

The round-trip time comprises all of the factors involved with a full-speed, non-stop, round-trip run as shown in the example in the right column.

In general, time intervals between elevators should be between 20 and 30 seconds; a waiting time of more than 35 seconds is usually considered unsatisfactory.

Action During Round-Trip Run	Time in Seconds
1. Passenger operates call button, doors open	3
2. Passenger enters car, operates floor button	2
3. Doors close	3
4. Car travels to upper floor	7
5. Doors reopen (starting before car stops) 3 less 1 premature opening =	2
6. Passenger leaves car	2
Total time to serve one passenger	19
7. Doors close	3
8. Car returns to original floor	7
Total Round-Trip Time	29

The *location of elevators* is critical to the efficiency of pedestrian traffic flow in a building. Elevators should be centrally located and easily accessible from all building entrances. The best arrangement is to place the elevators in an alcove off the main corridor, to reduce traffic conflicts. With groups of up to three elevators, the cars are best placed in a row; with four elevators or more, they are best grouped in banks opposite one another. In general, when more than eight elevators are needed, the best arrangement is a combination of local and express traffic banks.

Door arrangements on elevator cars may vary somewhat, with adequate width and rapid operation being necessary for efficiency. Very small apartment house elevators may have swinging doors, but higher-capacity installations require sliding doors to facilitate passenger loading. Doors that open to one side may be either single-speed or two-speed, the latter having a second panel telescoping alongside the first.

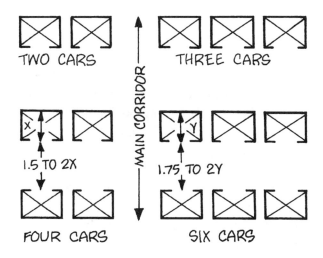

ELEVATOR CAR ARRANGEMENTS

Center-opening doors may also be single-speed or two-speed, with the latter arrangement comprising a total of four panels. Center-opening doors operate more efficiently than side-opening doors, since they make possible speedier passenger loading and unloading. In general, the optimum-sized door is 3'-6" wide, which allows two persons to enter or leave an elevator simultaneously.

ELEVATOR DOOR ARRANGEMENTS

Special design considerations may be required for elevators, depending on the unique function of a building. For example, hospital elevator cars should be large enough to accommodate beds, wheelchairs, and stretchers (5'-4" × 8'-4"), and have a capacity of 3,500 pounds or more. Restaurants and department stores require separate passenger and service elevators; and for industrial buildings, shift changes and the movement of large equipment must be taken into account. Other special situations include hotels (baggage); prisons (security); theaters (peak loads); professional buildings (high visitor population); and courthouses (user separation).

FREIGHT ELEVATORS

Freight elevators are used to vertically transport equipment, materials, and goods, rather than passengers. In low-rise buildings, hydraulic elevators are appropriate, but electric elevators are generally more economical for lifts exceeding 50 feet. Generally, freight elevators have a less finished appearance, lower speed, and greater capacity than passenger elevators. Depending on the building height, standard speeds vary between 75 and 200 fpm, but they may be greater for smaller capacity elevators. Freight elevators are available in capacities from 2,500 to 25,000 pounds or more; some can carry fully loaded trailer trucks and even railroad cars.

The American Standard Safety Code for Elevators defines the classes of freight elevators as follows:

Class A General Freight. Loaded by hand truck. No single piece of freight to exceed one-quarter capacity load of elevator, based on 50 pounds per square foot of platform area.

Class B Motor Vehicle Garage Elevator. Automobiles and trucks only, based on capacity of 30 pounds per square foot of platform area.

Class C Industrial Truck Loading. Must be able to support impact load and weight of truck. Capacity not less than 50 pounds per square foot of platform area.

Service elevators used in residential, commercial, and institutional buildings are usually passenger elevators that have been modified to handle oversize loads or hand trucks. They commonly have abuse-resistant interiors and are equipped with horizontal sliding doors, in contrast to the vertical biparting doors used in freight elevators. Service elevators must comply with code requirements for carrying passengers, and their size is generally determined by the largest or bulkiest load that is anticipated to be carried.

Sidewalk elevators are freight or supply lifts that rise to an upper level by opening hatch doors located in the ground floor. Years ago these were commonly placed in sidewalk areas; however, most municipal codes prohibit this practice today. Sidewalk elevators are either hydraulic or electric, two stories maximum, and they travel at about 25 fpm.

DUMBWAITERS

Dumbwaiters are hoisting and lowering devices, very much like small elevators, used to vertically transport materials and supplies, but never people. They are distinguished from freight elevators by limitations found in elevator safety codes; namely, car platforms may not exceed nine square feet in size, nor can the car height exceed four feet. Thus, dumbwaiters are quite small: their capacity never exceeds 500 pounds. They may be automatically powered (controlled by push buttons from the landing, not the cab), or they may be manually operated by pulling on ropes. In either case, they have very few safety

features, as their principal purpose is material handling.

Dumbwaiters are used for a variety of service-related functions, such as distributing mail in office buildings, delivering books in libraries, and transporting food and supplies in restaurants and hospitals.

Vertical conveyors are used to distribute a continuous flow of materials (never people) throughout multistoried buildings. In several different ways they bear a resemblance to other forms of vertical transportation. For example, they are mechanically similar to escalators in that they operate with a continuous chain which is driven by an electric motor. They are also similar to dumbwaiters in that they are small, carry relatively light loads, and operate at slow speeds. Vertical conveyors, like elevators, are enclosed in fire-resistant shafts.

Vertical conveyors carry trays or shelves spaced at regular intervals along the conveyor, with up loads on one side and down loads on the other. In most cases they are used to distribute paper work or light supplies.

ESCALATORS

An escalator, sometimes called a moving stairway, is a mechanical device on which passengers are transported along an incline from one floor to another. They provide rapid, comfortable, and continuous vertical travel without the long waiting periods frequently associated with elevators. Escalators are used to move large numbers of people from floor to floor quickly, efficiently, safely (safer than stairs), and at a relatively low cost of operation.

Escalators are made up of custom-built steel trusses that are fitted between floors, an

PARALLEL

CRISSCROSS

ESCALATOR ARRANGEMENTS

endless belt that contains the steps, and synchronized handrails. The normal angle of incline is approximately 30 degrees, and the operating speed is either 90 fpm or 120 fpm along the incline.

Escalators are rated by speed of operation in feet per minute and by nominal width, which is measured at approximately hip level. The two standard widths are 32 and 48 inches; the first allows a parent and child to share the same step, while the second allows two adults to ride side-by-side. Escalator capacity, expressed in passengers per hour, ranges from 4,000 to 5,000 passengers per hour on a 32-inch-wide 90 fpm escalator, to 8,000 to 10,000 passengers per hour on a 48-inch-wide escalator traveling at 120 fpm.

Because escalators are continuously running and unidirectional, pairs of escalators are necessary for two-way service, one for up traffic and one for down traffic. The conventional arrangements used are either parallel or criss-cross; the latter is preferred, as it is a more compact arrangement with lower structural requirements and hence lower cost.

Escalators are not generally accepted as legal exits, as their unidirectional travel may increase, rather than reduce, the hazards of emergency exiting. Furthermore, escalators are difficult to enclose, although they may be made fire-resistant with rolling shutters and deluge-type sprays.

As with elevators, escalators should be located so that most people entering a building can see them. They should be in the path of the heaviest expected traffic, centrally located, and with ample space at floor levels. For years, department stores have utilized escalators to move large groups of shoppers and steer them towards specific merchandise. However, in recent times escalators have also been installed in transportation terminals, convention halls, hotels, office buildings, theaters, sports arenas, and other buildings that must transport large numbers of people in a minimum amount of time.

Moving ramps are a form of vertical transportation closely related to escalators; the principal difference, of course, is that moving ramps have a continuous tread, rather than individual steps. They incline up to about 15 degrees, and when flat, they are referred to as moving sidewalks. Moving ramps are about 40 inches wide and have speeds that vary between 140 and 180 feet per minute. They allow pedestrians to move swiftly, as one may continue to walk along the moving treadway, doubling one's speed. Moving ramps provide an effective means of transporting and directing large numbers of people quickly, as for example, at airport terminals; and their use appears to be increasing.

CONCLUSION

The future of elevatoring promises to be imaginative and exciting, if the recent past is any indication. Over the last several years, a new concept of elevatoring multipurpose buildings has developed, in which separate groups of elevators serve the different areas of a building. For example, in the John Hancock Center in Chicago, one group of elevators serves the 40 stories of offices below, while a separate group is used for the 44 stories of apartments above.

A method of reducing space requirements in tall buildings is the use of double-deck elevators traveling in a single vertical shaft. The two compartments of the elevator are loaded simultaneously; for example, during early morning rush hours, passengers destined for odd-numbered floors enter the bottom deck, and those for even-numbered floors enter the upper deck. When the elevator stops, passengers from both decks are discharged simultaneously. Elevator controls have also moved into the computer age, with microcomputers that continuously scan the system to make it more efficient.

Dramatic and decorative glassed-in elevator cars are also currently used in a number of installations where the view in motion provides a thrilling experience. In contemporary hotels, such as the Hyatt Regency Hotels in Atlanta and San Francisco, occupants of large atrium-lobbies share the excitement of movement, as spectators, with the elevator passengers. Similar observation-type elevator cars are sometimes used on the exterior of buildings, providing the passengers with panoramic views of the urban landscape.

LESSON 9 QUIZ

1. The maximum usable speed of an elevator is generally limited by
   A. considerations of safety.
   B. car capacity.
   C. counterweight/load ratio.
   D. building height.

2. In the design of a three-story commercial building with a maximum height of 45 feet, the architect wishes to have a constant roof silhouette with no projections above the 4-foot-high parapet. Consequently, the architect should choose
   A. an electric elevator with geared traction and operating machinery at the basement level.
   B. a gearless electric elevator with operating machinery in a four-foot-high roof structure.
   C. a hydraulic elevator with operating machinery in a four-foot-high penthouse.
   D. a hydraulic elevator with operating machinery located in the elevator pit.

3. The recommended speed of a passenger elevator in a 20-story building should be about
   A. 200 feet per minute.
   B. 300 feet per minute.
   C. 800 feet per minute.
   D. 1,000 feet per minute.

4. Every fire door that is part of a fire stairway exiting system must open
   A. in the direction of travel.
   B. into the enclosed stairway.
   C. toward the flight leading down.
   D. toward the building exterior.

5. In which of the following ways do freight elevators generally differ from passenger elevators?
   I. They are never used by people.
   II. They are slower.
   III. They have greater capacity.
   IV. They require fewer safety features.
   V. Their doors operate differently.
   A. I, II, and III   C. II, IV, and V
   B. II, III, and V   D. I, III, and IV

6. In order to connect two levels whose difference of elevation is two feet, a handicapped ramp must be at least
   A. 10 feet long.   C. 24 feet long.
   B. 12 feet long.   D. 30 feet long.

7. What safety device on an electric elevator provides life safety protection in the event of a power failure?
   A. A governor
   B. An automatic brake
   C. The interlocks
   D. The car bumpers

8. The principal advantage in the use of moving ramps is

   A. speed.   **C.** safety.

   B. comfort.   **D.** convenience.

9. In determining the total number of elevators required in a new building, an architect should consider the

   I. total number of floors.

   II. estimated volume of traffic.

   III. number of hours of operation.

   IV. elevator roping system.

   V. elevator car size.

   A. II and V   **C.** I, II, and V

   B. I, III, and IV   **D.** II, III, IV, and V

10. Escalators are most effectively used in situations that require

    A. low cost.

    B. high speed.

    C. considerable life safety.

    D. considerable user capacity.

BUILDING CODES

by John A. Raeber, FAIA, FCSI, CCS

INTRODUCTION

One of the first steps in designing any facility is to determine governmental requirements applicable to the facility. Building construction is limited by a variety of regulatory conditions that are typically enumerated in various codes adopted by agencies charged with specific tasks relating to public health, safety, and welfare.

Building codes define the allowable size of a building, both in area and in height, based on the degree of danger defined by the type of occupancies or uses anticipated in the building and on the types of construction. A building structure constructed of combustible materials would be limited in both size and height. A building structure constructed of noncombustible materials with proper fire ratings and a fully automatic sprinkler system could be built as large as the budget allows.

In addition, building codes define requirements for fire ratings, fire protection, egress, and accessibility. They also provide specific requirements for materials and methods of construction, usually prescriptive in nature, but sometimes related to performance characteristics such as structural design requirements for dead loads, live loads, snow loads, wind loads, rain loads, and seismic loads.

Specific information provided here relating to building codes is intended to be conceptual in nature and should be relevant to most building codes. In many cases identifiers are taken from the International Building Code but are consistent with recent editions of the original three model building codes used to create the IBC. The NFPA 5000 generally recognizes the same concepts defined here but may use different methods for identifying specific elements such as not assigning specific letters to occupancies (for example, Group A as Assembly, Group B as Business) and there are differences between the IBC and NFPA 5000 relating to specific requirements throughout the codes.

HISTORY

Ancient history presently suggests the Babylonian Code of Hammurabi, written some 4,000 years ago, as the original building code where it stated that if a building collapsed and killed the owner the builder would be put to death. In modern times, starting in the 19th century, requirements limiting the type of construction and sizes of buildings were originally defined by insurance companies. Losses of both life and property in buildings caused building owners to seek insurance, and insurance companies like the American Insurance Association developed requirements to minimize their losses. In the early 20th century communities saw the benefits of these requirements and began using them as the basis of requirements for their communities.

Over time officials involved in developing and enforcing building codes joined together in associations and began developing regional building codes that reflected the needs of their areas. One group of building officials out of the Chicago area developed a model building code with an emphasis on snow loads. Another group of building officials out of the Atlanta area developed a model building code with an emphasis on wind loads, especially the extreme winds in hurricanes. And, a group of building officials out of California developed a model building code with specific seismic load requirements.

As communications and travel improved, these groups shared their specific knowledge and many of the specific requirements relating to snow, wind, and seismic loads were identical in the three model building codes. Modifications were made to bring the three model building codes into a common code format and to minimize the differences. Still, requirements relating to the allowable size of the building and other requirements did vary between the model building codes until the adoption of the International Building Code in 2000 by the International Code Council.

Unfortunately, in 2002 the National Fire Protection Association (NFPA) published a series of codes referred to as the Comprehensive Consensus Codes (C3) including NFPA 5000, "Building Construction and Safety Code." So architects are once again faced with the possibility of local communities' adopting either of the two model building codes, the IBC or the NFPA 5000. The IBC seems to be the preferred model building code at this time but architects must verify which building code has been adopted as well as which edition of the code. The International Building Code presently has both an IBC 2000 Edition and an IBC 2003 Edition. The NFPA 5000, 2003 Edition is the first edition but will, like the IBC, be updated on a regular basis.

USE AND OCCUPANCY

The intended use or "occupancy" of a building provides the first major design consideration. Each occupancy relates to a specific type of concern such as the potential for panic in facilities where large numbers of people congregate, special concerns when there are young people in need of adult guidance in an emergency, concerns for the safety of people who might be sleeping, and facilities that might have special hazardous materials.

The International Building Code classifies ten major types of occupancies, with some having from two to five subclassifications. NFPA 5000 has similar occupancies but does not use the abbreviations (A, B, E, etc.).

Group A—Assembly: In facilities where more than 50 people gather for a common purpose such as entertainment, recreation, food or drink, there is potential that irrational action by one person could result in irrational action by many. This irrational action is called panic and one of the requirements of the assembly occupancy is that doors are required to swing in the direction of exit travel and to have panic hardware allowing the pressure on the face of the door to release any latch device.

Group B—Business: Professional and service facilities as well as drinking and dining facilities with fewer than 50 occupants are the safest space available because most of the occupants are familiar with their surroundings and are expected to be awake while in the building.

Group E—Educational: This occupancy is intended only where there are six or more children that require adult supervision during an emergency. Education facilities through the 12th grade are anticipated to have trained faculty and staff who know through fire drills the proper procedures to ensure life safety for all school occupants. Like assembly occupancies panic devices are required where there are 50 or more occupants.

Group F—Factory: Factories with moderate and low hazard materials and standard industrial use share many of the requirements for Group B – Business occupancy.

Group H—Hazardous: Facilities that involve the manufacturing, processing, generation, or storage of materials that constitute a physical or health hazard such as explosive, combustible, corrosive, or toxic materials have special limitations and requirements.

Group I—Institutional: These are facilities that house people day and night who are supervised 24 hours a day, seven days a week, either due to medical problems or due to incarceration for the public welfare such as hospitals, nursing homes, nurseries, sanitariums, jails, prisons, and reform schools. Some day care facilities are also considered institutional occupancies.

Group M—Mercantile: Facilities for display and sale of merchandise presently share the same requirements as Group B—Business.

Group R—Residential: These are facilities used for sleeping other than institutional facilities including both transient facilities such as hotels (R-1) and primarily permanent facilities such as apartment houses and dormitories (R-2), and also one and two family dwelling units (R-3).

Group R occupancies may well be the least safe occupancy as the occupants can be sleeping and there is no 24-hour supervision. A sleeping person could inhale sufficient smoke to suffer "smoke inhalation syndrome," which relates to a loss of oxygen supply to the brain that causes sufficient confusion to prevent the person from being able to open a door with a key. More people die in home fires every year than in any other occupancy.

Group S—Storage: These are facilities used for storage including garages, aircraft hangers, and helistops. People may work in these facilities.

Group U—Utility: These facilities are not intended for human occupancy, including private garages, carports, sheds, fences, stables, and towers.

TYPE OF CONSTRUCTION

Another key factor in determining the relative safety of a building is the type of construction. Two specific characteristics are considered—first, whether the structural materials are classified as noncombustible or combustible, and second, how long the structure can be anticipated to not collapse after a fire begins based on hours, for example, 4, 3, 2, or 1-hour fire rated construction.

Noncombustible Construction

Noncombustible construction requires structural components to be made of steel, concrete, masonry, or some other "limited combustible" materials, but not wood. Noncombustible types of construction may or may not have fire ratings for structural components. Both the IBC and NFPA 5000 consider Type I and Type II construction noncombustible.

Combustible Construction

Combustible construction includes facilities with structural components of wood or other materials determined to be combustible such as some plastics. Combustible types of construc-

tion may or may not have fire ratings for structural components. Both model codes consider Type III, Type IV, and Type V construction combustible.

Just as important to the type of construction as whether or not the primary structural materials are combustible is the amount of time the structural components can be expected to continue to support their loads without collapse after a fire starts.

Fire Rated Construction

The International Building Code requires their highest rated structure, Type IA, to be able to support their design loads for not less than three hours after a fire begins based on either experience or testing. NFPA 5000 requires a four hour rating for structural components in their highest-rated structure Classified as Type I (442). NFPA 5000's Type I (332) construction would be closer in type of construction to IBC Type IA. These noncombustible buildings are often allowed unlimited height and area because the fire personnel can fight the fire from inside the building without the danger of collapse.

Without becoming too detailed with code nomenclature, both the model codes have classifications for two-hour fire rated construction, one-hour fire rated construction, and non-fire rated construction. A non-rated building could collapse in less than one hour after a fire began, which would limit the height and area of the building available to allow fire personnel to fight the fire from the exterior only. Ideally one-hour fire rated construction is also limited in height and area to allow fighting the fire from outside.

Even the safest occupancy, Group B—Business, is limited to no more than five stories for one-hour fire rated and non-fire rated construction, and six stories where an approved automatic sprinkler system is provided.

BUILDING VOLUME—AREA AND HEIGHT

Building area and height is determined by the type of construction along with the occupancy based on Table 503 in the International Building Code and Table 7.4.1 in the NFPA 5000. Unlimited heights and areas are typical for noncombustible construction fire rated at three hours or higher, with the primary exceptions relating to Hazardous Occupancies. Two-hour fire rated noncombustible construction may include high-rise buildings, 75 feet or more to the highest occupied floor, with some exceptions.

Height restrictions are given in the tables based on both the number of stories allowed and on the maximum height of the building in feet. Both height limitations differ in the two codes.

The allowable areas in the two model codes appear to be the same to the extent the two are comparable. Moreover, the areas listed in the model codes are just the beginning as area increases are allowed for various reasons.

First, both codes allow area increases based on the percentage of accessible building frontage, because the greater the frontage the greater the ability for fire personnel to fight the fire from more than one direction. Second, they allow area increases based on having an automatic sprinkler system, and unlike earlier codes the increase is permitted even if used for height or story increases. Third, they allow area increases based on having more than one story.

FIRE

Collapse

One primary life safety concern during a fire is that the building or a part of the building may collapse during a fire. If a fire starts on the first floor of a high rise building, and it can be estimated to take several hours to evacuate the building and extinguish the fire, it is important that the structural components be capable of continuing to support the building during the evacuation of the building and while firefighters are extinguishing the fire.

Structural components are rated based on the length of time in hours they will continue to be structurally sound during a fire. Tests and experience establish typical fire ratings of one hour, two hours, three hours, and four hours. Heavy timber construction (Type IV) is an example of experience establishing a fire rating. Heavy timber is automatically considered one-hour fire rated. Heavy timber is defined as wood structural members with their smallest dimension nominal six inches or greater.

Containment and Compartmentation

The spread of fire in a structure also provides a means for assuring the safety of the occupants and provides fire personnel time to extinguish a fire. By providing a fire separation proven by test or experience to be able to slow the spread of fire, occupants can be assured safe egress, even if their path goes through a floor with an active fire. Firefighters can also establish staging areas from safe locations knowing they will be protected for at least a minimal amount of time.

Walls, partitions, shafts, floor-ceilings, and roof-ceilings are rated based on the same time ratings as structural components, one hour, two hours, three hours, and four hours. The key difference is that structural components are tested on to ensure the component maintains structural integrity where containment and compartmentation requires openings in the fire rated construction such as doors, windows, and penetrations, to be fire rated.

In some cases building components can be fire rated for both structural and containment reasons. The fire rating of a floor assembly in a high rise building would have to meet both requirements. An exterior wall located on or near the property line might also require both structural fire ratings to prevent collapse and containment fire ratings for protection from a fire in an adjacent building. An exterior wall facing a public way, however, would only require a structural fire rating, allowing for limitless unprotected glazed openings facing the public way.

Flame Spread

Wainscoting, paneling, or other finish applied structurally or for decoration, acoustical correction, surface insulation, or similar purposes and used for wall or ceiling finishes are required to be tested for flame spread and for smoke developed.

Flame Spread ratings are measured according ASTM E 84, also referred to as UL 992 and NFPA 255. But whatever is used to describe the test method, it is the "Steiner Tunnel Test."

Classifications:

- Class A—Flame Spread 0 to 25. (Former building codes referred to this as Class I.)
- Class B—Flame Spread 26 to 75. (Former building codes referred to this as Class II.)
- Class C—Flame Spread 76 to 200. (Former building codes referred to this as Class III.)

The International Building Code describes the flame spread requirements in Table 803.5.

NFPA 5000 lists flame spread requirements as part of the requirements for each occupancy. The following classifications are general and can vary based on the Occupant Group and on whether or not the facility is sprinklered.

- Enclosed Vertical Exitways (Stairs): Class A.
- Other Exitways (such as Corridors): Class B.
- Rooms in Assembly and Institutional Occupancies: Class B.
- Rooms in other Occupancies: Class C.
- Dwelling Units (R-3): Class C.

Smoke Developed/Smoke Development

ASTM E 84, et al. also tests for the amount of smoke developed during the flame spread test. Smoke developed shall be maximum 450 in all cases. Some of the older model building codes referred to this as "smoke density."

Floor Finishes

It's important to recognize that flame spread and smoke developed classifications are for wall and ceiling finishes only, not for floor finishes. Floor finishes are tested using different testing criteria, ASTM D 2859 or NFPA 253, the flooring radiant panel test. Both codes list Class I and Class II ratings with Class I being more resistant to spreading fire.

Typically Class I floor finish ratings are required in Institutional Occupancy vertical exits, exit passageways, and exit access corridors. Class II floor finish ratings are required in the same locations in other occupancies.

EGRESS—EXIT ACCESS, EXIT, EXIT DISCHARGE

"Means of Egress" is defined as a continuous and unobstructed path of travel from any occupied portion of a facility to a public way. Egress consists of three specifically defined parts: exit access, exit, and exit discharge.

Some egress components can be found in all three parts. A door within an office suite would be part of the exit access. A door into a fire stair would be part of the exit. And, a door leading from an egress court to a street would be part of the exit discharge. Stairs, railings, and ramps could also be found in any part of the means of egress.

Comparisons between the International Building Code (IBC) and NFPA 5000 become more difficult related to egress as the earlier model codes used to create the IBC had basic requirements with exceptions and special requirements for various occupancies in Chapter 10. NFPA 5000 is based largely on the NFPA 101 Life Safety Code, where there are some general requirements, but specific requirements are located as part of each occupancy in various chapters.

Occupancy Loads

The first step in designing egress for a facility is to determine the occupant load. Occupant loads are determined based on tables in the model codes, Table 1004.1.2 in the IBC and Table 11.3.1.2 in NFPA 5000. The tables list various occupancies or uses along with a numeric floor area to be used to determine the occupant load.

Both model codes indicate "Business" as allowing for no more than 100 square feet per occupant. Thus the occupant load factor for an architect's office with 3,000 square feet would be 30 occupants, 3,000 divided by 100. The square footage for business occupancies is required to be calculated based on gross square footage. Occupancies such as assemblies and educational classrooms allow calculations to be based on net floor area.

In order to determine egress occupancy loads it is important to calculate the loads for each defined area on a floor and then to determine the egress occupancy loads for the entire floor.

This can prove difficult in buildings such as speculative office buildings. Calculations would have to be based on anticipated occupancies, the gross area of the floor divided by 100. When the tenant floor plans are established the resultant calculations will undoubtedly differ because every office area not designed on a 100-square foot division would result in additional occupants.

Thus a 3,000-square foot floor would be designed with 30 occupants anticipated. But, if the floor were designed with 20 offices with a gross area of 110 square feet each, the total occupants from those offices alone would be 40 occupants. The remaining 800 gross square feet on the floor (3,000 minus 2,200) would result in an additional 8 occupants or more, depending on the configuration, and a total occupant load factor of 48 or more, more than a 60 percent increase.

Changing one or more of the offices (Business) to conference rooms (Assembly) would have an additional increase in occupant load. Changing the whole floor to a restaurant (Assembly) would result in an occupant load factor of 150 or more depending upon the net square feet used without fixed seats, bench, or booth seating, and how much of the floor would be the kitchen area.

Egress Width

Once the occupant load has been determined it is necessary to compute the egress width required. The total exit width is calculated by multiplying the occupant load factor by a decimal number based on the occupancy type with the result being divided by the required number of exits.

Thus in the IBC a stairway serving 1,000 persons in a Business Occupancy in a building without sprinklers would use the factor of 0.3 from Table 1005.1 resulting in $1,000 \times 0.3 = 300$ inches. As the model codes require not less than three separate exits located remotely from each other for occupant loads of 501 to 1,000, the 300 inches would be divided by three, resulting in a requirement that each of the three exit stairs be 100 inches wide.

The same calculation for doors would be based on a factor of 0.2 from IBC Table 1005.1, thus a total of 200 inches for the three exit doors, requiring each door to be not less than 66.67 inches wide. As exit doors are required to have not less than 32" clear width and not more than 48" nominal width, the design for the three doors would most likely result in three pairs of 36" wide doors.

It is important to note that there are major differences in the width factors in the IBC and NFPA 5000.

Exit Access

Exit access starts where an occupant is within a facility and continues until the occupant reaches the "Exit." In a restaurant it begins at any given seat. In an office it begins in any office or other occupied part of the office. Exit access requires consideration of the number of exits required for each space, the required separation of exits when more than one exit is required, travel distance to the closest exit, egress through intervening spaces, and corridors.

Number of Exits

When discussing the number of exits from a building it is typically easiest to assume that

each building and each floor in each building requires not less than two exits; each building and each floor in each building with an occupant load of 501 to 1,000 requires three exits; and each building and each floor in each building with an occupant load of more than 1,001 requires at least four exits. Additional exits may be required based on travel distance on each floor to an exit.

But frequently a space within a floor of building might also require two or more exits. The IBC requires any space in occupancies other than H and S to have a second means of egress when the occupant load exceeds 50. Thus assembly occupancies, such as conference rooms with tables and chairs, in a space of 750 square feet or more would require two means of egress (50 times 15). Similarly office occupancies with 5,000 square feet or more would require two means of egress (50 times 1,000). Although the concept is the same as in earlier model codes, the numbers have changed over the years.

Separation of Exits

Another requirement typical in the model codes is that when more than one exit is required the exits are required to be separated by a specific distance. Where two exits are required the separation is required to be not less than one half the maximum diagonal of the space or floor requiring two exits. Where more than two exits are required the additional exits are required to be located a reasonable distance apart so the others will be available if one becomes blocked.

Travel Distance

Measuring from the most remote point to the closest exit the typical maximum travel distance is 200 feet in buildings without a sprinkler system and 250 feet in buildings with a sprinkler system. Business occupancies allow up to 300 feet in buildings with sprinklers. Hazardous occupancies and institutional occupancies typically allow less travel distance; and some Factory, Storage, and Utility occupancies allow 300 feet typically and 400 feet in buildings with sprinklers.

Egress through Intervening Spaces

Travel to an exit often requires leaving one room and passing through intervening spaces before reaching an exit. The model codes limit the types of spaces allowed. Typically the IBC allows exiting through adjoining rooms or areas accessory to the area served as long as they provide a discernible path to an exit.

Types of spaces not allowed to intervene with an exit path include kitchens, storage rooms, closets, toilet rooms, and bathrooms although kitchens in dwelling units are not prohibited. Separate dwelling units and separate tenant spaces may not be part of the required path of travel to an exit.

Corridors

The final segment of an exit access is often a corridor leading to the exit. The standard corridor width is 44 inches, although specific areas have different requirements; for example, Educational occupancies serving 100 or more require 72-inch wide corridors.

A "dead end" is where a corridor continues beyond an exit but does not continue to another exit. The maximum dead end is 20 feet. This means no person would have to travel more than 20 feet in smoke before reaching an end and then turning around and having to retrace their steps to the corridor. There were no exceptions in the older model building codes. But, both the IBC and NFPA 5000 have a number of exceptions, including allowing Business occupancies with sprinkler systems a dead end as long as 50 feet.

Fire rated corridors are required in most occupancies without sprinkler systems, as well as in some

Institutional and in all Hazardous occupancies even with sprinklers. Fire rated corridors are typically required in unsprinklered buildings where the occupant load exceeds 30 and in unsprinklered Residential occupancies where the occupant load exceeds 10. Even with a sprinkler system Residential occupancies with an occupant load greater than 10 require a 0.5 hour fire-resistive rating.

Finally, fire-resistant-rated corridors are required to be continuous from the point of entry to an exit with no intervening rooms except foyers, lobbies, and reception rooms constructed with the same fire-resistant-rating as the corridor.

Exits

The exit is that part of egress that either takes the occupant from the building or floor to a vertical exit enclosure (stair), an exit passageway, a horizontal exit, or an exterior exit ramp or stairway.

Vertical exit enclosures are interior exit stairways and interior exit ramps. Typically vertical exit enclosures are required to be 2-hour fire rated when serving four or more stories including basements (but not mezzanines). Where serving fewer than four stories they are required to be 1-hour fire rated. In rare instances vertical exit enclosures can be non-fire-rated such as when in a single residential dwelling unit, but care should be taken to verify the applicability of the exception.

Exit passageways serve to connect multiple vertical exit enclosures where the stairs cannot be continuous. An example would be the passageway connecting an enclosed stairway in a tower to another stairway at the perimeter of the building pedestal. An exit passageway could also serve to connect an enclosed stairway to an exterior wall where the stair walls are not at the building perimeter. The important aspect of the exit passageway is to realize it must comply with the same basic requirements as the vertical exit enclosure, meaning it may not have toilet rooms, mechanical closets, or storage closets opening directly into the exit passageway. It is easy to confuse an exit passageway with a corridor that does not have the same restrictions.

Horizontal exits were originally used in Institutional occupancies to allow the moving of persons who were nonambulatory (patients) or persons who were being restrained (prisoners) without having to evacuate them from the building. The process gained acceptance and now typically one exit from a space can be a horizontal exit as long as the other exit is either an enclosed vertical exit or an exit directly to the outside. The horizontal exit divides a building or floor into separate compartments with a 2-hour fire-rated partition separating the floor from exterior wall to exterior wall.

Exterior exit ramps and stairways provide the fourth type of exit as long as the building is not more than six stories or 75 feet in height. The exterior exit ramps and stairways are required to be open on at least one side and are required to be separated from the building by fire rated construction matching that required for vertical exit enclosures.

Exit Discharge

The final segment of the means of egress is the exit discharge. The exit discharge can be as simple as the door leading from an vertical exit enclosure to the public street and as complex as the path of travel from a theater building at an amusement park to the public way including the path through another building used for selling and collecting entry tickets. Open areas connecting the exit door to the public way may require conformance with requirements for egress courts.

ACCESS FOR PERSONS WITH DISABILITIES—CODE VS. ACT OF DISCRIMINATION

Present model codes include specific requirements for ensuring access for persons with disabilities based on scoping requirements in the model code along with specific accessibility requirements in the International Code Council (ICC) and American National Standards Institute (ANSI) A117.1, the American National Standard for *Accessible and Usable Buildings and Facilities*.

The scoping requirements in the model code provide requirements for accessible routes; accessible entrances; parking and passenger loading facilities; dwelling units and sleeping units; special occupancies such as accessible assembly area seating; toilets and bathing facilities; kitchens; drinking fountains; elevators; lifts; storage; service facilities such as check-out aisles,; controls; operating mechanisms; and hardware, recreational facilities, and signage.

These scoping requirements typically tell when these design elements are required to meet the specific accessibility requirements in ICC/ANSI A117.1.

It is important to recognize that the requirements in the model building codes are the same as the requirements for height and area limitations, type of construction, fire ratings, egress, and general construction. Where these chapters are adopted by state or local authorities the building officials have both the right and the responsibility to enforce compliance. Citizens might have rights to disagree on the building official's interpretation, based on the actual wording of the state or local law, but they cannot bring a lawsuit against the property owner or design team based on failure to comply with the code unless there is a specific law permitting such a complaint (as there is in California).

The Fair Housing Act and the Americans with Disabilities Act are not building codes and are subject to totally different enforcement processes.

FEDERAL STANDARDS AND REQUIREMENTS: OSHA, FHAG, ADAAG, UFAS

The U.S. Government has developed several standards and requirements that impact building design and construction. Best known perhaps is the Occupational Safety and Health Act or OSHA. In addition there is the Safety Glass standard 16 CPR 1201, the Fair Housing Act, and the Americans with Disabilities Act; federal agencies often adopt specific standards and requirements for construction of buildings and spaces for their own use or under their jurisdiction.

OSHA and the related CalOSHA in California provide specific requirements for the workplace that include stairs, railings, ladders, and protection of openings.

The safety glass standard still exists but the basic requirements have long ago been adopted into the model building codes, which limit those interested in the federal standards to lawyers and those trying to prove a violation-caused injury.

The Fair Housing Act and Americans with Disabilities Act are new types of federal regulation. They are similar to the building code requirements for access for persons with disabilities but they are part of the nondiscrimination laws rather than a federal building code. This means that enforcement is done through the federal courts system based on complaints by persons who believe they have been discriminated against based on their disability.

The results are three complete sets of federal requirements for accessibility—FHAG, ADAAG, and UFAS. The Fair Housing Accessibility Guidelines (FHAG) provide requirements to ensure nondiscrimination in privately funded housing, The Americans with Disabilities Act Accessibility Guidelines (ADAAG) provide requirements to ensure nondiscrimination in facilities other than privately funded housing, including publicly funded housing. And, the Uniform Federal Accessibility Standards (UFAS) provides requirements for construction under four specific federal government agencies including the United States Postal Service (USPS), the Department of Defense (DOD), and the General Services Administration (GSA).

For those slightly confused about the relationship of UFAS and the Americans with Disabilities Act, UFAS is solely for federally funded projects, but is an option to the ADA Access Guidelines for state and local government projects. Only the ADA Accessibility Guidelines (ADAAG) defines access requirements to privately owned facilities.

STATE BUILDING CODES

In an attempt to provide uniformity throughout their communities, many states have adopted one of the model codes and mandated its use throughout the state. Adoption of a particular model code by a state does provide some uniformity; however, it is possible for both the state and a community within the state to adopt revisions and additions to the adopted model code. Although these additions and revisions should not conflict (the operative words are *should not*), they can still cause a major amount of confusion for architects.

Most states adopt one of the model code families with little revision. States such as California and Florida have extensive differences, causing their state codes to vary extensively from the model codes they were originally based upon.

CITY BUILDING CODES

Although states may mandate adoption of a specific model building code, the enforcement of the code is typically left to building officials in each community. And, sometimes local conditions mandate the need for local modifications.

Even when there is no state mandated model building code, most communities adopt one of the model code families with little revision except to the administrative chapters that describe the operations of the local building departments.

Some larger cities are in the habit of adopting revisions to the model codes, and in some cases they can totally rewrite the model code to their own requirements. Some cities have such extensive differences that their codes are sometimes not even similar to the model codes they were originally based upon.

PLANNING AND ZONING CODES

Planning and zoning codes are usually defined by specific local interests and conditions. The City and County of Saint Louis, Missouri, limits buildings in the downtown area to heights lower than their famous Gateway Arch. Rural communities with no sewer systems limit the number of buildings based on the amount of area needed for the septic system either as a function of how many acres are required per dwelling unit, or in some cases how many acres are required per bathroom. Because planning and zoning codes are not nationalized, architects must obtain them from the local officials and ascertain their impact to the project as early as possible.

Planning and zoning codes can restrict specific areas in the community to certain types of building occupancies (commercial, residential, light industrial, etc.). They can also restrict building types in specific areas (construction materials such as concrete, steel, masonry, or wood frame construction). They can limit the heights and allowable square footage of buildings within a particular area of the community, sometimes based on the type of fire fighting equipment available in that area. And, they can require open space, limit shadowing, and even place design requirements such as building (or glass) colors.

The original purpose of the planning and zoning codes related to limiting construction of highly combustible wood frame construction in cities that had gone through major fires around the turn of the century, such as Chicago and St. Louis, and the site of the great fire that followed the San Francisco earthquake of 1906. Later these planning and zoning codes were designed to prevent factories causing pollution from being built in the residential and commercial areas of a community. They also were intended to prevent construction on flood plains, seismic faults, and hillsides subject to landslides. At present it can sometimes be difficult to recognize the original purposes.

FIRE CODES AND FIRE ZONES

Fire code requirements are intended to provide for public health and safety related to management and use of existing structures in case of an emergency. Model fire codes are generally written with requirements for management rather than construction. But fire codes can provide design information regarding the locations, types, and sizes of fire extinguishers, sprinklers, and wet and dry standpipe systems.

Standpipe systems direct water to upper floors of a building to provide water to firefighters in a particular area without having to bring external hoses up the stairs or into interior building spaces. A dry standpipe has no water in it until the connection is made at an outside hose connection. A wet standpipe has water in it at all times. Sprinklers also have water or some fire suppressing chemical in the pipes at all times.

Fire zones are often established to recognize the type of firefighting equipment and trained personnel available in a particular area. Where a particular fire station is not designed for a hook-and-ladder truck, the height of buildings in that station's area may be limited to two or three stories so the fires could be fought from the ground and standard ladders. Fire zones are sometimes incorporated into the building code.

ICC/ANSI A117.1 ACCESSIBLE AND USABLE BUILDINGS AND FACILITIES

The ICC/ANSI A117.1 standards are not in and of themselves building regulations. However, when state and local authorities adopt the model building code including the chapters on accessibility they adopt the ICC/ANSI A117.1 standards as part of their regulatory authority.

Even when the model code chapters on accessibility are not adopted familiarity with the standards published in ICC/ANSI A117.1 can help architects make their buildings and facilities more accessible.

Although the various regulations and standards relating to accessibility may never be identical they do have a common purpose. Whether the enforcement is by a local authority or by a complaint by an aggrieved person, architects need to develop an understanding of more than the words and measurements involved in accessibility.

CONCLUSION

Public health, safety, and welfare are the responsibility of every architect. Public agencies and authorities should be seen as members of the design team interested in helping architects achieve the degree of safety necessary for that responsibility. They should not be viewed as outsiders nor as people who can take on architectural design responsibility.

Architects need to understand the concepts of the building codes, incorporate the codes into their designs, and be diligent in making sure the finished project is in compliance.

When starting a project, always look for compliance with the following:

- Occupancy/Use (A, B, E, F, H, I, M, R, S, U)
- Construction Type (I, II, III, IV, V)
- Allowable Area
- Allowable Height
- Separations and Shafts
- Fire Resistance
- Fire-Extinguishing Systems
- Means of Egress
- Access for Persons with Disabilities
- Engineering and Material Requirements

LESSON 10 QUIZ

1. Building codes are intended to protect which of the following?
   A. Public health
   B. Public welfare
   C. Public safety
   D. All of the above

2. What model building code is presently published in the United States?
   A. International Building Code
   B. Uniform Building Code
   C. National Building Code
   D. Standard Building Code

3. Which can be considered as the safety occupancy in the model building codes?
   A. Assembly
   B. Business
   C. Commercial
   D. Residential

4. Combustible types of construction include all but which of the following?
   A. Type II N
   B. Type III N
   C. Type V N
   D. Type V one hour

5. Which of the following factors are to be considered in determining the allowable area of a building?
   I.   Occupancy
   II. Type of Construction
   III. Percentage of building frontage accessible to a public way or open space
   IV. Automatic sprinkler system
   V.   Number of stories of building
   A. I, II, and IV
   B. I, II, III, and IV
   C. I, II, IV, and V
   D. I, II, III, IV, and V

6. Fire ratings including one hour, two hours, three hours, and four hours could be related to which of the following?
   A. The ability of a wide flange structural steel member with fireproofing to withstand fire without collapse for the designated time
   B. The ability of an exterior curtain wall to withstand fire for up to the designated time without collapse
   C. The ability of an enclosed vertical exit stair to maintain a safe passage for persons exiting the building without being exposed to fire for the designated time
   D. The ability of a door to prevent the spread of fire through the door opening for the designated time

7. What is the purpose of the Steiner Tunnel Test?

   A. To test waterproofing for tunnel construction under bodies of water

   B. To test the flame spread rating of finishes for interior walls and ceilings

   C. To test the fire ratings of interior finishes

   D. To test the wind loads on a curtain wall

8. Which of the following are considered the primary components of the "Means of Egress"?

   I. Exit access

   II. Exit door

   III. Exit

   IV. Exit corridor

   V. Exit discharge

   A. I, II, IV, and V

   B. II and IV

   C. I, III, and V

   D. I, II, III, IV, and V

9. The need for three exits can be based on which of the following?

   I. Occupancy type

   II Type of construction

   III. Number of occupants (more than 500 but not more than 1,000)

   IV. Travel distance to an exit

   V. Intervening rooms

   A. I and II   **C.** III and V

   B. III and IV   **D.** IV and V

10. Which of the following provide information for designing facilities accessible to persons with disabilities?

    I. ICC/ANSI A117.1

    II. FHAG

    III. ADAAG

    IV. UFAS

    V. IBC

    A. I, II, and III

    B. I, II, III, and IV

    C. II, III, and IV

    D. I, II, III, IV, and V

SUSTAINABLE DESIGN

11

by Jonathan Boyer, AIA

This section is meant to prepare you for the *"green" architecture, sustainability,* and *new material technologies* topics that NCARB has introduced to several of the multiple-choice divisions of the ARE 3.0.

INTRODUCTION

Architects can no longer assume that buildings function independently of the environment in which they are placed. In the late 1800s the machine age offered the lure of buildings that were self sufficient and independent of their natural surroundings—"The Machine for Living," as LeCorbusier proclaimed.

In the middle of the 20th century, the promise of endless and inexpensive nuclear energy lured architects into temporarily ignoring the reality of the natural elements affecting architectural design. Why worry about natural systems if energy was going to be infinite and inexpensive? Glass houses proliferated.

Energy is not free, the global climate is changing, and the viability of natural ecosystems is diminishing. The architect is designing structures that affect all these natural ecosystems. Much as Marcus Vitruvius wrote thousands of years ago that architects must be sensitive to the local environment, architects are returning to study the virtues of tuning to natural systems. Contemporary architects must combine their knowledge of the benefits of natural systems with the understanding of the selective virtues of contemporary innovative technologies.

This lesson focuses on the fundamental principles of environmental design that have evolved over the thousands of years that humans have been creating spatial solutions.

HISTORY OF SUSTAINABLE DESIGN

In early human history, builders of human habitats used materials that occurred naturally in the earth, such as stone, wood, mud, adobe bricks, and grasses. With nomadic tribes and early civilizations, the built environment made little impact on the balance of natural elements. When abandoned, the grass roof, adobe brick, or timber beam would slowly disintegrate and return to the natural ecosystem. Small human populations and the use of natural materials had very little impact on a balanced natural ecosystem.

But as human populations expanded and settlements moved into more demanding climates,

natural materials were altered to become more durable and less natural. In fact, archeological finds demonstrate some of the human creations that are not easily recycled into the earth; fired clay, smelted ore for jewelry, and tools are examples of designs that will not easily reintegrate into the natural ecosystem. These materials may be reprocessed (by grinding, melting, or reworking) into other human creations, but they will never be natural materials again.

As human populations expanded, there is strong evidence that some civilizations outgrew their natural ecosystem. When overused, land became less fertile and less able to support crops, timber, and domesticated animals necessary for human life. The ancient solution was to move to a more desirable location and use new natural resources in the new location, abandoning the ecologically ruined home site.

The realization that global natural resources are limited is an age-old concept. The term *conservation,* which came into existence in the late 19th century, referred to the economic management of natural resources such as fish, timber, topsoil, minerals, and game. In the United States, at the beginning of the 20th century, President Theodore Roosevelt and his chief forester, Gifford Pinchot, introduced the concept of conservation as a philosophy of natural resource management. The impetus of this movement created several pieces of natural legislation to promote conservation and increased appreciation of America's natural resources and monuments.

In the middle of the 1960s, Rachel Carson published *Silent Spring,* a literary alarm that revealed the reality of an emerging ecological disaster—the gross misunderstanding of the value and hazards of pesticides. The pesticide DDT and its impact on the entire natural ecosystem was dramatic; clearly, some human inventions were destructive and could spread harm throughout the ecosystem with alarming speed and virulence. Birds in North America died from DDT used to control malaria in Africa. Human creations were influenced by the necessities of the natural cycles of the ecosystem. Human toxic efforts could no longer be absorbed by the cycles of nature. Human activities became so pervasive and potentially intrusive that there needed to be a higher level of worldwide ecological understanding of the risk of disrupting the ecosystem.

Architects, as designers of the built environment, realize the ecological impact of their choices of architectural components, such as site selection, landscaping, infrastructure, building materials, and mechanical systems. The philosophy of sustainable design encourages a new, more environmentally sensitive approach to architectural design and construction.

There are many credos for the approach to a new, sustainable design. Some architectural historians maintain that the best architects (Vitruvius, Ruskin, Wright, Alexander) have always discussed design in terms of empathy with nature and the natural systems. Now it is evident that all architects should include the principles of sustainable design as part of their palette of architectural best practices.

PRINCIPLES OF SUSTAINABLE DESIGN

The tenets outlined below indicate why it is necessary to maintain the delicate balance of natural ecosystems.

1. In the earth's ecosystem (the area of the earth's crust and atmosphere approximately five miles high and five miles deep) there is a finite amount of natural resources. People have become dependent on elements such as fresh water, timber, plants, soil, and ore, which are processed into necessary pieces of the human environment.

2. Given the laws of thermodynamics, energy cannot be created or destroyed. The resources that have been allotted to manage existence are contained in the ecosystem.

3. All forms of energy tends to seek equilibrium and therefore disperse. For example, water falls from the sky, settles on plants, and then percolates into the soil to reach the subterranean aquifer. Toxic liquids, released by humans and exposed to the soil, will equally disperse and eventually reach the same underground reservoir. The fresh water aquifer, now contaminated, is no longer a useful natural resource.

There is a need to focus on the preservation of beneficial natural elements and diminish or extinguish natural resources contaminated with toxins and destructive human practices.

There are many credos for environmental responsibility. One, *The Natural Step,* was organized by scientists, designers, and environmentalists in 1996.

They were concerned with the preservation of the thin layer that supports human life in a small zone on the earth's surface: the ecosphere (five miles of the earth's crust) and the biosphere (five miles into the troposphere of the atmosphere).

Their principles are as summarized as follows:

1. Substance from the earth's crust must not systemically increase in the ecosphere.

    Elements from the earth such as fossil fuel, ores, timber, etc., must not be extracted from the earth at a greater rate than they can be replenished.

2. Substances that are manufactured must not systemically increase in the ecosphere.

   Manufactured materials cannot be produced at a faster rate than they can be integrated back into nature.

3. The productivity and diversity of nature must not be systemically diminished.

   This means that people must protect and preserve the variety of living organisms that now exist.

4. In recognition of the first three conditions, there must be a fair and efficient use of resources to meet human needs.

   This means that human needs must be met in the most environmentally sensitive way possible.

   Buildings consume at least 40 percent of the world's energy. Thus they account for about a third of the world's emissions of heat-trapping carbon dioxide from fossil fuel burning, and two-fifths of acid rain-causing carbon dioxide and nitrogen oxides.*

The built environment has a monumental impact on the use of materials and fuels to create shelter for human beings. The decisions about the amount and type of materials and systems that are employed in the building process have an enormous impact on the future use of natural resources. Architects can affect and guide those decisions of design to influence the needs of sustainability and environmental sensitivity.

---

* *Sources: David Malin Roodman and Nicholas Lessen, "Building Revolution: How Ecology and Health Concerns are Transforming Construction."* Worldwatch Paper *124 (Washington DC, Worldwatch Institute, 1995);*

Sandra Mendler & William Odell, The HOK Guidebook to Sustainable Design, (New York: John Wiley & Sons, Inc., 2000).

SUSTAINABLE SITE PLANNING AND DESIGN

Most architectural projects involve the understanding of the design within the context of the larger scale neighborhood, community, or urban area in which the project is placed.

If the building will be influenced by sustainable design principles, its context and site should be equally sensitive to environmental planning principles.

Sustainable design encourages a re-examination of the principles of planning to include a more environmentally sensitive approach. Whether it is called Smart Grow, sustainable design, or environmentally sensitive development practice, these planning approaches have several principles in common.

Site Selection

The selection of a site is influenced by many factors including cost, adjacency to utilities, transportation, building type, zoning, and neighborhood compatibility. In addition to these factors, there are sustainable design standards that should be added to the matrix of site selection decisions:

■ **Adjacency to public transportation**

   If possible, projects that allow residents or employees access to public transportation are preferred. Allowing the building occupants the option of traveling by public transit may decrease the parking requirements, increase the pool of potential employees and remove the stress and expense of commuting by car.

- **Flood plains**

  In general, local and national governments hope to remove buildings from the level of the 100-year floodplain. This can be accomplished by either raising the building at least one foot above the 100-year elevation or locating the project entirely out of the 100-year floodplain.

  This approach reduces the possibility of damage from flood waters, and possible damage to downstream structures hit by the overfilled capacity of the floodplain.

- **Erosion, fire, and landslides**

  Some ecosystems are naturally prone to fire and erosion cycles. Areas such as high slope, chaparral ecologies are prone to fires and mud slides. Building in such zones is hazardous and damaging to the ecosystem and should be avoided.

- **Sites with high slope or agricultural use**

  Sites with high slopes are difficult building sites and may disturb ecosystems, which may lead to erosion and topsoil loss. Similarly, sites with fertile topsoil conditions—prime agricultural sites—should be preserved for crops, wildlife, and plant material, not building development.

- **Solar orientation, wind patterns**

  Orienting the building with the long axis generally east west and fenestration primarily facing south may have a strong impact on solar harvesting potential. In addition, protecting the building with earth forms and tree lines may reduce the heat loss in the winter and diminish summer heat gain.

- **Landscape site conditions**

  The location of dense, coniferous trees on the elevation against the prevailing wind (usually west or northwest) may decrease heat loss due to infiltration and wind chill factor. Sites with deciduous shade trees can reduce summer solar gain if positioned properly on the south and west elevations of the buildings.

Alternative Transportation

Sites that are near facilities that allow several transportation options should be encouraged. Alternate transportation includes public transportation (trains, buses, and vans); bicycling amenities (bike paths, shelters, ramps, and overpasses); carpool opportunities that may also connect with mass transit; and provisions for alternate, more environmentally sensitive fuel options such as electricity or hydrogen.

Reduction of Site Disturbance

Site selection should conserve natural areas, and restore wildlife habitat and ecologically damaged areas. In some areas of the United States, less than 2 percent of the original vegetation remains. Natural areas provide a visual and physical barrier between high activity zones. Additionally, these natural areas are aesthetic and psychological refuges for humans and wildlife.

Storm Water Management

There are several ways by which reduced disruption of natural water courses (rivers, streams, and natural drainage swales) may be achieved:

- Provide on-site infiltration of contaminants (especially petrochemicals) from entering the main waterways. Drainage designs that use swales filled with wetland vegetation is a natural filtration technique especially useful in parking and large grass areas.

- Reduce impermeable surface and allowing local aquifer recharge instead of runoff to waterways.

- Encourage groundwater recharge.

Ecologically Sensitive Landscaping

The selection of indigenous plant material, contouring the land, and proper positioning of shade trees may have a positive effect on the landscape appearance, maintenance cost, and ecological balance. The following are some basic sustainable landscape techniques:

- Install indigenous plant material, which is usually less expensive, to ensure durability (being originally intended for that climate) and lower maintenance (usually less watering and fertilizer).

- Locate shade trees and plants over dark surfaces to reduce the "heat island effect" of surfaces (such as parking lots, cars, walkways) that will otherwise absorb direct solar radiation and retransmit it to the atmosphere.

- Replace lawns with natural grasses. Lawns require heavy maintenance including watering, fertilizer, and mowing. Sustainable design encourages indigenous plant material that is aesthetically compelling but far less ecologically disruptive.

- In dry climates, encourage xeriscaping (plant materials adapted to dry and desert climates); encourage higher efficiency irrigation technologies including drip irrigation, rainwater recapture, and gray water reuse. High efficiency irrigation uses less water because it supplies water directly to the plant's root areas.

Reduction of Light Pollution

Lighting of site conditions, either the buildings or landscaping, should not transgress the property and not shine into the atmosphere. Such practice is wasteful and irritating to the inhabitants of surrounding properties. All site lighting should be directed downward to avoid "light pollution."

Open Space Preservation

The quality of residential and commercial life benefits from opportunities to recreate and experience open-space areas. These parks, wildlife refuges, easements, bike paths, wetlands, or play lots are amenities that are necessary for any development.

In addition to the aforementioned water management principles, the following are principles of design and planning that will help increase open-space preservation:

- **Promote in-fill development** that is compact and contiguous to existing infrastructure and public transportation opportunities.

  In-fill development may take advantage of already disturbed land without impinging on existing natural and agricultural land.

  In certain cases, in-fill or redevelopment may take advantage of existing rather than new infrastructure.

- **Promote development that protects natural resources** and provides buffers between natural and intensive use areas.

  First, the natural areas (wetlands, wildlife habitats, water bodies, or flood plains) in the community in which the design is planned should be identified.

  Second, the architect and planners should provide a design that protects and enhances the natural areas. The areas may be used partly for recreation, parks, natural habitats, and environmental education.

  Third, the design should provide natural buffers (such as woodlands and grasslands) between sensitive natural areas and areas of intense use (factories, commercial districts, housing). These buffers may offer visual, olfactory, and auditory protection between areas of differing intensity.

Fourth, linkages should be provided between natural areas. Isolated islands of natural open space violate habitat boundaries and make the natural zones seem like captive preserves rather than a restoration or preservation of natural conditions.

Fifth, the links between natural areas may be used for walking, hiking, or biking, but should be constructed of permeable and biodegradable material. In addition, the links may augment natural systems such as water flow and drainage, habitat migration patterns, or flood plain conditions.

■ **Establish procedures that ensure the ongoing management of the natural areas** as part of a strategy of sustainable development.

Without human intervention, natural lands are completely sustainable. Cycles of growth and change including destruction by fire, wind, or flood have been occurring for millions of years. The plants and wildlife have adapted to these cycles to create a balanced ecosystem.

Human intervention has changed the balance of the ecosystem. With the relatively recent introduction of nearby human activities, the natural cycle of an ecosystem's growth, destruction, and rebirth is not possible.

Human settlement will not tolerate a fire that destroys thousands of acres only to liberate plant material that reblooms into another natural cycle.

The coexistence of human and natural ecosystems demands a different approach to design. This is the essence of sustainable design practices, a new approach that understands and reflects the needs of both natural and human communities.

AHWAHNEE PRINCIPLES

In 1991, in the Ahwahnee Hotel in Yosemite National Park, a group of architects, planners, and community leaders met to present community principles that express new, sustainable planning ideas. These principles are summarized below.

Preamble

Existing patterns of urban and suburban development seriously impair our quality of life. The symptoms are: more congestion and air pollution resulting from our increased dependence on automobiles, the loss of precious open space, the need for costly improvements to roads and public services, the inequitable distribution of economic resources, and the loss of a sense of community. By drawing upon the best from the past and the present, we can plan communities that will more successfully serve the needs of those who live and work within them. Such planning should adhere to certain fundamental principles.

Community Principles

1. All planning should be in the form of complete and integrated communities containing housing, shops, workplaces, schools, parks, and civic facilities, essential to the daily life of the residents.

2. Community size should be designed so that housing, jobs, daily needs, and other activities are within easy walking distance of each other.

3. As many activities as possible should be located within easy walking distance of transit stops.

4. A community should contain a diversity of housing types to enable citizens from a wide range of economic levels and age groups to live within its boundaries.

5. Businesses within the community should provide a range of job types for the community's residents.

6. The location and character of the community should be consistent with a larger transit network.

7. The community should have a center focus that combines commercial, civic, cultural, and recreational uses.

8. The community should contain an ample supply of specialized open space in the form of squares, greens, and parks, whose frequent use is encouraged through placement and design.

9. Public spaces should be designed to encourage the attention and presence of people at all hours of the day and night.

10. Each community or cluster of communities should have a well-defined edge, such as agricultural greenbelts or wildlife corridors, permanently protected from development.

11. Streets, pedestrian paths, and bike paths should contribute to a system of fully connected and interesting routes to all destinations. Their design should encourage pedestrian and bicycle use by being small and spatially defined by buildings, trees, and lighting, and by discouraging high speed traffic.

12. Wherever possible, the natural terrain, drainage, and vegetation of the community should be preserved with superior examples contained within parks or greenbelts.

13. The community design should help conserve resources and minimize waste.

14. Communities should provide for the efficient use of water through the use of natural drainage, drought tolerant landscaping, and recycling.

15. The street orientation, the placement of buildings, and the use of shading should contribute to the energy efficiency of the community.

Regional Principles

1. The regional land-use planning structure should be integrated within a larger transportation network built around transit rather than freeways.

2. Regions should be bounded by and provide a continuous system of greenbelt/wildlife corridors to be determined by natural conditions.

3. Regional institutions and services (government, stadiums, museums, and so forth) should be located in the urban core.

4. Materials and methods of construction should be specific to the region, exhibiting a continuity of history and culture and compatibility with the climate to encourage the development of local character and community identity.

Implementation Principles

1. The general plan should be updated to incorporate the above principles.

2. Rather than allowing developer-initiated, piecemeal development, local governments should take charge of the planning process. General plans should designate where new growth, in-fill, or redevelopment will be allowed to occur.

3. Prior to any development, a specific plan should be prepared based on these planning principles.

4. Plans should be developed through an open process and participants in the process

should be provided visual models of all planning principles.

Source: Local Government Commission's Center for Livable Communities, http://lgc.org/clc/.

USGBC—U.S. GREEN BUILDING COUNCIL

Incorporated as a nonprofit trade association in 1993, the U.S. Green Building Council (USGBC) was founded with a mission "to promote buildings that are environmentally responsible, profitable and healthy places to live and work." It is formed of leaders from across the building industry who head a national consensus for producing a new generation of buildings that deliver high performance inside and out.

The core of the USGBC's work is the creation of the Leadership in Energy and Environmental Design (LEED) green building rating system. LEED provides a complete framework for assessing building performance and meeting sustainability goals. Based on well-founded scientific standards, LEED emphasizes state of the art strategies for sustainable site development, water savings, energy efficiency, materials selection and indoor environmental quality. LEED recognizes achievements and promotes expertise in green building through a comprehensive system offering project certification, professional accreditation, training, and practical resources.

USGBC committees are actively collaborating on new and existing LEED standards, including a standard for homes, neighborhood development, and commercial interiors.

Their Web site is: *www.usgbc.org.*

ARCHITECTURAL PROCESS

After the planning process has been concluded, and the site has been selected, the architectural team will begin to focus on the project, including the project's buildings and related infrastructure.

Traditionally, the architect is faced with four components to every design decision: cost, function, aesthetics, and time. The new paradigm adds *sustainability* to this list.

The ingredients of the normal process have been discussed previously, but the new ingredient, sustainability, changes the meaning of all these pieces of the architectural process.

Cost

As architects put together budgets for their clients, they are always concerned with the first costs of the design components—the initial cost to purchase and install the design element.

Sustainable design has made the economic decision process more holistic. The decision to select a design element (such as a window, door, flooring, exterior cladding, or mechanical system) is now concerned with the "life cycle" cost of the design.

Life-Cycle Costing

Life-cycle costing is concerned not only with the first cost, but the operating, maintenance, periodic replacement, and residual value of the design element.

For example, two light fixtures (A and B) might have different first cost: Fixture A has a 10 percent more expensive first cost than B. But when the cost of operation (the lamps use far less energy per lumen output) and the cost of replacement (the bulbs of A last 50 percent longer than the bulbs of Fixture B) is evaluated,

Fixture A has a far better life-cycle cost and should be selected.

In this kind of comparison, the life-cycle cost may be persuasive; the extra cost of Fixture A may be recovered in less than two years due to more efficient operation and replacement savings. In this situation the architect justified Fixture A to the owner, who benefits from a more energy-efficient lighting that continues to save the owner operating costs for the life of the building.

Matrix Costing

While designing a typical project, the architect faces numerous alternate decisions, a process that may be both intriguing and complex.

Sustainable design adds an ingredient to the matrix of decisions that may actually help the composition.

For example, decisions that allow the improved efficiency of the building envelope, light fixtures, and equipment may permit the architect to allow the engineer to reduce the size of the HVAC system, resulting in a budgetary trade-off. The extra cost of the improved envelope may be economically balanced by the diminished cost of the mechanical system.

This type of economic analysis, which evaluates cost elements in a broad matrix of interaction, is a very valuable architectural skill. The ability to understand the interaction between different building systems in a creative and organized fashion can differentiate an excellent from a simply adequate architectural design.

Function

Functionality is one of the primary standards of architectural design. If the building does not perform according to the client's needs, then the building design has failed.

Years ago, the design element could perform at the highest level regardless of its impact on the environment or energy use. The fact that many industrial and residential buildings are operating in 2003 much more efficiently than 1960 is evidence that the building design and construction profession is learning how to tune buildings to a higher degree of energy operation. But, with diminishing natural resources and increasing pollution of the environment, even more efficient design is necessary.

Today, architects will include sustainability in the selection of optimal functional design components.

For example, a roof system must be able to withstand a variety of weather conditions, be warranted to be durable a minimum of years, be able to be applied in a range of weather conditions, and have a surface with reflectivity that does not add to the urban heat effect.

Time

The schedule of a project is always a difficult part of the reality of the design process. Time is a constraint that forces a systematic and progressive evaluation of the design components.

The sustainable component of the architectural process may add to the amount of time the architect will spend on the research for the project.

The architect may spend more time on a sustainable design with the result being a more integrated, sustainable project.

Aesthetics

The aesthetic of a project is the combination of the artistry of the architect and the requirements of the project.

Sustainable design has the reputation of emphasizing function and cost over beauty and appeal.

It is the architect's responsibility to keep all the design tools in balance. A project without aesthetic consideration will fail the client, its user, and the potential client who may be deciding between the normal design and one that considers a broader, integrated, sustainable approach.

Sustainability

The fifth point is a new component that leads to a new approach to the design process.

Sustainable designs should have five goals:

1. Use less
2. Recycle components
3. Use easily recycled components
4. Use fully biodegradable components
5. Do not deplete natural resources necessary for the health of future generations

STANDARDS FOR EVALUATION

How can we objectively evaluate the quality of a sustainable project?

The architect is faced with responding to many standards and regulations in the course of assembling a design. Building codes, life safety standards, fire code, zoning regulations, and health and sanitary regulations are some of the many municipal, state, and federal standards that an architect must evaluate in the course of any project.

Sustainability is a new filter for the design process and there are several organizations that have offered checklists for evaluating the inclusion of environmentally sensitive elements into the project.

One of the measures of performance is LEED (Leadership in Energy & Environmental Design), which is sponsored by the USGBC (U.S. Green Building Council). This standard was developed in the 1990s by a consortium of building owners, architects, suppliers, engineers, contractors, and governmental agencies.

The goal of LEED and similar environmental design standards is to introduce new sustainable approaches and technologies to the construction industry. LEED is a voluntary environmental rating system that is organized into six categories:

1. Sustainable sites
2. Water efficiency
3. Energy and atmosphere
4. Materials and resources
5. Indoor air quality
6. Innovation and design practice

LEED covers the range of architectural decisions, including site design, water usage, energy conservation and production, indoor air quality, building materials, natural lighting, views of the outdoors, and innovative design components.

The LEED point award matrix is a mixture of teaching, persuasion, example, and incentive. It is good checklist for the entire project team to evaluate the quality of sustainable design decisions for the complete project—from initial planning through final construction, maintenance, and training procedures.

These categories combine *prerequisites* (basic sustainable practices such as building commissioning, plans for erosion control, or meeting minimum indoor air quality standards) with optional *credits* (water use reduction, heat island reduction, or measures of material recycled content).

Most of the credits are performance based—solutions based on system performances against an established standard such as American Society of Heating, Refrigeration and Air Conditioning Engineers (ASHRAE). ASHRAE has created one of most widely recognized standards of energy design that is used by mechanical engineers and architects.

For example, one credit (under the Energy and Resources category) is "Optimize Energy Performance."

The number of points for this credit depend on how the architectural and engineering team can optimize the design of the building's energy systems against the ASHRAE 90.1 standards.

The possible design solutions include optimizing the heating, cooling, fans, pumps, water, and interior lighting systems.

In the graduated point matrix for a new building, if the team improves the performance (against ASHRAE standards) by 15 percent they receive one point and if they manage to improve by 60 percent they receive 10 points.

LEED describes suggested results but allows the architectural team to find a variety of solutions. The LEED certification awards range from Bronze at 40 percent compliance to Platinum at 81 percent compliance. The LEED certification is innovative and rigorous, and currently there are fewer than a half dozen platinum buildings in the United States.

THE SUSTAINABLE DESIGN PROCESS

Is a sustainable design organized and implemented differently from a conventional design?

The Design Team

What kind of design team is necessary for a sustainable project?

The scope of a sustainable design invites an expanded team approach, which may include the following:

■ Architects or engineers (structural, MEP) with energy modeling experience

■ A landscape architect with a specialty in native plant material

■ A commissioning expert (if LEED employed)

■ An engineer/architect with building modeling experience

The design team for a sustainably designed project tends to have a larger pool of talent than a typical architectural project. Wetlands scientists, energy efficient lighting consultants, native plant experts, or commissioning engineers are examples of the additional talent that may be added to sustainable design projects.

As with any architectural design, there is a hierarchy of design goals:

■ *Initial imperatives* such as budget, timing, image, and program necessities

■ *Subjective goals* such as a functionally improved and more pleasing work environment, pleasing color schemes, and landscaping that complements the architecture

■ *Specific goals* such as more open space, more natural light, less water usage, and adjacency to public transportation

And with the inclusion of sustainability there may be additional goals:

■ *Initiatives that are specific to sustainability* such as fewer toxins brought into the space, daylighting in all spaces with people occupancies, less overall energy consumed, less water usage, adjacency to public transportation, and improved indoor air quality

- Desire to exceed existing standards such as ASHRAE, USGBC, or American Planning Association (APA)

RESEARCH AND EDUCATION

Is additional education and research necessary for a sustainable project?

Yes. Innovative HVAC systems, durable yet nontoxic materials, recycled materials, recyclable materials, native plant material, energy efficient lighting, and controls are examples of design components that are not normally designed and installed by general contractors and architectural consultants on typical projects.

Education of the Client

Sustainable design requires a new way of examining the architectural design process. Concepts such as life-cycle costing, recycled versus recyclable materials; non-VOC (volatile organic compounds) substances; daylighting; and alternate energy sources are among the several new concepts that the architect should discuss with the client before the design process commences.

It is critical that the client understands the sustainable process and is sympathetic to its potential economic and environmental benefits.

Education of the Project Team

Once the project has been assigned to an architect, but before the design process begins, the project team (architect, engineer, contractor, consultants, and owner) should assemble and discuss the project scope and objectives with all the project team members.

Establishing Project Goals

Among the many items included in the scope of work (including the extent of work, program elements, budget, and schedule) are the objectives for sustainable design.

For example, the architect and owner might establish goals for several environmental areas such as:

- X percent reduction of energy usage from the established norm (see "Benchmarking" later in this section)
- Improved lighting (less energy used and more efficient dispersal of indirect light with less glare)
- Nontoxic and low VOC paint and finishes
- Increased recycled content in materials such as carpeting, gypsum wallboard, ceiling tiles, metal studs, and millwork
- High-efficiency (energy star) appliances
- Wood elements are all certified wood products
- Daylighting in all work/occupied spaces

As the leader of the project team, it is the architect's responsibility to include sustainable goals with the rest of the project scope of work.

A detailed explanation of the benefits of these sustainable design elements to all of the project team will ensure that they fully understand the design potential and economic implications of these concepts.

Verify Extent of Work

Sustainable design involves a more comprehensive approach to pre-project planning.

The LEED certification process will require record keeping and verification of the source of materials—a process that is beyond the normal design and construction work. For purposes of selecting a contractor and consultants, the team should be briefed on these additional obligations.

For example, the demolition process (if LEED certified) will require verification that materials have been sorted and delivered to an approved recycling organization. By contrast, the normal demolition process does not require recycling or verification that each material is sorted by type.

Clearly establishing the extent and type of effort required for each member of the sustainable design team is critical. The extent and type of effort will affect each member's ability to participate and their fees for services and construction work.

Energy and Optimization Modeling

Building shape, orientation, fenestration location, roof color, envelope configuration, and HVAC system efficiency are some of the variables in sustainable design projects that can be fine-tuned with DOE-2 (U.S. Department of Energy's building analysis program) and other computer energy modeling programs.

The "fine tuning" of a project's energy components is one of the elements in the architect's design matrix that affects the final appearance, cost, and performance of the final design.

Energy modeling will not govern the final design. Issues such as compatible scale, color, texture, and functionality are still part of the architect's palette. But energy modeling is one additional factor that the architect will employ as part of the "best practices" approach to architecture.

In addition, modeling can assist in the cost analysis of a project. The fact that the modeling program is interactive helps the architect simultaneously adjust design elements to demonstrate alternate energy efficient solutions.

For example, energy modeling might allow the architect to demonstrate to the team that a more durable, aesthetically pleasing, and energy efficient building skin could be economically justified by reducing the size and cost of the mechanical system.

The ability to visually and numerically quantify the efficacy of trading certain design elements may be an effective tool for the architect when discussing the building design with the consultants and owner.

The Bid and Specification Process

The requirements of a sustainable design will often vary from a normal project.

For example, the millwork section of bid documents will normally specify the finish material, configuration of the design and methods of attachment, delivery, and installation. But the requirement of non-VOC glues and non-VOC substrate may confuse a potential bidder and cause that bidder to increase the bid price unnecessarily.

To facilitate the bidding and construction process, the architect should include the following:

- Simple definitions of sustainable elements—for example, what "VOC," "certified" wood product, or "daylighting" mean
- Explanations of specific characteristics of sustainable elements—for example, specifically state the standard that must be met (for example, Green Label Testing Program Limits, carpet's total VOC limit, that is, formaldehyde 0.05 (mg/m2)
- References of specific regulatory agency's information (name, address, e-mail, phone, and so on)—for example, the Carpet and Rug Institute, *www.carpet-rup.com*, (800) 882-8846

■ Examples of suppliers that could meet the sustainable standards indicated—in the case of sustainable products, there are at least two approaches to a list of suppliers for products:

1. Limit the installer to three to five suppliers of a product that is known to satisfy the sustainable design specifications.

   This approach assures the architect that the product will meet specified standards.

   (Note, however, that with the constantly changing nature of the emerging sustainable design market, a limited list could limit competition and the diversity of creative alternatives.)

2. Identify a list of qualified suppliers, but permit the bidder/contractor to submit alternative suppliers who satisfied the sustainable design criteria. This approach creates a more competitive environment, but it will require more effort of the architect to properly review and qualify the bids.

Changes and Substitutions

Every project is faced with the reality of time and budgetary pressures. And, in those instances, there may be situations when one product or design element may not be available in the form originally specified.

Sustainable designed projects require more stringent architectural supervision to ensure that original design standards are met. For example, in the rush to project completion the installer may claim that paints used for "touch up" of damaged areas are so small that they may be installed with normal, higher-VOC paints. This minor transgression might jeopardize the integrity of the project and the ability to receive certification for LEED credits in certain areas.

ENERGY EVALUATION

In the climates of North America, buildings need some form of purchased energy (electricity, natural gas, oil) in order to operate. The architect works with his or her team to design strategies that may reduce the amount of purchased energy, reduce operating costs, and reduce the nation's dependence on imported fossil fuels.

The following are some design strategies that the sustainable design approach might employ to improve a building's energy performance. These elements are listed and briefly described.

Solar Design

Solar design is the age-old system of using sunlight or solar radiation to supply a portion of the building's heat energy. By a combination of techniques such as window and skylight design, location of internal thermal mass, and internal organization of the building's functions, solar design may replace some of the fossil fuel needed for heating and cooling buildings.

Passive solar systems are those systems that permit solar radiation to fall on areas of the building that benefit from the seasonal energy conditions of the structure.

For example, some North American buildings are designed to reduce solar radiation gains from sunlight in the summer. Passive solar design relies on inherent qualities of the building's fenestration, massing, and orientation to capture sunlight.

Passive solar systems are usually categorized into direct or indirect gain systems:

Direct gain systems, as the title implies, are those systems that allow solar radiation to flow directly into the space needing heat. A process commonly known as the "greenhouse effect" allows much of the sunlight that passes through the glass of the fenestration to be retained in the material it strikes (stone, concrete, wood, etc.) inside the building. Thus, south facing windows allow solar radiation to be directly gained and used inside the building.

Indirect gain systems operate when the sunlight first strikes a thermal mass that is located between the sun and the space. The sunlight absorbed by the mass is converted to thermal energy (heat) and then transferred into the living space.

There are basically two types of indirect gain systems: thermal storage walls and roof ponds. The difference is essentially the location—roof verses wall materials.

Passive solar design might employ several architectural strategies to facilitate the design:

1. *Architectural sun control devices.* Overhangs or shading devices that have been designed to permit winter solar radiation from entering the building interior while blocking the higher angled, summer solar radiation from entering the building. Deciduous trees often perform the same function of permitting winter sunlight to enter and blocking much of the summer solar radiation with branches and leaves. Other examples include shutters; vertical projections or fins; awnings; trellises (especially with shading vegetation); and sunscreens (some with PV panels that both gather sunlight to convert into electricity and shade unwanted radiation from interior space in the warm months).
2. *Light-colored roof systems.* Light-colored roofing materials reflect sunlight and reduce the amount of radiation that is absorbed through the roof into the interior space. Colors with higher reflectance (albedo) factors are preferred. For example, some cities in the United States require roof materials to have a minimum albedo rating of .65 (65 percent of the solar radiation is reflected back into the atmosphere). The urban heat island effect, caused by roofs, roads, and parking areas that absorb solar radiation during the day and retransmit the stored heat during the afternoon and evening, can be modified with light-colored roof systems.

By designing these surfaces with light-colored and reflective material, the amount of heat energy stored in these materials is diminished and the urban heat island effect is reduced. Grass or vegetated roof areas have good insulating value and may also reduce the urban heat island effect and provide cooling through evapotranspiration.

3. *Optimized building glazing systems.* Orientation, light transmittance factors, and U-value are all factors architects consider in selecting glazing. Glass that is low-E (emissivity) is desirable because it is coated with a material that allows a maximum amount of sunlight to be transferred through the glass and not reflected back into the atmosphere.

Lighting

The illumination of the interior of a sustainably designed building requires a holistic approach that balances the use of artificial and natural lighting sources.

Daylighting

Properly filtered and controlled solar radiation may provide a valuable source of illumination to a building interior. This process is called "daylighting" (simply having properly designed fenestration that allows natural sunlight to replace or dramatically reduce the need for artificial lighting).

Because unwanted sunlight (particularly in summer months) can also add to the internal heat load of a building, the architect must be careful to allow only beneficial sunlight and reduce unwanted solar heat gain. There are several techniques for controlling daylighting:

1. Overhangs, fins, and other architectural shading devices

2. Sawtooth (not bubble) skylight design, which allows the glass to face north for illumination, not south for solar heat gain

3. Interior window shading devices, which allow solar gain during cool months, and the blocking of solar radiation during the warmer seasons

4. Light shelves, which permit the daylight to reflect off the ceiling and penetrate farther into the interior without affecting views outside

Higher Efficiency Light Fixtures

In addition to a daylighting strategy, light fixtures that are more efficiently designed reduce energy cost and increase comfort, such as the following:

■ Fixtures that use fluorescent or HID lamps, which provide more illumination per watt than incandescent lighting.

■ Fixtures that are designed to diffuse or bounce the illumination off the ceilings or internal reflectors, which are more efficient; cause less glare (especially in an environment with computer monitors); and save operating costs.

■ Fixtures that have higher efficiency (T-8) fluorescent bulbs, which produce more

lumens per watt and thereby diminish the heat generated by lighting.

■ Fixtures that offer dimming or multiple switching capability, which permit the architect a more energy efficient lighting design. Dimming or multiple switching fixtures allow the architect to design lighting patterns that blend nicely with daylighting opportunities. For example, an office with perimeter fenestration allows daylighting supplemented with overhead lighting that can be dimmed or reduced. The interior spaces, which are too far from the perimeter for daylighting, may be controlled with switches or dimmers that allow relatively higher levels of illumination. The result is an even illumination pattern, which saves on artificial lighting costs, by relying on daylighting at the perimeter.

■ Fixtures that use higher efficiency lamps such as fluorescent, high intensity discharge (HID) sulfur lighting (exterior only).

■ Fluorescent fixtures that use high efficiency electronic ballasts.

Additionally, the architect may avoid less efficient incandescent lighting where possible; install task lighting to supplement diffused ambient lighting; and install LED (light emitting diode) lighting for exit signs. LED lighting lasts longer than incandescent and is far less expensive to operate.

Lighting Sensors and Monitors

Where possible, lighting costs can be diminished by installing light monitors that sense occupancy conditions. As long as the room contains people, the lights will remain on. If people leave, the sensor will wait for a few minutes, then shut off all the lighting in the room.

Lighting sensors can be designed to operate with a preference for motion, heat (from people), or desired time of occupancy.

Lighting Models

Computer lighting models are one option that allows the architect to simulate the levels of sunlight that penetrate into a building design, depending on the building location, varying times of year, fenestration orientation, and design.

By incrementally altering fenestration (skylights, windows, or light transport systems) and the artificial lighting system, the architect may optimize the daylighting and artificial lighting systems for the building.

Benchmarking

The U.S. Department of Energy provides "benchmark" information of total energy consumption in BTUs/SF for various kinds of buildings in the United States. These standards, or benchmarks, can be useful in the measuring of energy efficiency standards for various types of buildings:

For example:

- Average for all office buildings (pre-1990)   104.2
- Average for all office buildings (1990–1992)   87.4
- Average for all educational buildings (pre-1900)   87.2
- Average for all educational buildings (1990–1992)   57.1
- Average for all laboratory buildings (pre-1990)   319.2
- Average for all health care buildings (pre-1990)   218.5

Source: U.S. Department of Energy, Commercial Building Energy Consumption and Expenditures.

Benchmarking is a good way to alert the design team to the base energy standards for their design. It's a good place to start and ultimately a standard to beat. And, one can see from some of the comparisons (office and educational buildings), that some energy efficiency is occurring.

COMMISSIONING

Commissioning is an organized process to ensure that all building systems perform interactively according to the intent of the architectural and engineering design, and the owner's operating needs.

Commissioning usually includes all HVAC and MEP systems, controls, ductworks and pipe insulation, renewable and alternate technologies, life safety systems, lighting controls and daylighting systems, and any thermal storage systems. Commissioning also verifies the proper operation of architectural elements such as the building envelope, vapor and infiltration control, and gaskets and sealant used to control water infiltration.

Commissioning is a process required for LEED certification, but is a recommended procedure for any building involved with sustainable design procedures.*

* Source: Commissioning Requirements for LEED Green Building Rating, Version 8. February 5. 1999; Sandra Mendler and William Odell, The HOK Guidebook to Sustainable Design, New York, John Wiley & Sons, Inc.: 2000, p. 71.

INNOVATIVE TECHNOLOGIES

Besides the aforementioned issues of solar design, improved lighting systems, improved HVAC systems, and improved building massing and envelope design, there are several "innovative technologies" that the architect can offer to the project team for consideration.

Ground Water Aquifer Cooling and Heating (AETS)

One alternative to full air-conditioning with chillers, which make heavy demands on electricity, is the aquifer thermal energy storage, which uses the differential thermal energy in water from an underground well to cool a building during summer and heat a building in the winter.

This is an efficient a relatively low-cost system, but it may require approval from the local environmental authority before installation.

Geothermal Energy

Where appropriate, heat contained within the earth's surface causes macro-geological events (such as underground geothermal springs or lava formations) that may be tapped to produce heat for adjacent structures.

In select locations this heat energy can be transferred and conveyed to supplement a building's heating demand.

Wind Turbines

Small-scale wind machines used to generate electricity can be mounted on buildings or in open space nearby. These systems share several advantages:

- Relatively cost-effective
- Tested and established technology

- Systematic started-up
- Relatively high output

These systems share several disadvantages:

- Need a relatively high mast
- Require substantial structural support
- Present potential for noise pollution
- Visually intrusive

Photovoltaic (PV) Systems

The basis of the PV systems is the concept that electricity is produced from solar energy when photons or particles of light are absorbed by semiconductors.

Most PV systems are mounted to the building (either on the roof or as shading devices above fenestration). Currently, PV systems are not cost effective. But with promised government subsidy necessary to achieve an economy of scale, PVs may be a viable method of electrical production in the United States, Japan, and Germany in the near future.

Fuel Cells

Even though Sir William Grove invented the technology for the fuel cell in 1839, it has only recently been recognized as a potential power source for the future. The fuel cell claims to be the bridge between the hydrocarbon economy and the hydrogen-based society.

Fuel cells are electrochemical devices that generate direct current (DC) electricity similar to batteries. But, unlike batteries, they require a continual input of hydrogen-rich fuel. In essence, fuel cells are reactors that combine hydrogen and oxygen to produce electricity, heat, and water. They are clean, quiet, and emit no pollution when fed directly with hydrogen.

At the moment, fuel cell technology is still not cost effective for the commercial building market. Still, there seems to be a general feeling that hydrogen-based energy reactors will soon be an optional energy source.

Biogas

Biogas is produced through a process that converts biomass, such as rapid-rotation crops and selected farm and animal waste, to a gas that can fuel a gas turbine. This conversion process occurs through anaerobic digestion—the conversion of biomass to gas by organisms (like bacteria) in an oxygen-free environment.

Biogas has several advantages: it has relatively high energy production; it lends itself to both heat and power production; it creates almost zero carbon dioxide emissions; it virtually eliminates noxious odors and methane emissions; and it protects ground water and reduces the landfill burden.

Small-Scale Hydro

Harnessing the energy from moving water is one of the oldest energy production systems in the world. In some locations, small-scale hydro power is a efficient and clean source of energy and is devoid of environmental penalties associated with large scale hydro projects. It allows small scale, local energy production, with relatively low cost.

Ice Storage Cooling Systems

One of the problems for energy supply companies is that the highest demand for electricity often coincides with the highest cooling demand.

The utilities would prefer to "flatten the curve" (to even out or flatten the measure of average daily energy demand). The fewer the number of peaks (high points of energy demand), the less the utilities have to bolster their power supply with expensive, supplemental fuels.

One way to reduce this peaking problem is to supplement a building's cooling capacity with an ice storage system.

An ice storage system has three components: a tank with liquid storage balls, a heat exchanger, and a compressor for cooling. The essence of the ice storage system is that the chilling and freezing of the ice balls occurs at night (when the cost of energy is lower due to lower demand). During the day, the cool temperatures, stored in the ice, are transmitted into the building's cooling system.*

CONCLUSION

The knowledge of environmental systems has become essential to the architect's design palette. Buildings that take advantage of natural systems such as sun, wind, rain, ground water, topography, and climate are more elegant solutions. Architectural designs that incorporate natural systems, in conjunction with contemporary technologies, are in the tradition of architects providing spatial solutions with the most innovative contemporary thinking available.

Buildings with this approach operate more efficiently, integrate effectively into their local environment, and tend to produce spaces that are more pleasing to work and live. Knowledge of an integrated or holistic design principals is not a limitation but another set of tools to produce humane, efficient, healthy, and aesthetically compelling architecture.

Source: Peter F. Smith, Sustainability at the Cutting Edge (Jordan Hill, Oxford: Architectural Press, an Imprint of Elsevier Science, 2003.

LESSON 11 QUIZ

1. Sustainable design is primarily concerned with which of the following issues?

   I.   Economics

   II. Aesthetics

   III. Environment

   IV. Mechanical systems

   A. III

   B. I, II, and III

   C. I and III

   D. All of the above

2. The *Natural Step* is an approach to the environment that follows which of the following principles?

   I.   The biosphere affecting humans is a relatively stable and resilient zone that includes five miles into the earth's crust and five miles into the troposphere.

   II. Improved technologies have dramatically increased the number and quantity of available natural resources.

   III. Toxic substances released into either the sea or atmosphere will only influence areas adjacent to the toxic source.

   IV. Using building materials that are recycled is an adequate sustainable design approach.

   A. I

   B. II

   C. II and IV

   D. None of the above

3. The planning phase of a sustainably designed architectural project should include which of the following elements?

   I.   Native landscaping that is aesthetically pleasing and functional

   II. Designing structures in the floodplain that can resist the forces of flood waters

   III. Consideration of sun orientation, topographic relief, and the scale of adjacent buildings

   IV. Locating projects within existing neighborhoods that are adjacent to public transportation

   A. I and II

   B. I and III

   C. I, III, and IV

   D. All of the above

4. The Ahwahnee principles include which of the following ideas?

   I.   Communities with only residential use should be relegated to areas outside the central business district.

   II. Preserved open spaces should be either wildlife habitats or recreational areas.

   III. Transportation planning should include roads, pedestrian paths, bike paths, and mass transit systems.

   IV. Job creation and economic diversity is a desired goal.

   A. I

   B. II, III, and IV

   C. III and IV

   D. None of the above

5. Life-cycle costing is an economic evaluation of architectural elements that includes which of the following factors?

I. First cost

II. Maintenance and operational costs

III. Repair costs

IV. Replacement cost

A. I

B. II, III, and IV

C. II and IV

D. All of the above

6. LEED, the name of a program that environmentally evaluates sustainable projects, is a checklist that is concerned with which of the following?

I. Indoor air quality

II. Storm water

III. Innovative energy systems

IV. Aesthetic design

A. I

B. I, II, and III

C. II and III

D. All of the above

7. Which of the following is a consultant who might be employed in a sustainable design project?

I. Wetlands engineer

II. Energy commissioner

III. Landscape architect

IV. Energy modeling engineer

A. I

B. I and II

C. II, III, and IV

D. All of the above

8. Sustainable design may require research and education that is beyond a normal architectural project. Which of the following is part of this process?

I. Energy modeling

II. Education of the client

III. Art selection

IV. Selection of energy efficient appliances

A. I and IV

B. I and II

C. I, II, and IV

D. All of the above

9. Sensitivity to the nuances of site conditions is key to sustainable design. Which of the following are site conditions the architect should examine in the design process?

I. Solar orientation

II. Decorative landscaping

III. Scale and style of adjacent structures

IV. Ground water conditions

A. I and II

B. I, III, and IV

C. I and III

D. All of the above

10. Sustainably designed architecture requires attention to which of the following building elements?

I. Solar shading devices

II. Urban heat island effect

III. Increased parking

IV. Fenestration and glazing

A. I, II, and IV

B. I and IV

C. I and II

D. All of the above

The following glossary defines a number of terms, many of which have appeared on past exams. While this list is by no means complete, it comprises much of the terminology with which candidates should be familiar. You are therefore encouraged to review these definitions as part of your preparation for the exam.

A

Accelerator   A substance, such as calcium chloride, added to a concrete mix to speed up its setting and strength development.

Acoustics   The science of sound and sound control.

Acrylic   A noncrystalline thermoplastic with good weather resistance, shatter resistance, and optical clarity; sometimes used for glazing.

Admixture   A prepared substance added to concrete to alter or achieve certain characteristics.

Aggregate   The chemically inert element of concrete, usually consisting of sand, crushed rock, and/or gravel.

Air Entrainment   The incorporation of tiny air bubbles into concrete or mortar to improve its workability and resistance to freezing.

Alkyd   A synthetic resin used as a vehicle for paint.

Alloy   A substance generally composed of two or more metals that have been intimately mixed.

Asbestos Cement   A material consisting of a mixture of portland cement and asbestos fiber. Although resistant to fire, it is considered a health hazard.

Ashlar   A building stone that has been shaped and smoothed into a rectangular form for use in masonry construction.

Asphaltic Concrete   A mixture of asphaltic cement and aggregates, used as a paving material, which is spread and rolled while hot.

ASTM   American Society for Testing and Materials.

B

Backfill   Earth that is replaced around a foundation or retaining wall after the concrete forms have been removed.

Balloon Framing   A method of framing wood stud walls in which the studs are continuous for the full height of the building, which is usually two stories, with the joists bearing on a ribbon let into the studs.

Baluster   A vertical support for a handrail.

Balustrade   A complete railing system, consisting of a top rail, supporting balusters, and sometimes a bottom rail.

Bar Chair   A device used to support reinforcing bars during the placing of concrete.

Base Shoe   A quarter round trim piece used to cover the joint between the finish flooring and the base.

Batter Boards   Horizontal boards offset from the building line and set prior to excavation, used to indicate a specific location, such as the corner of a building.

Bearing Capacity   The unit load, in pounds or kips per square foot, that can be safely supported by the soil.

Bed Joint   The horizontal mortar joint in masonry work.

Bitumen   A substance derived from petroleum or coal used to resist water penetration, such as asphalt or coal-tar pitch.

Blind Nailing   Driving nails in such a way that the nail heads are not visible.

Board Foot   A unit of measure for lumber equal to the volume of a board 12" × 12" × 1".

Book Matching   A way of placing successive veneers sliced from the same flitch so that alternate sheets appear as mirror images.

Brass   An alloy of copper and zinc that is corrosion resistant and very workable.

Bridging   Crossed braces used between joists to stabilize them.

Bronze   An alloy of copper and tin.

BTU   British Thermal Unit: the amount of heat required to raise one pound of water 1 degree Fahrenheit.

Bullnose   The rounding of an exposed edge, such as a tile or wood trim piece.

Butt   A hinge applied to the edge of a door in which only the butt end remains visible.

C

Caisson   A waterproof box-like structure in which construction work can be done below water level.

Camber   A slight upward curve built into a member to compensate for deflection.

Cant Strip   A beveled strip used to avoid a sharp bend in roofing material.

Capillary Action   The tendency of water to move into small spaces, regardless of gravity.

Caulking   The application of a compound to seal the joint between two materials or surfaces.

Cement   A material that is able to unite nonadhesive materials into a solid mass.

Ceramic Veneer   Terra cotta facing applied as a finish wall material.

Chase   A recessed space or passage through a wall or other element to accommodate pipes or ducts.

Cofferdam   A watertight, temporary structure placed under water and pumped dry to allow construction work to be performed.

Cold Joint   A joint formed when a concrete surface hardens before the next batch of concrete is placed against it.

Collar Beam   A horizontal tie beam connecting two opposite rafters at a level above the wall plates.

Combustible   Capable of burning.

Concrete   A mixture of fine and coarse aggregates, portland cement, and water.

Control Joint   A groove in a concrete structure made to predetermine the location of cracks.

Coping   A protective cap of brick, stone, or concrete used at the top of a wall to prevent water penetration.

Cricket   A flashing saddle used on a sloping roof to divert water around a chimney.

Culls   Rejected material whose quality is too low to be used.

Curing   Maintaining concrete at the proper moisture and temperature after it is cast.

Cut and Fill   Earth that is removed (cut) and earth that is added (fill) in grading.

D

Dado   A rectangular grooved wood joint. Also, the lower part of a wall below a molding or other trim.

Dampproofing   The materials and methods used to prevent moisture from penetrating a building at or below grade.

Decibel   A logarithmic measure of sound intensity level.

Double Glazing   Two sheets of glass with an air space between, to insulate against the passage of heat or sound.

Dry Pack   To fill a confined space with a damp concrete mixture, by packing in tightly.

Dry Rot   Timber decay due to fungus, in which pockets of dry powder develop.

Drywall A masonry wall built without mortar. Also, an interior wall or ceiling of gypsum wall board construction.

E

Earthwork *See* Grading.

Efflorescence The whitish powder of crystallization, caused by water soluble salts, which comes to the surface when water evaporates from brick.

Elastomer A material having the qualities of rubber.

Enamel A smooth and hard pigmented paint that uses varnish as the vehicle.

Entrained Air Tiny air bubbles intentionally incorporated into mortar or concrete during mixing to resist freezing action.

Epoxy A synthetic resin having excellent adhesive properties.

Escutcheon A metal plate around a knob and/or keyhole of a door.

Excavation The digging or removal of earth.

Expansion Joint The complete separation, from top of footing to the roof, of adjacent building parts to allow for expansion and contraction caused by temperature changes.

F

Fire Brick Brick made from fire clay that has great resistance to high temperatures.

Fireproof Describing construction that will not burn or is highly resistant to fire.

Firestops Horizontal blocks placed between studs to resist the spread of fire.

Flame-Spread Rating A classification of finish materials indicating the rate at which flame will spread.

Flashing The application of an impervious material to prevent water penetration at joints formed by different materials or surfaces.

Flitch A large timber from which veneers are cut.

Footing The part of a foundation that spreads the load over a large area of soil.

Forms The molds into which concrete is placed until it has hardened.

Foundation The part of a building's structure that transmits the building's load to the underlying soil.

Furring Wood or metal strips used to make a plane surface; also a cavity within a wall or ceiling.

G

Galvanic Action The deteriorating reaction between dissimilar metals that are in contact in the presence of moisture.

Galvanizing The process of applying a coating of zinc to iron for protection against corrosion.

Glazing The work of installing glass in a frame.

Glulam A glued laminated timber used structurally.

Grading Removing and/or adding earth in order to bring the ground surface to a specified elevation or profile.

Grillage A framework of horizontal members used to spread a structural load over a larger area.

Grout A fluid mixture of portland cement, sand, and water used to fill joints and cavities of masonry or tile.

Grubbing The removal from a site of unwanted roots, stumps, and so forth, during excavation.

Gunite Pneumatically applied concrete.

Gutter A trough at the edge of a roof used to carry off rainwater.

Gypsum   Hydrated calcium sulfate, from which gypsum plaster and plasterboard are made.

Gypsum Board   A prefabricated form of plaster used in place of conventional three-coat interior plaster.

H

Hand of Door   Convention relating to door swing, used when ordering door hardware.

Header Course   A masonry course in which the flat, short ends of the units are exposed.

Hinge   A device on which doors, windows, cabinets, and so forth, turn or swing, to open and close.

Hip   The exterior edge formed by the meeting of two adjacent sloping roof surfaces.

Hollow Core   Describing a door in which veneer faces are glued to an inner skeleton framework.

Honeycomb   A void left in concrete that is poorly mixed or placed.

Hospital Tip   Rounded top edge on a hinge, designed for cleanliness and to avoid catching garments.

I

Insulating Glass   *See* Double Glazing.

Insulation   A material that provides high resistant to sound transmission or heat flow.

Intumescent Paint   Paint that swells up when exposed to excessive heat and thus resists flame spread.

J

Jack Rafter   A short rafter between hip rafter and eave or between valley and ridge.

Jalousie   A window or door blind made of fixed or movable horizontal slats.

Jetting   Placing piles using high pressure water jets.

K

K Value   The thermal conductivity of a material.

Kalamein Door   A type of fire-resistive door that has a solid wood core covered with sheet metal.

Keene's Cement   A quick-setting gypsum plaster used in areas exposed to moisture.

Kerf   A cut or notch in a material.

L

Laitance   Mortar or grout scum on the surface of concrete.

Latch   A beveled fastening device that automatically slides into position when the door is closed.

Ledger   Horizontal member supporting joists. Also sometimes called ribbon, girt, purlin, or stringer.

Lewis Bolt   A round threaded metal device with a bell-shaped end that is used to anchor stone.

Lock   A mechanical fastening device with a rectangular locking bolt that is projected manually or with a key.

M

Mandrel   Solid core used in driving a shell pile into the ground. When the mandrel is removed, the shell is filled with concrete.

Mastic   A permanently plastic waterproof adhesive material used in sealing joints.

Matrix   The binding or cementing material in mortar, concrete, or terrazzo.

Modular   Describing a system composed of standardized units or sections used for simplified construction or flexibility.

Monel   An alloy of nickel and copper that is resistant to corrosion and used for roofing, kitchen equipment, etc.

Mortar   A mixture of cement, lime, sand, and water used to bond bricks or stone in masonry work.

Mullion   A vertical member between windows or doors.

Muntin   A short, secondary member within a window frame, either vertical or horizontal.

N

Neat   Describing cement or plaster that has been mixed with water only, without sand or lime.

Needle Beam   A short beam passed through a wall to provide temporary support.

O

Oil Canning   The wavy distortions of glass or metal panels, often seen in curtain wall construction.

P

Panic Hardware   A door-latching assembly that will open the door if subjected to pressure.

Parging   The application of plaster to the back of masonry walls.

Particle Board   A manufactured panel of wood particles and binders that is bonded together under heat and pressure.

Perlite   A lightweight volcanic rock used as an aggregate in lightweight concrete or plaster.

Perm   The unit of water vapor transmission, equal to the flow of one grain of water vapor through one square foot of surface per hour under the pressure of one inch of mercury.

Permeability   The property of permitting passage of water vapor through a material without causing rupture or displacement.

Pervious   Permitting leakage or flow of water.

Pigment   The solid component of paint, consisting of finely ground material, which gives the paint its color.

Pile   A vertical member driven into the ground to support the vertical load of the structure above.

Pith   The heart center of a log.

Plaster   A mixture of portland cement (exterior plaster) or gypsum (interior plaster) with sand and water, which is applied in layers, or coats, which harden and dry.

Platform Framing   A method of framing wood stud walls in which the studs are one story in height and the floor joists bear on the top plates of the wall below.

Portland Cement   The cementitious binder used to make concrete and mortar.

Putty Coat   The final smooth coat of interior plaster.

R

R Factor   A measure of thermal resistance.

Raked Joint   A mortar joint that has been cleaned of mortar for about 3/4 inch back from the face.

Reglet   A slot in which roofing material or flashing is inserted, generally in a vertical wall surface.

Reverberation   The persistence of sound in an enclosed space after the source has stopped.

Roping   The arrangement of cables used to hoist an elevator.

Rowlock   A masonry course in which the units are laid on edge, with their ends exposed.

S

Sabin   The unit of sound absorption, equivalent to the absorption of one square foot of open window.

Sash A frame in which the panes of a window or door are placed.

Screed A strip of material placed at intervals along a wall to be plastered to gauge the thickness of the plaster.

Sealant Material used to prevent the passage of liquid across a joint or opening.

Shakes Hand-split wood shingles.

Sheepsfoot Roller A large-toothed roller used for the compaction of soil.

Sheeting Vertical construction used to temporarily hold the face of an excavation during construction.

Shellac A solution of refined lac resin and denatured alcohol used as a clear coating.

Shoring Temporary support for a portion of a building.

Sleeper A horizontal member used to support a structure above, such as one of the wood strips between a concrete slab and finish wood floor.

Slump Test A test for mixed concrete to determine consistency and workability.

Slurry A soupy mixture of water and clay, or water and portland cement.

Soil A natural material, formed of decomposed and disintegrated parent rock, that can support plant life.

Soil Boring Log A graphic representation of the soils encountered in a test boring.

Sound Transmission Class A rating for the evaluation of a particular construction cross-section in the transmission of air-borne sound.

Stile The upright or vertical edge of a door or window.

Stretcher A brick laid with its length parallel to the length of the wall.

Stucco A mixture of sand, portland cement, lime, and water, that may be tinted and applied as an exterior plaster finish.

T

Terne Plate Steel coated with lead and tin used for roofing and flashing.

Terrazzo Flooring material made from small chips of marble set in cement and polished.

Test Boring A hole drilled into the ground, from which samples of undisturbed subsurface soils are obtained for laboratory inspection and testing.

Test Pit An excavation made to expose the subsurface soils for in-place examination.

Tremie A pipe or tube used to deposit concrete under water.

U

U Factor The thermal conductivity of a wall section, expressed in BTUs per hour per degree Fahrenheit per square foot.

Urethane A synthetic resin from which paints and insulation foams are manufactured.

V

Valley The interior trough formed by the intersection of two sloping roof surfaces.

Vapor Barrier An airtight layer used to prevent moisture from a warm interior from passing into and condensing within a cold wall or ceiling area.

Vehicle The liquid portion of a paint that holds the pigment or solids in suspension.

Vermiculite A lightweight aggregate used in lightweight concrete or plaster.

Vitrification The fusion of a clay product after firing, which makes it impervious.

W

Warp Distortion of timber during seasoning caused by changing moisture content.

Water-Cement Ratio The ratio of water to cement in a concrete mix, which is the main factor which determines concrete strength.

Waterproof Impervious to water or water vapor, even under pressure.

Water Stop A device used at a joint as a sealant, usually to prevent the passage of water.

Water Table The level below that the earth is fully saturated with water.

Weatherstripping The means employed to make exterior openings weathertight.

Weep Holes Small openings left in retaining walls, sills, aprons, foundations, etc., which permit water to drain.

Wythe Each individual vertical tier of masonry in a cavity wall.

BIBLIOGRAPHY

The following list of books is provided for candidates who may wish to do further research or study in Building Design/Materials and Methods. Most of the books listed below are available in college or technical bookstores, and all would make welcome additions to any architectural bookshelf. In addition to the course material and the volumes listed below, we advise candidates to review regularly the many professional journals, which are available at most architectural offices.

A Dictionary of Building
Scott
Penguin Books

Architectural Graphic Standards
Ramsey and Sleeper
John Wiley and Sons

Basic Building Data
Graf
Van Nostrand Reinhold

Building Construction
Huntington and Mickadeit
John Wiley and Sons

Building Construction Handbook
Merritt
McGraw Hill Book Co.

Building Construction Illustrated
Ching
Van Nostrand Reinhold

Construction Materials
Hornbostel
John Wiley and Sons

Construction Principles, Materials and Methods
Schmitt, Olin, and Lewis
American S&L Institute Press

Dictionary of Architecture and Construction
Harris
McGraw Hill

Fundamentals of Building Construction Materials and Methods
Allen, Edward
John Wiley and Sons

Standards for Access for Persons with Disabilities
ANSI A117.1
American National Standards Institute

Materials and Methods for Contemporary Construction
Hornbostel and Hornung
Prentice Hall

International Building Code
International Code Council

QUIZ ANSWERS

Lesson 1

1. C Subsurface water should be diverted away from a building's foundation by means of drainage tiles laid in a gravel bed. Foundations should be placed above, not below, the water table (A), and contours are modified during rough, not finish, grading (B).

2. B See page 13.

3. A A mat footing distributes vertical loads over the entire building area and is used when soil conditions are poor.

4. D When upper soils have low bearing capacity, piles may be used to transmit a building's loads to deeper, firmer soils.

5. B Asphalt paving is applied either hot or cold (D is incorrect) over an aggregate base (B). It is two to three inches thick (A is incorrect), and joints are not required (C is incorrect).

6. D See page 7.

7. A Roots are dug out, or grubbed, and topsoil is stockpiled before rough grading is done. After rough grading, batter boards are placed and excavation for footings is performed.

8. D Boat footings are used where the underlying soil has a low bearing capacity, jetted piles are rarely used, and wood piles are used for light to moderate loads. The only appropriate choice is structural steel piles.

9. C As load is placed on a footing, it compresses the soil and reduces the soil's void volume. Although this results in settlement, it is not necessarily differential settlement.

10. B This is a question in which all the answers are at least partially correct. However, the most inclusive answer is B, to determine the character of the soil.

Lesson 2

1. C The purpose of a control joint is to create a weakened section, so that shrinkage cracking will occur at the joint, rather than in a random fashion.

2. A As hot weather tends to shorten concrete's setting time, one would add a retarding agent to the mixture. This would counteract the weather's effect by lengthening the setting time.

3. B See page 29.

4. A Lightweight concrete, whether structural or nonstructural, provides good thermal insulation (I) and resistance to fire (III). It has low density (II is incorrect) and relatively high cost (IV is incorrect), and it is easy to handle and place (V is incorrect). The correct combination of answers is found in choice A.

5. D The strength of concrete depends on a number of factors, but primarily on the water-cement ratio.

6. C After concrete is placed, the proper humidity and temperature must be maintained for some time in order to assure satisfactory hydration of the cement. For this purpose, a number of methods may be employed, including covering the concrete with a membrane (A), supplying additional moisture by spraying (B), and covering the concrete with moist sand (D). Blowing with fans (C) is not normally done, as this would probably result in excessive evaporation of water, which is precisely what curing attempts to avoid.

7. D The concrete pour in this question was improper for two reasons: it was dropped from an excessive height, and it was deposited at one point, instead of uniformly along the form. Both of these procedures tend to cause segregation of the mix, and no further treatment will solve this problem. The only solution, therefore, is to remove and discard the concrete.

8. **B**   Concrete is strong in compression, but weak in tension. Therefore, reinforcing steel is embedded in the concrete to resist tension, while the concrete itself resists compression. The combination of the two materials is known as reinforced concrete.

9. **D**   The maximum size of coarse aggregate permitted is 1/5 of the narrowest dimension between forms, or 1/3 of the thickness of slabs, or 3/4 of the minimum space between reinforcing bars. Thus, III and V are correct (choice D).

10. **B**   Precast concrete offers a number of advantages, including better quality control (A), all-weather construction (C), and often, greater economy (D). While precast concrete can be steam cured, which provides better quality control, the curing time is not necessarily reduced (B).

Lesson 3

1. **C**   See page 49.

2. **A**   This is an easy question, as it is apparent that glass block is the only material listed that is able to transmit light.

3. **C**   Face brick is more uniform in size and color than building brick. Its durability and weather resistance are the same as building brick of the same grade (A and B are incorrect). Face brick is only available in certain sizes, textures, and colors (D is incorrect).

4. **A**   Concrete block is usually less expensive per square foot of wall than brick (I). Concrete blocks are also much faster to erect than brick because of their larger size: one concrete block has the same volume as 8 or 12 bricks (IV). Because they are larger and

heavier, concrete blocks are harder to handle (II is incorrect). Blocks are not easier to reinforce (III is incorrect), and in general, they are less attractive than brick (V is incorrect).

5. **B**   Efflorescence is a whitish powder that sometimes comes to the surface when water evaporates from brick or other masonry. Choices A, C, and D all help to keep water from penetrating the masonry and therefore tend to reduce efflorescence. Wetting the masonry units (B) may be desirable, particularly for brick, but is does nothing to reduce efflorescence.

6. **D**   Hydrated lime is used in a mortar mixture to improve workability and water retentivity, although it reduces the strength of the mortar (A and B are incorrect, D is correct). C is also incorrect.

7. **B**   The variations in the color and hardness of brick are caused by the varying characteristics of the clays from which they are made (II) and the temperatures at which they are fired (IV).

8. **D**   See the sketch on page 44.

9. **D**   Water tends to collect and remain in troweled joints, so it is likely that if left alone the mortar would eventually deteriorate, causing leaks and loose units. It is important that joints be well filled, tightly compacted, and of the proper shape. Troweled joints are a poor choice on an exterior wall, for they collect water, while weather-struck joints shed water. Adding mortar to an existing joint (C) is always poor practice, so the only alternative is to redo the wall.

10. **D**   None of the first three choices provides the weather resistance of a proper mortar joint. Plastering the wall is a reasonable alternative, but it changes the architectural

character and may not be acceptable to the owner and/or architect. Rebuilding the wall is still a better choice.

Lesson 4

1. **B** Heavy timber construction consists of wood beams, girders, and columns that are very large, as specified by the building code. Such construction is fire resistant because massive wood members burn very slowly.

2. **C** Insects, decay, and fire are continual risks to wood construction. Keeping underfloor wood members dry and well ventilated (I) reduces the risk of damage from insects or decay. Intermittent wetting provides a favorable environment for decay, but complete submersion in water (II), so that air is excluded, minimizes the possibility of decay. Decay-resistant species of wood, such as redwood, are often used for members close to the earth, but these are generally softwood, not hardwood (III is incorrect). Surface coatings are usually ineffective in preventing termite infestation (IV is incorrect). V is correct: the use of intumescent paint reduces the rate of flame spread.

3. **A** Wood trusses, laminated beams, and girders are all possible substitutes for conventional joists, but their use would be impractical and far more expensive than providing additional joists.

4. **C** Nails and other metal fasteners were not massed produced until the 19th century, which completely changed all types of wood joinery.

5. **A** See page 64.

6. **D** Wood with a moisture content of 30 percent is considered unseasoned, or green, and will shrink if used in construction.

7. **A** See page 69.

8. **C** See page 69.

9. **B** Plainsawed lumber has a more distinctive grain pattern than quartersawed or rift cut. Factory and shop lumber refers to lumber used for remanufacture, not to grain pattern.

10. **D** All of the listed factors affect the strength of a wood member.

Lesson 5

1. **C** Cast iron has a high carbon content and is strong in compression, but weak in tension.

2. **A** Among the metals listed, bronze is most resistant to galvanic deterioration. Refer to the list on page 80–81.

3. **D** Steel is the most widely used metal in building construction, including those items classified as miscellaneous metalwork.

4. **C** Open web steel joists are shop-fabricated (III), small, lightweight, standardized steel trusses (I and II). They are strong in the vertical direction, but weak in the flat, horizontal direction (IV is incorrect).

5. **B** Steel is strong and relatively inexpensive (I and III). However, it is susceptible to corrosion and lacks fire resistance (IV and V). Steel usually requires a great deal of precise shop fabrication (II is incorrect).

6. **A** Aluminum has all the properties listed, except high resistance to galvanic action. See page 83.

7. **D** Lightweight metal framing systems have all of the advantages listed, except fire resistance. Although metal is incombustible, it loses so much strength when exposed to

a severe fire that it may fail or deform excessively.

8. **B**   Galvanizing iron and steel protects it against deterioration from corrosion.

9. **B**   Metal decking can support live and dead loads, can serve as permanent formwork, and is usually corrugated or ribbed (I, IV, and V are correct). Decking is usually welded to the supporting members (II is incorrect). Whether plain or galvanized, metal decking must have a covering of concrete for permanent weather protection (III is incorrect).

10. **D**   An advantage to using aluminum is that complex sections, such as those used for window assemblies, can easily be produced by extrusion. In this process, a heated billet of aluminum is squeezed through a die to produce the desired shape in any length.

Lesson 6

1. **C**   Tile roofs are heavy, permanent, and fireproof (I, III, and IV). However, they are expensive (II is incorrect), and they are only suitable for relatively steep roof pitches (V is incorrect).

2. **B**   Slabs on grade are often placed over a granular fill several inches thick in order to prevent ground water from being drawn into the slab by capillary action.

3. **C**   Loose fill is an inappropriate insulation because the fill would tend to slide along the sloping surface and accumulate at the low end. Such insulation should only be used in flat air spaces, such as attics, or in completely filled wall cavities.

4. **A**   Vapor barriers should always be installed on the warm or room side of construction, in this case just above the finish ceiling. Vapor barriers are never installed between rafters, because the sheet must be continuous to be effective in preventing the passage of water vapor.

5. **C**   Expansion joints cannot reduce, prevent, or cause movement due to temperature change. Their purpose is to provide a complete separation, which will permit movement, while maintaining structural integrity and weathertightness.

6. **A**   See page 96.

7. **D**   Condensation can be controlled by using insulating glass (I), applying a vapor barrier (II), and providing ventilation (V). Attic insulation (III) is used for thermal control, not condensation control. And perimeter drain tiles (IV) are used to carry ground water away from a structure.

8. **B**   See the sketch on page 96.

9. **B**   Flashing is used to provide a seal and prevent water penetration at joints and intersections, such as those in choices A, C, and D. The standing seams of a sloping metal roof form a seal and therefore do not require flashing (B).

10. **D**   Referring to the table on page 102, one can see that the R value for a one-inch plastic panel is 6.00, which is greater per inch of thickness than any other type shown.

Lesson 7

1. **B**   Patterned glass obscures vision and reduces light transmission.

2. **C**   Skylight glazing must be safe from breaking and falling, which might endanger occupants. Laminated, tempered, or wired glass are appropriate to specify for skylights.

3. **D**   A tactile finish is used on operating hardware on doors leading to areas that might be dangerous to blind people.

4. **C** Aluminum door and window sections are strong and durable (B and D are incorrect), and have relatively low initial expense (A is incorrect). However, special precautions must be taken to prevent galvanic action (C).

5. **B** Referring to the table on page 114, the glazing permitted in a Class B labeled fire door is 100 square inches. Dividing this area by the four-inch width of glazing results in a maximum allowable height of 25 inches.

6. **B** Revolving doors can carry a continuous two-way flow of pedestrian traffic (IV is incorrect, V is correct). Very little cold (or warm) outside air is permitted to enter the building (III is correct). However, revolving doors do not provide for emergency exiting or handicapped access (I and II are incorrect).

7. **A** See page 116.

8. **A** Plastic substitutes for glass are available in transparent sheets (C is incorrect), are fire-resistant (B is incorrect), and are usually more expensive (D is incorrect). However, plastic is generally less durable than glass (A is correct).

9. **C** Panic hardware is used on exit doors to quickly and easily open the doors in case of emergency. Knurled knobs (A) are used as a tactile finish to warn blind people that the doors lead to a dangerous area. A lever handle (B) is a horizontal handle used to open a door and is not suitable for emergency exiting. A fusible link (D) melts in case of fire, thereby closing a door or damper to prevent the spread of fire.

10. **D** Wood windows are relatively inexpensive, durable, and widely available (II, IV, and V). However, they require periodic maintenance and are not fire-resistive (I and III are incorrect).

Lesson 8

1. **C** Asphalt tile, terrazzo, and elastomeric-type flooring lack resilience, while cork flooring is highly resilient.

2. **D** Vermiculite is an expanded mica used as an insulating fill or as aggregate in a plaster mix to make it fire-resistant and lightweight.

3. **B** Statements I, II, and V are advantages of using a suspended acoustical tile ceiling system. Statements III and IV are incorrect: acoustic tiles are fragile and provide no fire rating.

4. **D** A plumb surface is created by attaching metal furring channels to the concrete walls, over which metal lath and plaster are applied. Applying lath directly to rough concrete would not result in a smooth, plumb surface. Also, because of potential moisture penetration, using gypsum or plywood would be risky.

5. **B** Gypsum board, or drywall construction, has many advantages over wet plaster, but greater durability is not one of them. Usually, wet plaster applied in three coats is thicker, more dense, and more durable.

6. **C** The most important factor in painting work is surface preparation. The surface must be clean and dry if the paint is to perform satisfactorily.

7. **C** Ceramic tiles are permanent, waterproof, durable, and easily maintained (A, B, and D are incorrect). However, they are more costly than Keene's cement plaster.

8. **A** The scratch coat is the first plaster coat (I), and its ingredients are correctly described in statement II. It is generally applied over gypsum lath or metal lath (III is incorrect), it may be applied by hand or machine (IV is incorrect), and it is about 1/4 inch thick (V is incorrect).

9. A Wood flooring is durable, comfortable, attractive, and easy to maintain. However, all wood is susceptible to swelling and shrinkage caused by changes in humidity (A), and therefore, sufficient expansion space must be provided at the floor's perimeter. Wood flooring generally has a hard, dense surface to withstand heavy wear (B is incorrect). Wood floors tend to burn very slowly in case of fire (C is incorrect), and some types of wood flooring are very resistant to the effects of oil, grease, and mild chemicals (D is incorrect).

10. B Floor finishes such as urethane are applied directly to concrete, wood, or metal to produce a hard, durable, wear-resistant, easily maintained, greaseproof floor finish.

Lesson 9

1. D The maximum usable speed of an electric elevator varies from about 300 to 1,800 feet per minute, and is limited by the building height, as acceleration and deceleration require a substantial distance.

2. D Buildings less than 50 feet high, or five stories high, generally have hydraulic, rather than electric, elevators. Hydraulic elevators require no penthouse and are simpler and less expensive to install.

3. C Refer to the table on page 151.

4. A Fire stairs required for emergency exiting must have fire doors that open in the direction of emergency travel.

5. B Freight elevators are generally slower and have greater capacity than passenger elevators. They may also have different types of doors. Freight elevators often carry people as well, and must have the same safety features as passenger elevators.

6. C The maximum slope permitted for a handicapped ramp is 1:12. Thus, if the difference of elevation is 2 feet, the length of the ramp must be at least 12 × 2 feet, or 24 feet.

7. B The main brake is mounted on the motor shaft of the elevator machine and stops the car automatically in case of a power failure. The governor measures and limits the elevator speed. The interlocks prevent the lobby door from opening when the elevator car is elsewhere. And the car bumpers, located at the bottom of the shaft, stop the car if it should over-travel at low speed.

8. A Moving ramps allow pedestrians to move swiftly: if one continues to walk along the moving ramp, one's speed will be doubled.

9. C The number of elevators required in a new building is determined by the number of floors (I), volume of traffic (II), and size and capacity of the elevator cars (V). Elevator traffic is computed for peak traffic periods and is not based on the number of hours of operation (III is incorrect), and the elevator roping system is not related to the number of elevators required (IV is incorrect).

10. D Although all four answers have some degree of truth, escalators are most effectively used where large numbers of people must be moved quickly.

Lesson 10

1. D All of the above. Building codes are intended to protect the public health, safety, and welfare.

2. A The two model building codes published in the United States are the International Building Code and the National Fire Protection Association (NFPA) 5000. The other three model building codes, Uniform, National, and Standard were discontinued when the International Building Code was published.

3. **B** Business occupancies are considered the least dangerous because the occupants should be familiar with their surroundings and are expected to be awake while in the building. Assembly occupancies have an increased potential of panic; residential occupancies have an increased potential for problems due to people's sleeping in the facility. There is no commercial occupancy.

4. **A** Type II N is considered noncombustible construction. The rest are all considered combustible.

5. **D** Building area is determined by the occupancy and type of construction with the resultant area increased based on percentage of building frontage accessible to a public way or open space, whether or not the building has an automatic sprinkler system, and the number of stories of the building.

6. **A** Wide flange structural steel members with fireproofing can be fire rated relating to potential collapse for one, two, three, or four hours. Exterior curtain walls are not capable of withstanding fire in any application. Enclosed vertical exit stairs are only rated as one hour or two hours. Doors are fire rated for 20 minutes, 30 minutes, 45 minutes, one hour, 90 minutes, two hours, or three hours.

7. **B** The Steiner Tunnel Test, also known as ASTM E 84, UL 992, and NFPA 255, is used to determine the flame spread rating of finishes for interior walls and ceilings.

8. **C** The means of egress consists of three elements, the exit access, the exit, and the exit discharge. Exit doors could be included in any of the three. Corridors are part of the exit access with comparable elements being the exit passageways for the exit, and exit courts for the exit discharge.

9. **B** Three exits are required where there are more than 500 occupants and four exits are required where there are more than 1,000 occupants. Other areas typically require only two exits but where the path to the first exit exceeds the allowable travel distance a third exit would be required.

10. **D** The ICC/ANSI A117.1 American National Standard "Accessible and Usable Buildings and Facilities," the Fair Housing Accessibility Guidelines (FHAG), the Americans with Disabilities Act Accessibility Guidelines (ADAAG), the Uniform Federal Accessibility Standards (UFAS), and the International Building Code, Chapter 11, all provide information for designing facilities accessible to persons with disabilities.

Lesson 11

1. **D** All of the above. The holistic approach to sustainably designed projects encourages the design team to examine the impact of environmental, economic, mechanical, and aesthetic architectural decisions.

2. **D** None of the above.

Choice I is not correct. The zone of the earth that supports human life (five miles into the earth's crust and five miles into the atmosphere) is an extremely fragile ecosystem. This biosphere that has evolved over millions of years has been dramatically affected by the growth of human activity in the last 150 years.

Choice II is not correct either. While innovative technologies are improving energy efficiency of some building systems, the vast majority of the built environment is energy inefficient.

Choice III is also not correct. Toxic substances have the tendency to expand and affect large areas. For example, the air above the Great Lakes contains evidence of DDT, a toxic pesticide banned in the United States decades ago. It was discovered that DDT is captured in the jet stream bringing toxic materials from far away continents, which still use toxic pesticides.

Choice IV is not correct. While recycling is helpful, it is just the beginning of the sustainable design process. The principles of sustainable design say that we need to have more building products that can be recycled and are biodegradable to create a more sustainable ecosystem.

3. **C I, III, and IV**

Choice I is correct. Designing with native landscaping is preferred to using exotic or imported plant types. Indigenous plants tend to survive longer, use less water, and cost less.

Choice II is not correct. Placing any structure in a floodplain, even those that resist floodwater, is not desirable. Placing buildings in a floodplain can increase flooding further down stream.

Choice III is also correct. Buildings sensitive to the benefits of solar orientation and passive and active solar gain techniques save energy and are more visually aligned with local climatic conditions.

Choice IV is correct as well. In-fill development and proximity to a variety of transportation options are design principles that benefit the inhabitants and their environment.

4. **C III and IV**

I is not correct. Communities that are only residential are not encouraged. Mixed-use development (combining housing, retail,

open space, and commercial) is a preferred sustainable design.

II is not correct. Open space should not be designed only for recreation and wild life habitat. Additional uses such as environmental education, storm water retention, flood control, wetlands drainage, and so on, should be considered in sustainable planning.

III is correct. The Ahwahnee principles support a wide range of interconnected transportation to encourage many options for travel.

IV is also correct. Development that permits opportunities for a diverse number of jobs is a key goal of the Ahwahnee principles.

5. **D All of the above**

I is correct. While first cost is not the primary concern of life cycle costing, it is one of the economic factors considered.

II is also correct. The cost of maintenance is part of the evaluation.

III is correct as well. The durability of a product or system is considered in the cost of repair and part of the overall evaluation.

IV is correct because the comparison of product or system life is one of the factors evaluated in life cycle costing.

6. **B I, II, and III**

I is correct. LEED has several options for improving IAQ (Indoor Air Quality) including filtering the air system and installing low VOC (Volatile Organic Compound) paints and caulking.

II is also correct. Methods to store, recirculate, and locally distribute rainwater are encouraged.

III is correct as well. Innovative solutions to energy conservation such as fuel cells, photovoltaic panels, and gas turbine energy production are encouraged in the LEED accreditation system.

IV is incorrect. Unfortunately, the LEED system awards no points awards for designs with strong aesthetics.

7. **D**   All of the above

All of these consultants (wetlands engineer, energy commissioner, landscape architect, and energy modeling engineer) might be necessary for the holistic approach to sustainable design. The landscape architect should have experience with local, native plant design.

8. **C**   I, II, and IV

I is correct. Computer programs that allow energy modeling of design options allow the architect a quick method of evaluating numerous different solutions.

II is also correct. It is extremely important that the client be able to understand the value of sustainable design solutions.

III is not correct. Art selection is at the client's discretion.

IV is correct. Locating the most energy efficient appliances, plumbing fixtures, and office equipment will improve the energy efficiency of the entire project.

9. **B**   I, III, and IV

I is correct. Solar orientation can affect many architectural design elements including massing, landscaping, fenestration, and building skin design.

II is not correct. Landscape design should be functional as well as visually pleasing. Landscape design for purely visual impact is not consistent with the sustainable design approach.

III is also correct. Architectural design that understands the context (scale, color, style, texture) of adjacent structures is sympathetic to the sustainable design philosophy.

IV is correct as well. Understanding all site conditions, and their potential to assist building's energy systems is helpful. For example, ground water connected to a heat pump is a good source of supplemental energy for cooling and heating a building.

10. **A**   I, II, and IV

I is correct. Solar shading, whether from landscaping or architectural elements, can regulate the insulation to increase winter light and reduce warm summer sunlight.

II is also correct. Urban heat island effect is the tendency of a building roof to absorb solar radiation during the day and then emit heat radiation during the evening. Roof systems with grass or light colored roofing material reduce the urban heat island effect.

III is not correct. Sustainable design encourages approaches that reduce the area allocated to parking.

IV is correct. The type, location, and size of building fenestration are key aspects of architectural design for sustainable projects.

The examination on the following pages should be taken when you have completed your study of all the lessons in this course. It is designed to simulate the Building Design/Materials and Methods division of the Architect Registration Examination. Many questions are intentionally difficult in order to reflect the pattern of questions you may expect to encounter on the actual examination.

You will also notice that the subject matter for several questions has not been covered in the course material. This situation is inevitable and, thus, should provide you with practice in making an educated guess. Other questions may appear ambiguous, trivial, or simply unfair. This too, unfortunately, reflects the actual experience of the exam and should prepare you for the worst you may encounter.

Answers and complete explanations will be found on the pages following the examination, to permit self-grading. **Do not look at these answers until you have completed the entire exam**. Once the examination is completed and graded, your weaknesses will be revealed, and you are urged to do further study in those areas.

Please observe the following directions:

1. The examination is closed book; please do not use any reference material.

2. Allow about one hour to answer all questions. Time is definitely a factor to be seriously considered.

3. Read all questions *carefully* and mark the appropriate answer on the answer sheet provided.

4. Answer all questions, even if you must guess. Do not leave any questions unanswered.

5. If time allows, review your answers, but do not arbitrarily change any answer.

6. Turn to the answers only after you have completed the entire examination.

GOOD LUCK!

EXAMINATION ANSWER SHEET

Directions: Read each question and its lettered answers. When you have decided which answer is correct, blacken the corresponding space on this sheet. After completing the exam, you may grade yourself; complete answers and explanations will be found on the pages following the examination.

1. Ⓐ Ⓑ Ⓒ Ⓓ
2. Ⓐ Ⓑ Ⓒ Ⓓ
3. Ⓐ Ⓑ Ⓒ Ⓓ
4. Ⓐ Ⓑ Ⓒ Ⓓ
5. Ⓐ Ⓑ Ⓒ Ⓓ
6. Ⓐ Ⓑ Ⓒ Ⓓ
7. Ⓐ Ⓑ Ⓒ Ⓓ
8. Ⓐ Ⓑ Ⓒ Ⓓ
9. Ⓐ Ⓑ Ⓒ Ⓓ
10. Ⓐ Ⓑ Ⓒ Ⓓ
11. Ⓐ Ⓑ Ⓒ Ⓓ
12. Ⓐ Ⓑ Ⓒ Ⓓ
13. Ⓐ Ⓑ Ⓒ Ⓓ
14. Ⓐ Ⓑ Ⓒ Ⓓ
15. Ⓐ Ⓑ Ⓒ Ⓓ
16. Ⓐ Ⓑ Ⓒ Ⓓ
17. Ⓐ Ⓑ Ⓒ Ⓓ
18. Ⓐ Ⓑ Ⓒ Ⓓ
19. Ⓐ Ⓑ Ⓒ Ⓓ
20. Ⓐ Ⓑ Ⓒ Ⓓ
21. Ⓐ Ⓑ Ⓒ Ⓓ
22. Ⓐ Ⓑ Ⓒ Ⓓ
23. Ⓐ Ⓑ Ⓒ Ⓓ
24. Ⓐ Ⓑ Ⓒ Ⓓ
25. Ⓐ Ⓑ Ⓒ Ⓓ

26. Ⓐ Ⓑ Ⓒ Ⓓ
27. Ⓐ Ⓑ Ⓒ Ⓓ
28. Ⓐ Ⓑ Ⓒ Ⓓ
29. Ⓐ Ⓑ Ⓒ Ⓓ
30. Ⓐ Ⓑ Ⓒ Ⓓ
31. Ⓐ Ⓑ Ⓒ Ⓓ
32. Ⓐ Ⓑ Ⓒ Ⓓ
33. Ⓐ Ⓑ Ⓒ Ⓓ
34. Ⓐ Ⓑ Ⓒ Ⓓ
35. Ⓐ Ⓑ Ⓒ Ⓓ
36. Ⓐ Ⓑ Ⓒ Ⓓ
37. Ⓐ Ⓑ Ⓒ Ⓓ
38. Ⓐ Ⓑ Ⓒ Ⓓ
39. Ⓐ Ⓑ Ⓒ Ⓓ
40. Ⓐ Ⓑ Ⓒ Ⓓ
41. Ⓐ Ⓑ Ⓒ Ⓓ
42. Ⓐ Ⓑ Ⓒ Ⓓ
43. Ⓐ Ⓑ Ⓒ Ⓓ
44. Ⓐ Ⓑ Ⓒ Ⓓ
45. Ⓐ Ⓑ Ⓒ Ⓓ
46. Ⓐ Ⓑ Ⓒ Ⓓ
47. Ⓐ Ⓑ Ⓒ Ⓓ
48. Ⓐ Ⓑ Ⓒ Ⓓ
49. Ⓐ Ⓑ Ⓒ Ⓓ
50. Ⓐ Ⓑ Ⓒ Ⓓ

1. Which type of glass is appropriate to use in areas exposed to fire hazards?

    A. Heat-absorbing glass

    B. Heat-strengthened glass

    C. Wired glass

    D. Tempered glass

2. Masonry joints that lack sufficient mortar are often repaired by adding fresh mortar while the surrounding mortar is still green. This process is called

    A. raking.

    B. pointing.

    C. troweling.

    D. jointing.

3. Spandrel glazing in a curtain wall system should be

    A. double-strength glass.

    B. tempered glass.

    C. heat-absorbing glass.

    D. heat-strengthened glass.

4. Life-cycle costing is an economic evaluation of architectural elements that include which of the following factors?

    I. First cost

    II. Maintenance and operational costs

    III. Repair costs

    IV. Replacement cost

    A. I

    B. II, III, and IV

    C. II and IV

    D. All of the above

5. In laying a conventional wood strip tongue-and-groove floor, the strips are usually attached to the subfloor by blind nailing. With regard to the last strip, closest to the wall, it is

    A. attached with waterproof mastic.

    B. attached by face nailing.

    C. also attached by blind nailing.

    D. not attached, but left loose for expansion.

6. The slump test is used to measure the

    A. compressive strength of concrete.

    B. tensile strength of concrete.

    C. soundness of concrete aggregates.

    D. workability of concrete.

7. Which of the following features are required in an elevator car in order for the car to comply with the ANSI handicapped standards?

    I. Self-leveling device

    II. Door reopening device

    III. Emergency communication system

    IV. 36-inch-high car control buttons

    V. Hard, non-slip floor surface

    A. I and II   C. II, IV, and V

    B. I, III, and V   D. I, II, III, and IV

8. Structural steel members are to be used in a structure where they will be exposed to severe weather conditions. The members have been cleaned and prepared at the mill, where a priming coat of red-lead alkyd-based primer has been applied. After they are in place, you should specify a finish coat of

    A. coal-tar enamel.

    B. alkyd enamel.

    C. oleoresinous paint.

    D. Any of the above

9. With reference to the detail shown below, which of the following statements is most correct?

   A. The foundation drain is placed in gravel fill in order to minimize the cracking or breakage of individual drain tiles.

   B. The waterproof rigid insulation between the concrete slab and foundation wall may be omitted in areas where the minimum daytime winter air temperature remains above freezing.

   C. The granular fill beneath the slab may consist of crushed stone, coarse slag, or gravel.

   D. Even with the waterproof membrane placed as shown, floor coverings may be damaged by the rise of capillary moisture from the ground.

10. Referring to the drawing of the previous question, what is the most obvious error in the detail, considering conventional practices?

    A. The foundation drain should be located just below the bottom of the footing.

    B. The finish grade should slope away from the foundation wall.

    C. The waterproof membrane should be located below the granular fill.

    D. The finish grade should be set at least 12 inches below the finish slab level.

11. Prior to the 18th century, iron was used only sparingly, for fastenings or in decorative ways. All of the reasons below account for this limited use *EXCEPT*

    A. it offered poor resistance to weather exposure.

    B. it lacked classical precedents and therefore was unpopular.

    C. it could not be produced in large sizes or in great quantity.

    D. iron ore was scarce and difficult to mine.

12. Concrete made from Type IV low-heat portland cement would be most appropriately used

    A. in massive concrete pours.

    B. for general overall use.

    C. during very cold weather.

    D. in high alkaline areas.

13. Bulb tees are generally used

    A. in foundation work involving caissons.

    B. in underpinning as a form of temporary support.

    C. in gypsum concrete roof deck construction.

    D. as water stops in below-grade concreting.

14. At the conclusion of a workday, a masonry wall remains unfinished. As the weather report calls for a rainstorm that evening, you should advise the contractor to

  A. cover the exposed top of the unfinished wall with loose boards or roofing paper.

  B. protect the exposed top with a positive waterproof cover, securely weighted down and hung over each side of the wall at least two feet.

  C. ignore the rain, unless the temperature drops below 40 degrees.

  D. ignore the rain, as masonry, whether finished or not, cannot be harmed by water.

15. Combustible types of construction include all but which of the following?

  A. Type II N

  B. Type III N

  C. Type V N

  D. Type V one hour

16. The planning phase of a sustainably designed architectural project should include which of the following elements?

  I.   Native landscaping that is aesthetically pleasing and functional

  II. Designing structures in the floodplain that can resist the forces of flood waters

  III. Consideration of sun orientation, topographic relief, and the scale of adjacent buildings

  IV. Locating projects within existing neighborhoods that are adjacent to public transportation

  A. I and II

  B. I and III

  C. I, III, and IV

  D. All of the above

17. The need for three exits can be based on which of the following?

  I.   Occupancy type

  II. Type of construction

  III. Number of occupants (more than 500 but not more than 1,000)

  IV. Travel distance to an exit

  V.   Intervening rooms

  A. I and II   **C.** III and V

  B. III and IV   **D.** IV and V

18. Which of the following statements concerning fire doors is NOT true?

  A. Class A fire doors are rated for 3 hours and are not permitted to have windows in them.

  B. A 1-1/2-hour-rated fire door may be either Class B or Class D, and is permitted to have up to 100 square inches of wired glass per leaf.

  C. Class E doors are rated 3/4-hour fire resistance in exterior walls with up to 720 square inches of wired glass.

  D. Carpeting is not permitted to pass under any fire door, regardless of the rating of the door, the flame spread rating of the carpet, or whether the door is arranged to be held open by a magnetic release device to permit self-closing in the event of fire.

19. An incombustible building material is one that

  A. has at least a one-hour fire rating.

  B. is not made of wood, fabric, or paper.

  C. will not burn.

  D. will smolder but not support flames.

20. With reference to the detail shown below, the cant strip is indicated as a continuous filler piece cut on a 45-degree angle. The purpose of this angle is to

A. provide a moderate bend in the roofing sheets and thereby avoid potential damage to the roofing.

B. assure that roofing water will run off the gravel stop and flow away from the roof edges, toward the drains.

C. avoid 90-degree angle creases or pockets in which water may collect and possibly freeze in the winter.

D. conserve material, as two cant strips may be cut from a single rectangular block.

21. Sustainably designed architecture requires attention to which of the following building elements?

I.   Solar shading devices

II. Urban heat island effect

III. Increased parking

IV. Fenestration and glazing

A. I, II, and IV

B. I and IV

C. I and II

D. All of the above

22. Among the following statements concerning glued laminated timber, which is true?

A. Laminated members are manufactured from the longest pieces of lumber commonly available.

B. Laminations may vary in thickness, but in no case are they ever less than 1-1/2 inches thick.

C. Glued laminated timbers in straight lengths can readily span 60 feet or more.

D. The classification for the finest appearance of glued laminated members is "architectural" grade.

23. According to the ANSI handicapped standards, objects projecting from walls, such as public telephones, which are mounted between 27 and 80 inches above the finished floor, may not protrude more than 4 inches into passageways. Objects lower than 27 inches, such as trash receptacles, may protrude

A. an equal amount.

B. no amount at all.

C. a variable amount.

D. any amount.

24. An abundance of native stone was used in ancient Egyptian architecture because

A. it was relatively easy to handle.

B. it was low in cost, relative to other materials.

C. it was the most stable and permanent material available.

D. it had a high insulating value.

25. Which of the following statements concerning the water-cement ratio of a concrete mix is NOT true?

 A. The water-cement ratio is based on volume, not weight.

 B. A low water-cement ratio reduces the shrinkage of concrete and increases its durability.

 C. The strength of concrete remains the same for a given water-cement ratio, irrespective of the amount of aggregate.

 D. Provided there is sufficient water to hydrate the cement and to avoid air being trapped because the mix is too stiff to compact thoroughly, the strength of concrete increases as the water-cement ratio increases.

26. Building codes are intended to protect which of the following?

 A. Public health

 B. Public welfare

 C. Public safety

 D. All of the above

27. Aluminum window sections are frequently coated with methacrylate lacquers or strippable plastic coatings prior to installation in a rough-framed structure. The purpose of these temporary coatings is to

 A. minimize corrosive damage from galvanic action.

 B. minimize corrosive damage from alkalies.

 C. reduce deterioration caused by normal weathering.

 D. keep the sections clean until construction is completed.

28. Clay roofing tiles are generally attached by means of

 A. steel or hardened steel nails.

 B. annular or helical nails.

 C. copper or aluminum roofing nails.

 D. elastic cement or mastic.

29. In which of the situations described below would you most likely employ a needle beam?

 A. To support the spandrel section in a conventional metal curtain wall

 B. To support the load above an opening cut into an existing masonry wall

 C. To support vertical plywood forming sections for poured-in-place concrete walls

 D. To support cantilevered roof loads in exposed plank-and-beam construction

30. Gypsum partition tiles, otherwise known as plaster blocks, are frequently used for lightweight, fire-resistant interior partitions. Such units are generally held together with

 A. gypsum mortar.

 B. portland cement mortar.

 C. waterproof mortar.

 D. type A or B mortar.

31. At the intersection of a wall and ceiling, one might specify a wooden trim shape known as a

 A. crown mold. C. corner bead.

 B. casing mold. D. chair rail.

32. If an Underwriters' Laboratories 1-1/2-hour B label were attached to a door, you would know that

 A. the door required an automatic closing device.

 B. glazed openings would not be allowed in the door.

 C. Both of the above statements are true.

 D. Neither of the above statements is true.

33. Along which line in the diagram above should a vapor barrier be located?

 A. II only   C. I or II

 B. III only   D. III or IV

34. LEED, the name of a program that environmentally evaluates sustainable projects, is a checklist that is concerned with which of the following?

 I. Indoor air quality

 II. Storm water

 III. Innovative energy systems

 IV. Aesthetic design

 A. I

 B. I, II, and III

 C. II and III

 D. All of the above

35. Metal casement windows, regardless of the manufacturer, are generally available in identical stock sizes. The standard dimensions of these windows are based on

 A. standard metric measurements.

 B. a standard four-inch module.

 C. standard brick masonry modules.

 D. traditional English measurements.

36. If you specified the use of an intumescent paint, you would expect the coating to

 A. inhibit rust on ferrous metal surfaces.

 B. provide dampproofing on concrete or masonry above grade.

 C. resist abrasion and impact when used on floor surfaces.

 D. retard the spread of fire and the effects of intense heat.

37. The apartment building on the Rue Franklin in Paris, designed by Auguste Perret, is famous as the first such building to

 A. eliminate all decorative ornament.

 B. employ reinforced concrete framing.

 C. reach great heights using load-bearing masonry walls.

 D. make use of extensive glass areas.

38. Among the following factors, which are considered distinct advantages in the use of escalators?

I.   They operate continuously.

II. They have low power consumption.

III. They are dependable in the event of fire.

IV. They are architecturally flexible.

V. They are relatively quiet.

A. I, II, and IV   **C.** I, II, and III

B. I, II, and V   **D.** III, IV, and V

39. Shown below is a section through a terrazzo floor installation. The purpose of the neoprene filler is to

A. allow for expansion, contraction, or structural movement.

B. provide a waterproof joint at a point of stress in the floor.

C. provide a durable accent strip of contrasting color and texture.

D. provide a preformed cold joint for pouring a large area of terrazzo.

40. In built-up composition roofing systems, one of the principal causes of roofing failure is the presence of blisters, which may be caused by

I.   air between the roofing felts.

II. moisture in the roofing insulation.

III. moisture in the roof deck.

IV. air between the roofing felt and the roof deck.

A. I only   **C.** I, III, and IV

B. II and III   **D.** I, II, III, and IV

41. What are the actual dimensions of a nominal 8" × 8" × 16" concrete masonry unit?

A. 8" × 8" × 15-5/8"

B. 8" × 7-5/8" × 15-5/8"

C. 7-5/8" × 7-5/8" × 15-5/8"

D. 8" × 8" × 16"

42. Which of the following paints would you select if low-flame-spread rating were the most important consideration?

A. Acrylic latex

B. Polyester-epoxy

C. Alkyd

D. Polyurethane

43. Which of the following features apply to the Crystal Palace in London, built in 1851?

I.   It was the first building to employ iron framing.

II. It was the first building to exhibit great spans.

III. It was standardized and prefabricated.

IV. It was, in 1851, the largest building in the world.

V. It was completely fireproof.

A. I and II   **C.** I, II, and V

B. III and IV   **D.** III, IV, and V

44. Select the correct statements.

I. The principal factors affecting the strength of concrete are the water-cement ratio and the extent of hydration.

II. Air-entrained concrete is more resistant to freezing and thawing than non-air-entrained concrete.

III. Concrete having a low water-cement ratio is stronger and more resistant to freezing and thawing than concrete with a high water-cement ratio.

IV. The length of time during which concrete is moist-cured affects its strength and watertightness.

V. Excessive bleeding tends to make the surface of concrete weak.

A. I, III, and V   **C.** II, IV, and V

B. I, II, and IV   **D.** I, II, III, IV, and V

45. A section through steel floor decking is shown above. What is the purpose of the deformations in the deck?

A. They simplify the fabrication of the deck.

B. They improve the safety of the decking during construction by making the surface non-skid.

C. They lock the concrete slab and decking together to achieve composite action.

D. They increase the section modulus of the decking.

46. The clear space between a handrail or grab bar used by the handicapped and the wall on which it is installed should be no less than

A. 1-1/2 inches.

B. 3 inches.

C. 6 inches.

D. 10 percent of its height from the floor.

47. A school district has asked you to reduce the heat loss for a 35-year-old classroom building. The construction of the exterior walls is eight-inch hollow concrete block with no interior finish. Natural light consists of 3-foot by 5-foot wood sash window frames with single glazing in the masonry walls, and these constitute approximately 15 percent of the exterior wall surface. Without preparing a detailed study, you suggest that the most important first step is to

A. apply rigid insulation and gypsum board to the interior surface of the exterior walls.

B. replace all single glazing with double glazing.

C. caulk around all the windows and doors.

D. re-grout the masonry walls.

48. A new building is being constructed adjacent to an existing building whose footings are shallower than those planned for the new structure. The foundation for the new building should be constructed

A. in the usual way, as the existing building's footings will be minimally disrupted.

B. to the same depth as the footings in the existing building.

C. after the footings of the existing building have been extended down to the depth of the footings of the proposed building.

D. in two steps: first on the three non-adjacent sides and then on the remaining side.

49. What is the desirable interval for elevators in a high-rise office building?

    A. 5 seconds   **C.** 2 minutes

    B. 30 seconds   **D.** 5 minutes

50. In the detail of an aluminum skylight frame illustrated below, an arrow is shown pointing to an L-shaped extrusion. The purpose of this extrusion is to

    A. strengthen the bending resistance of the overall section.

    B. provide a means for removal of condensate.

    C. provide an integral ledge on which sun-control panels may be supported.

    D. provide a backup safety ledge capable of supporting the glass panel above.

The examination answers and explanations will be found on the following pages.

Do not look at the answers until you have completed the exam.

1. **C** Wired glass is sheet or plate glass into which a thin wire mesh has been embedded. It has great resistance to impact and resists shattering when exposed to high heat. Therefore, it is used in fire doors, exterior walls, vertical shafts, and areas leading to fire escapes.

2. **B** Because the lack of a full bed or head of mortar can cause a masonry joint to leak, incomplete joints must be repaired while the mortar is still fresh. This process is called pointing. When similar repairs are made to old work, the process is referred to as tuck pointing.

3. **D** Heat-strengthened glass is plate or patterned glass to which a colored ceramic glaze has been fused. It is strong, opaque, and used almost exclusively in panels for spandrel glazing in curtain wall construction.

4. **D** *I* is correct: While first cost is not the primary concern of life cycle costing, it is one of the economic factors considered. *II* is correct: The cost of maintenance is part of the evaluation. *III* is correct: The durability of a product or system is considered in the cost of repair and is part of the overall evaluation. *IV* is correct: The comparison of product or system life is one of the factors evaluated in life cycle costing.

5. **B** Conventionally laid wood strip floors are blind nailed in order to conceal the nails and tightly drive each strip closer to the preceding strip. At the wall, however, there is no room to drive a nail at a 45-degree angle. The final strip, therefore, is generally face nailed. It is also set about 1/2 inch away from the wall in order to allow for expansion.

This space is usually covered by the wood base.

6. **D** The standard slump test measures the workability of concrete. The slump of a standard cone of fresh concrete is measured, and the stiffer the mix the less the slump.

7. **A** All elevators used by the public must comply with the ANSI handicapped standards. For example, all cars must operate automatically, which includes self-leveling devices (I) that align cars with floor landings within a 1/2 inch tolerance, as well as door reopening devices (II) that automatically function if the door becomes obstructed by an object or person. However, elevator cars do not require emergency communication systems (III), and car control buttons may be mounted up to 54 inches, not 36, above the floor (IV). Finally, elevator car floors may be covered with any stable and regular finished surface, including carpet and padding (V); however, such carpeting should have a short pile (1/2 inch maximum) and be firmly installed. The correct combination of features is found in answer A.

8. **B** The finish of ferrous metals is of particular concern, as steel is susceptible to corrosion when exposed to air and moisture. Under these circumstances, alkyd-based paint is preferred over oil-based because it dries faster, harder, and with greater resistance to the weather. Furthermore, it is generally advisable for all coats of paint to be of the same base type. Incidentally, coal-tar enamel (A) should be specified where steel is installed underground or in water. In that case, the primer should also be a coal-tar product.

9. C The only true statement is correct answer C. The gravel fill in which the drain tiles are set (A) provides a porous material through which water may flow to the open joints between the tiles and then away from the building. The waterproof joint between slab and wall (B) provides a positive seal, as well as thermal insulation for the slab. It is sometimes omitted in temperate areas, but only when the temperature remains above freezing during the night, as well as the day. Finally, the capillary rise of ground moisture (D) should be effectively stopped by the waterproof membrane barrier; that is, in fact, its very purpose. Furthermore, capillary action rarely occurs in coarse granular fills, such as the one indicated in the detail shown.

10. B In the control of surface ground water, the finish grade should be set at least six inches below the slab level, as shown (D). However, the grade should be sloped away from the foundation at all sides (correct answer B), in order to protect the structure. If the drain were set below the footing (A), there would be danger of undermining the footing from the flow of running water. Therefore, foundation drains are always placed as shown. Finally, the waterproof membrane should never be set below the granular fill (C), because the purpose of the fill is drainage, insulation from the soil below, and most importantly, the reduction of capillary action.

11. D Iron did not become an important construction material until it could be produced in great quantity. When the Englishman Abraham Darby developed the blast furnace around 1750, mass production became possible. Prior to that time iron was difficult to produce in quantity (C), and it was also unpopular because of its poor resistance to weather (A) and its lack of historical precedent (B). Iron ore was plentiful, however, and relatively simple to mine. At first, mass-produced iron was used for machines, utensils, and rails, and shortly thereafter, the first cast iron bridges were constructed in England.

12. A Portland cement is manufactured in several types, each with characteristics that make it preferred for a particular set of conditions. For example, the low-heat cement of this question would be suitable where slow setting is desired and where the heat generated by ordinary cements would be excessive and lead to serious cracking. This situation often exists in massive concrete work (correct answer A). For general use (B) one would use Type I (normal). During very cold weather (C) one would use Type III (high early strength) in order to generate greater heat and offset low temperatures. In alkaline areas (D) the best choice would be Type V (sulfate-resisting), which is better able to withstand chemical attacks from sulfates found in the ground or in some building materials. While the different types of cement have different rates of strength gain, they all eventually reach about the same strength.

13. C Bulb tees are used in gypsum concrete construction as structural sub-purlins. The bulb tees are fastened to the primary framing and provide support for the form boards that receive the gypsum concrete. They also anchor the deck against uplift forces, restrict deck movement due to temperature changes, and provide lateral bracing for the roof structure. Gypsum concrete roof decks are lightweight, they set rapidly (30 minutes), and when used over gypsum or mineral fiber form boards, they are classified as noncombustible.

14. B An unprotected, partially finished masonry wall that may be saturated by rain can cause problems. The wall may take months to dry out, and during this drying period, efflorescence may appear on the wall surface. If there is a threat of rain, the wall should be positively protected, as described in correct answer B. Incidentally, when the outside temperature drops below 40 degrees (C), no further masonry work should be performed unless adequate precautions are taken against freezing.

15. A Type II N is considered noncombustible construction. The rest are considered combustible.

16. C Choice I is correct: Designing with native landscaping is preferred to using exotic or imported plant types. Indigenous plants tend to survive longer, use less water, and cost less. Choice II is not correct: Placing any structure in a floodplain, even those that resist floodwater, is not desirable. Placing buildings in a floodplain can increase flooding further downstream. Choice III is also correct: Buildings sensitive to the benefits of solar orientation and passive and active solar gain techniques save energy and are more visually aligned with local climatic conditions. Choice IV is correct as well: In-fill development and proximity to a variety of transportation options are design principles that benefit the inhabitants and their environment.

17. B Three exits are required where there are more than 500 occupants and four exits are required where there are more than 1,000 occupants. Other areas typically require only two exits but where the path to the first exit exceeds the allowable travel distance a third exit would be required.

18. B Fire door requirements are covered in Chapter 43 of the UBC, as well as corresponding sections of other building codes. Class A doors (three-hour rating) are used in openings in fire walls or division walls between buildings or sections of buildings. Class B doors (1-1/2 -hour rating) are used in openings in enclosed vertical shafts, such as stairs or elevators. Class D doors are also rated 1-1/2 hours, but are intended for severe fire exposure in exterior walls, and no glass is permitted. Statements A, C, and D are true, while statement B, the correct answer, is false.

19. C There are few definitions as clear as that for incombustible. It simply means incapable of igniting or supporting combustion when exposed to fire, usually at an air temperature of 1,200 degrees. An incombustible building material, therefore, is simply one that will not burn.

20. A In the application of built-up composition asphalt roofing materials, the use of angled cant strips is standard procedure. The reason for this is stated in correct answer A. When 15# felts are bent at a 90-degree angle, they have a tendency to crack or rupture. The resulting weakness, when combined with the natural shrinkage and expansion due to weather and other movements of the building, may produce serious roofing failures. Cant strips are generally cut from wood or manufactured from a variety of lightweight, inexpensive materials.

21. **A**   I is correct: Solar shading, whether from landscaping or architectural elements, can regulate the insulation to increase winter light and reduce warm summer sunlight. II is also correct: Urban heat island effect is the tendency of a building roof to absorb solar radiation during the day and then emit heat radiation during the evening. Roof systems with grass or light colored roofing material reduce the urban heat island effect. III is not correct: Sustainable design encourages approaches that reduce the area allocated to parking. IV is correct: The type, location, and size of building fenestration are a key aspect of architectural design for sustainable projects.

22. **C**   In the same order as the statements, laminated members are generally manufactured from short and narrow lengths of lumber. One of the great advantages is that these small pieces may be end-joined to form almost any length desired with no loss in strength. Concerning the thickness of lumber used, laminations rarely exceed two inches in thickness, but they may be thinner. In the case of some curved members, for example, where the bending radius is short, 3/4-inch-thick laminations are often used. The next statement (C) is the correct answer. Simply-supported single spans of 60 feet or more are not uncommon. In the form of arches or simple trusses, clear spans may reach 100 feet or more in length. The last statement is false. The very best appearance grade is called "premium," which is specif-

ically intended for use in exposed construction. In descending order of appearance grade, next comes "architectural" grade and then "industrial" grade.

23. **D**   Objects that project from walls constitute a hazard to those with sight disabilities. Therefore, projections are limited to four inches when such hazards are mounted between 27 and 80 inches from the floor. When located below 27 inches, however, wall-mounted projections are easily contacted by a hand-held cane before the blind person reaches the object. Therefore, the ANSI standards permit these objects to protrude any amount, so long as the object does not reduce the clear minimum width of an accessible route.

24. **C**   The ancient Egyptians employed stone because it was available and its use resulted in stable and permanent structures. The immense stone blocks were difficult to handle (A), but the vast armies of unpaid laborers, prisoners, and slaves solved that problem, as well as the problem of cost (B). Finally, stone does have a high value of insulation appropriate for a warm climate (D), but that quality was incidental to the ancient Egyptians.

25. **D**   All of the statements are true with the exception of the last one. As the water-cement ratio increases, the strength of the concrete decreases. The densest and strongest concrete, therefore, is obtained by using a workable mix with the lowest water-cement ratio that will enable the mix to be thoroughly compacted.

26. **D**   All of the above. Building codes are intended to protect the public health, safety, and welfare.

27. B Aluminum is highly resistant to corrosion from normal weathering because of the tough film of aluminum oxide that rapidly forms on exposed surfaces. It is subject to attack by alkalies, however, and must therefore be protected from contact with wet concrete, mortar, and plaster. Various temporary plastic coatings are used for this purpose. Aluminum is also subject to galvanic action (A), and therefore where it comes in contact with other metals, the meeting surfaces should be insulated by gasketing or by painting with asphaltic or bituminous paint.

28. C The most important consideration in the selection of roofing nails is that they be non-corrosive, such as copper or aluminum (correct answer C). The danger in using steel nails (A) is that they may eventually rust, discolor the tiles, or even corrode to the point of failure. Annular or helical nails (B), whether manufactured from a non-corrosive metal or not, have great holding power, but strength of this magnitude is generally unnecessary. Elastic cement (D) is often used to seal a roof tile joint, but it does not have sufficient holding power for roof tile application.

29. B A needle beam is used in the situation described in correct answer B. A hole is cut into an existing masonry wall, through which the needle beam is placed at right angles to the wall. Each end of the beam is supported at some distance from the wall and serves as temporary support while the required opening is cut. After the new lintel or arch is formed, the needle beam is removed and the original hole is patched. Needling may require more than one temporary beam if the opening is very wide.

30. A Non-load-bearing partitions are made from either solid or cored gypsum blocks that are 12 inches high, 30 inches wide, and from 1-1/2 to 6 inches thick. They are generally set on a waterproof base course and joined by a mortar consisting of one part neat, unfibered gypsum to three parts sand (correct answer A). Portland cement mortar (B) is used for brick or concrete block construction and is classified as type A, B, or C (answer D), depending on its resistance to weather exposure.

31. A A number of patterns and dimensions of trim are produced in a variety of hard and soft woods, for both interior and exterior use. Each was originally developed for a specific appearance when covering the joint where two surfaces meet. At a wall and ceiling intersection, for example, a crown mold is often used (correct answer A). Casing molds are used around openings, corner beads are used at exterior corners, and chair rails are applied at the midheight of walls to protect them from furniture damage.

32. D The door label designating a 1-1/2-hour fire-resistive rating is used in class B openings, generally in vertical stairwells. For that designation, the fire assembly (door frame, hardware, etc.) is required to be self-closing. This means that it is equipped with a mechanical closer that insures closing and latching after being opened. An automatic closing device, on the other hand, is used on a fire assembly that may remain open, but will close automatically if subjected to an increase in temperature. This is required for a three-hour fire-resistive rating. Glazed openings in a class B assembly are permitted, providing they do not exceed 100 square inches. The correct answer therefore is D, as neither statement applies to the door label described.

33. B   The amount of water vapor that the air can hold increases with the temperature. Within a building, this moisture can come from mechanical equipment, perspiration, and even breathing. The amount of moisture held in the air is usually expressed as relative humidity. The temperature at which the air becomes saturated and vapor condenses is known as the dew point. Although air in a room is generally well above its dew point, the temperature of some surfaces is not, and that is why we usually see condensation first appearing on the inside of windows, which may be cold. Because vapor flows from high to low pressure, it can pass through porous construction, cool to its dew point, and condense as water within the structure. This can be prevented by the use of a vapor barrier. The barrier itself, usually a plastic film or metal foil, must be at a temperature above the dew point, and therefore it is always installed on the warm or room side of the construction beneath the interior finish (correct answer B).

34. B   I is correct: LEED has several options for improving IAQ (Indoor Air Quality) including filtering the air system and installing low VOC (Volatile Organic Compound) paints and caulking. II is also correct: Methods to store, recirculate, and locally distribute rainwater are encouraged. III is correct: Innovative solutions to energy conservation such as fuel cells, photovoltaic panels, and gas turbine energy production are encouraged in the LEED accreditation system. IV is incorrect: Unfortunately, the LEED system awards no points for designs with strong aesthetics.

35. C   The standard sizes of metal casement windows are all based on brick masonry modules (correct answer C), as these windows were originally developed for use in brick wall construction.

36. D   Intumescence is the formation of a charred, foamlike material on a coated surface that has been subjected to intense heat. Paints that are able to sacrifice themselves and form this char are called intumescent paints (correct answer D). These special paints are formulated to protect underlying flammable surfaces by insulating them from the intensity of heat, thus delaying ignition. Generally, the fire is not extinguished, but merely retarded. However, delaying the flame spread by even 15 to 30 minutes may save many lives in the evacuation of a school or hospital. Concerning the other choices, other coatings are available that satisfy these special requirements.

37. B   Perret's eight-story apartment building, built in 1903, was the first to use reinforced concrete frame construction. Although the concrete columns and beams were sheathed in terra cotta, the structure was revealed to a degree unprecedented in domestic architecture. The infilling panels were ceramic tile decorated in relief, and the building's glass areas were more extensive than usual for that time.

38. B   Among the many advantages of escalators are those factors listed in correct answer B. Escalators are not, however, dependable in the event of a fire. Their mechanisms may be damaged and they may fail to operate. Escalators may employ fire-protective devices, such as a sprinkler system or rolling steel shutters that close a stairwell, but these devices are difficult to incorporate in an open area, and thus, are not commonly used. Escalators are also not very flexible architecturally, as they are custom made for each installation, and once positioned, they are almost never moved to another location.

39. A What is shown is an expansion-type dividing strip, the purpose of which is described in correct answer A. This type of strip is manufactured from a variety of expandable materials, which are used wherever such joints are required. The joint width depends on the total anticipated structural movement.

40. D Blisters may be caused by all of the factors listed (correct answer D). Most of the moisture comes from exposure during construction or from poured roof decks that have not had enough time to dry adequately before the application of roofing. Blisters may also result from failure to cement the felts securely to each other, to the insulation, and to the deck, all of which create air bubbles.

41. C A concrete masonry unit is specified by its width, height, and length, in that order. The actual dimensions are generally 3/8 inch less, to allow for a mortar joint. The correct dimensions are therefore shown in answer C.

42. A Of the types of paint in this question, only acrylic latex (correct answer A) is completely solvent-free, and therefore presents no flammability hazard in either storage or application. Polyester-epoxy combines the physical toughness, adhesion, and chemical resistance of epoxy with the color retention and clarity of polyester. Alkyd paints are made by combining synthetic materials with various vegetable oils to produce clear, hard resins. Polyurethane contains flammable solvents but is highly resistant to abrasion, impact, and chemicals.

43. B The Crystal Place was designed by Joseph Paxton to house the Great Exhibition of 1851 in London. Although it employed cast iron framing (I), and exhibited great spans (II), it was not the first building to do so, as it was preceded by several bridges, factories, and warehouses. It was, however, standardized, prefabricated, and erected in only three months (III); and in 1851, it was the largest building the world had ever seen (IV), enclosing nearly a million square feet. Finally, the Crystal Place was not fireproof (V), and in fact, the entire iron and glass structure was totally destroyed in a rapid fire in 1937.

44. D All of the statements are true and therefore D is the correct answer.

45. C The decking shown and the concrete floor slab placed over it act together as a composite member (correct answer C). This type of action is made possible by the deformations in the deck, which function as mechanical connectors between the slab and deck.

46. A Handrails and grab bars that are required by the ANSI handicapped standards must have a diameter of gripping surface between 1-1/4 and 1-1/2 inches. When they are mounted adjacent to a wall, the clear space between the handrail or bar and wall must be no less than 1-1/2 inches (correct answer A). In addition, the gripping surfaces must be continuous and free of any sharp or abrasive element.

47. A Although all of the choices are valid and might be implemented to reduce the heat loss in this old building, the most important first step is to reduce the U factor in that portion of the building envelope that constitutes 85 percent of the exterior wall surface. In this case, applying insulation and gypsum board to the interior surface of the exterior walls will reduce its U value from approximately .56 to .24 (correct answer A). Similarly, double glazing (B) will reduce the U factor from 1.13 to .45; however, it affects only 15 percent of the building envelope, and therefore it would be a secondary consideration. Caulking at windows and doors (C) as well as re-grouting the masonry walls (D) will reduce or eliminate leakage, or infiltration, and these are additional considerations in reducing heat loss.

48. C No excavation for the new footings should be started until the footings of the existing building are first extended down to the level of the proposed building's footings. This is accomplished by using temporary supports, such as timber shores or steel needle beams, to carry the weight of the existing building until the new and lower foundation is in place. When the entire weight of the existing wall is transferred to the new section of the foundation, the shoring and underpinning are removed and the foundation for the new building may proceed. The new work is generally performed on all sides simultaneously.

49. B Interval is defined as the average time between successive departures of cars from the main floor or lobby of a building. Although the requirements and functions of high-rise buildings vary, the accepted interval for good service in the average building is 30 seconds.

50. B The L-shaped extrusion forms a continuous condensate gutter (correct answer B). Under certain temperature conditions, moisture vapor, or humidity, changes to liquid through condensation. Generally, moisture vapor flows from high to low pressure independent of air flow. The formation of condensation is particularly prevalent during winter months on glass surfaces that are heated on one side. In a skylight, this moisture must be removed by condensation gutters or else the moisture may cause damage in other parts of the structure.

INDEX